U.S. Domestic and National Security Agendas

U.S. Domestic and National Security Agendas

INTO THE TWENTY-FIRST CENTURY

Edited by

Sam C. Sarkesian

and

John Mead Flanagin

Foreword by
Richard E. Friedman

UA
23
.U2

Contributions in Military Studies,
Number 152

GREENWOOD PRESS
Westport, Connecticut • London

Library of Congress Cataloging-in-Publication Data

U.S. domestic and national security agendas : into the twenty-first
century / edited by Sam C. Sarkesian and John Mead Flanagin :
foreword by Richard E. Friedman.
     p.   cm. — (Contributions in military studies, ISSN 0883–6884
; no. 152)
   Includes bibliographical references and index.
   ISBN 0–313–28870–4 (alk. paper)
   1. National security—United States—Congresses. 2. United
States—Politics and government—1993- —Congresses. I. Sarkesian,
Sam Charles. II. Flanagin, John Mead. III. Series.
UA23.U2   1994
355'.033073—dc20   93–21499

British Library Cataloguing in Publication Data is available.

Library of Congress Catalog Card Number: 93–21499
ISBN: 0–313–28870–4
ISSN: 0883–6884

First published in 1994

Greenwood Press, 88 Post Road West, Westport, CT 06881
An imprint of Greenwood Publishing Group, Inc.

Printed in the United States of America

The paper used in this book complies with the
Permanent Paper Standard issued by the National
Information Standards Organization (Z39.48–1984).

10 9 8 7 6 5 4 3 2 1

Contents

Figures and Tables

Foreword

Political instability in the former Soviet Union, the increase in ethnic hostilities, the expansion of Islamic fundamentalism, and the potential for increased international terrorism are factors that make the world a dangerous place. Although the threat of global war between superpowers has abated, the threat of major regional conflict has increased. The United States is in a period of transition when the nature of the threat to U.S. national security is less clear than it was in the Cold War era. This is a time when strategic analysis must address a complex array of functional issues and regional perspectives against the backdrop of profound economic changes.

In the United States and among states of the G-7 (Britain, Canada, France, Italy, Germany, Japan, and the United States), economic realities are a major consideration in the formulation of strategy. The amount of money available for traditional national security objectives has diminished. However, the prevailing desire to address domestic needs first will be frustrated by the continuing challenges presented by an unstable international environment. Problems are infinite and resources are finite.

A workshop was held September 17–19, 1992, to analyze the changing relationships between domestic politics and national security. The workshop, co-sponsored by the Robert R. McCormick Tribune Foundation, the Strategic Studies Institute of the U.S. Army War College, and the National Strategy Forum, was held at the McCormick Tribune Foundation's Cantigny Conference Center. Top academicians from the Department of Defense, analysts from leading think tanks, and prominent scholars from major universities came together for an extensive examination of the shifting alignment between domestic and international problems. The discussions centered on strategic questions, recognizing the constraints of economic factors and the dominance of domestic requirements. National strategy was considered in its broad dimensions: economics, technology, history, demographics, industrial policy, international trade, and intelligence gathering. The chapters in this book—which constitute the output of the workshop—demonstrate that strategy must integrate multiple factors and that traditional threat assessment is not sufficient.

Three themes were developed in the workshop: the strengths and weaknesses of the Base Force concept, the need to strike a balance between available means and strategic ends, and the role of the United States as the sole military superpower. Each of these themes raised numerous questions based upon present and future problems.

The questions that were posed, the discussions that addressed the issues raised, and the strategic principles involved are identified and analyzed by the authors of the chapters in this book. There are no conclusive answers to the array of complex problems, but the creative and thoughtful analyses presented herein will be helpful to policymakers and informed citizens.

The Base Force concept originated in the latter stages of the Bush Administration. Does the Base Force concept realistically confront the challenges that are facing the United States? What lessons were learned from the Persian Gulf War regarding mobilization and deployment and the Total Force blend of regular army, reserves, and the National Guard? U.S. military forces are going through a period of profound change, including base closings, manpower reductions, and adaptations to new personnel policies. Will the force be ready for another unforeseen crisis comparable to that in the Persian Gulf region?

Strategy is the balancing of means and ends. Since the end of the Cold War, there has been a strong and growing movement toward neo-isolationism in the United States. Neo-isolationists conclude that the United States is overextended and that we are squandering domestic resources (means) for ill-defined international purposes (ends). The view tends to oversimplify complex issues, and in times of economic scarcity the notion that we should turn away from international commitments is attractive. However, it is increasingly difficult to distinguish between domestic and international politics. As the global economy and technology base become more tightly integrated, it is important to remember that international stability is also a "means" to the "end" of domestic prosperity. The United States cannot restore and maintain domestic vitality by neglecting international concerns such as trade, natural resources, the environment, and demographics.

We are in the beginning phase of accommodating to the reality that the United States is the sole military superpower. The outstanding performance of U.S. military forces in the Persian Gulf War is instructive. In context, the force that routed the Iraqi military was built, equipped, and trained to fight the U.S.S.R. An irony is that the U.S. National Training Center at Fort Irwin, California, resembles the Persian Gulf terrain more closely than the European battleground that was the planning regime during the Cold War. The key point is that the United States could not predict the onset of the Persian Gulf conflict, and it is unlikely that the United States will be able to predict the next major regional conflict. One primary planning premise is that the United States will not have a military force designed to defeat a superpower—it will have something less. The crises in Somalia and former Yugoslavia illustrate the volatility of the new security environment and how difficult it is to answer questions of whether, how, and when the United States should intervene in regional conflicts. A decision to intervene must be justified on strategic grounds and political feasibility. It must be based upon U.S. strategic goals that are consistent with the strategic goals of our allies. Future crises are likely to carry a wide range of conflicting considerations. For example, the humanitarian motivation for intervention in Bosnia must be balanced by sensitivity to the traditional relationship between Russia and Serbia, the concern for political stability in Russia, and the effect that more intensive intervention by the United States in the former Yugoslavia would have on Russian internal politics and the desire for a U.S. relationship with a stable Russia.

There is a spate of contemplated military base closings that will have severe, adverse economic impact on many regions within the United States. These closings also raise questions about the strategic manpower reserve of the U.S. armed forces. Elsewhere, defense contractors must close down production facilities. What will happen to industrial surge capacity, and will research and development continue at a level that will ensure U.S. superiority in military technology? Base Force envisions a minimum level of reconstitution capacity. Will it be available when it is needed? The issues implicit in these questions are addressed by the authors of the chapters in this book. There are no definitive answers. However, creative and thoughtful analysis will provide a basis for resolving these problems.

This provocative book and the ideas advanced within it are the result of a group effort. In addition to recognizing the contributions of the authors, special thanks are due to Neal Creighton, President and Chief Executive Officer; and Richard Behrenhausen, Vice President and Chief Operating Officer of the Robert R. McCormick Tribune Foundation. Two workshop coordinators were instrumental to the success of this project. They are Colonel John Auger, of the Strategic Studies Institute at the Army War College; and Professor Sam C. Sarkesian, of Loyola University Chicago, who chairs the Academic Advisory Council of the National Strategy Forum.

Richard E. Friedman
National Strategy Forum

Preface

The post–Cold War period has ushered in a complex relationship between domestic and external affairs. Combining changes in the international arena with those occuring in American domestic politics, the security landscape has turned into a confusing and often unpredictable mosaic of conflicts, threats, humanitarian issues, human rights, refugee problems, and regional and international power projections. Complicating this landscape are the changes taking place in American demographics and public opinion about foreign involvement, conflict characteristics, and domestic priorities. Questions regarding the linkage and intermix between domestic politics and policy and national security have become clouded and undefined.

To examine these matters, a workshop in September 1992 at Cantigny, Illinois, focused on "U.S. Domestic and National Security Agendas: Into the Twenty-First Century." The workshop, conducted by the National Strategy Forum and supported by the Robert R. McCormick Tribune Foundation and the U.S. Army War College, brought together military professionals, academics, and government representatives. A series of papers were presented covering three broad areas: Domestic Issues: Shaping the National Security Agenda; The Domestic and International Security Landscapes: Contradictions and Complexities; and National Security: Into the Twenty-first Century. These papers covered subjects ranging from a study of the American economy and defense budget, arms control, and the Gulf War to the national security establishment, Total Force Policy and civil-military relations. Most of these papers have been included in this volume. In addition, the introductory chapter offers a broad landscape of the domestic and national security linkages, and the concluding chapter identifies the major themes emerging from the chapters and provides commentary about the future.

No attempt has been made by the editors to structure or reshape the papers to fit a particular theme or format. We believe that each author brings a unique perspective to the subject. This uniqueness, combined with the authors' intellectual insights, is an important dimension in examining the broader subject of domestic and national security agendas and in offering a variety of perspectives.

We also acknowledge that the scope of this book does not include all the major issues of domestic and national security agendas. It was never intended to be so comprehensive in scope that *all* major areas were examined, even if this could be done in one volume. We believe that the book offers a detailed map of the subject with important reference points that can serve as a framework for future study of the subject.

We recognize that the international system is in transition. This is also the case with U.S. strategic orientation and force structuring. All of this will surely have an impact on the intermix of domestic and national security agendas. Complicating our view of this transition is that, at this writing, it is not clear what the final shape of the Clinton Administration will be in terms of domestic politics and the American political system.

Thus, this book appears at a time when the national security landscape remains clouded and the direction and policies of the Clinton Administration are unclear and untested. Nonetheless, it is important that the debate and examination of the domestic and national security agendas begin in earnest. We believe that this volume not only can assist in the debate, but brings to bear the views of authorities on various aspects of the subject.

Finally, rather than wait for an unfolding of the strategic landscape in clearer terms, we believe that it is important to try to come to grips with the issues now, even if later developments challenge assessments made here. External events and strategic issues do not necessarily wait for the design of U.S. national security strategy. Thus, there must be some reference point or framework to set the stage for responding to the strategic landscape as it evolves. We make no apologies for this effort.

Part I

Introduction

I

The Strategic Landscape, Domestic Imperatives, and National Security

Sam C. Sarkesian

Throughout the Cold War period, American domestic and national security agendas were linked primarily by superpower issues and ideological challenges. While some areas in the domestic arena had little to do with national security, the fear of nuclear war and the continuous challenge of Marxist-Leninist ideology constantly reminded Americans of a dangerous world. The victory of the Chinese Communists, the Korean War, and Vietnam, among other events, periodically and dramatically brought national security issues into the domestic arena with a vengeance. The security landscape seemed relatively clear and predictable. The clear adversary was the Soviet Union—the Evil Empire. International politics were driven mainly by East-West issues emerging from the confrontations between the United States and the U.S.S.R.

The post–Cold War international environment, however, has dramatically changed the security landscape. As a result, the United States has entered into what is an agonizing period of reappraisal and rethinking with regard to its national security posture. All of this is complicated by the difficulty in drawing clear distinctions between domestic and national security policy. The 1992 presidential election campaign set the stage for the complexities that emerged in 1993. Not only did a new administration come to office, but in 1993 national security issues emerged from the shadows of the 1992 presidential campaign to virtually overshadow domestic issues. That election seemed to be based primarily on the American economy and domestic issues, almost precluding any serious debate on the international issues and American national security. This was the case even though one of the more compelling security issues was (and is) U.S.-Russian relationships. Many Americans also turned inward as the fear of strategic nuclear war with the Soviet Union faded with the dissolution of the Evil Empire. Indeed, some argued that military force had lost its utility; economic power was the real mover of world events. But as Somalia, Bosnia-Herzegovina, and other hot spots in the world seemed to demonstrate, economics cannot substitute for military power.

Notwithstanding the efforts of some to distance the U.S. domestic agenda from national security, even a cursory view of the changing national security landscape reveals numerous points of contact linking domestic and national security issues. These range from the redeployment of most of the U.S. military to the continental United States, the impact of the redeployment on local communities, and changing civil-military relations to global economic interdependence, linkages between drug lords and revolutionary groups, and the notion of peacetime engagements that include using the U.S. military for humanitarian assistance both at home and abroad. In 1992, some in Chicago even suggested using military forces—the National Guard—to police a high-crime housing project. Unfortunately, few if any of these notions were debated in the 1992 election campaign. After focusing on the changing domestic political arena, one author concluded, "There is a strong preference for domestic over foreign policy issues, supported in turn by voting patterns in favor of members of Congress identified with these issues."[1] But world events are not likely to allow the United States and the American people to focus solely or even primarily on the domestic environment.

Indeed, whether one focuses on the Cold War or the post–Cold War era, important domestic issues are inextricable from the national security agenda. In discussing the "features" of the evolving strategic landscape, John Chipman has written, "These features of the evolving international system fix the framework within which strategic action may or may not take place. . . . The first of these is the now obvious intermingling of domestic and international security."[2]

The purpose of this introductory chapter is to paint a picture of the landscape and draw an overlay of the critical points of contact between domestic and national security agendas. Chapters that follow examine in more detail many of these changes, focusing on the linkage between domestic and national security agendas.

A brief historical review is followed by an examination of three major areas: the military and society, the nature of conflicts, and the concept of national security. These categories are not intended to be inclusive of all points of contact between domestic and national security agendas. But they are three important categories in shaping the conceptual framework for a systematic study of domestic and national security agendas. Finally, conclusions will focus on what needs to be done to come to grips with national security in the new era and how national security and domestic agendas are linked even in an era of diminished fears of major wars.

HISTORICAL OVERVIEW

While the general outlines of the evolution of U.S. national security establishment and policy process are reasonably well known to most, it is useful to review these in order to identify major features.[3] Until World War II, national security policy was a small part of the American foreign policy establishment. Isolationism and rejection of "old world" politics drove American policy concerns and with it only a passing attention to national security issues. Indeed, the U.S. military was a small force, a reflection of the traditional American view of the fear of standing armies that is embedded in the American psyche. This was reinforced by the efforts to remain distant from Old World issues. America's security concerns were primarily shaped by interests in Latin America and to some extent by interests in selected areas in the Pacific.

As is well recognized, World War II produced a dramatic change in America's standing as a world power and in national security perspectives. The emergence of the superpower era, nuclear weaponry, the United Nations and a host of regional organizations, and a world generally divided by East-West confrontations changed the domestic and national security equation. Distinctions between domestic and national security agendas became less clear, as did distinctions between foreign and national security policy.

The Initial Period

The creation of a variety of national security institutions in the aftermath of World War II, including the National Security Council, the Central Intelligence Agency, and the Department of Defense, highlighted the changed domestic structure. "The Cold War with the Soviet Union that followed World War II firmly entrenched the national security state."[4] At the same time, the federal budget and resources devoted to nonmilitary programs had to be weighed against the needs of the defense budget, the maintenance of a larger military establishment, and research and development of sophisticated weaponry. With the emergence of a military industrial complex, due to its close connection with the domestic economy, employment and economic growth became characteristic of the period. Reinforcing this linkage between national security and domestic agendas was the perception by many Americans of the Soviet Union as a distinct threat, both militarily and ideologically.

The linkage could be seen also in domestic social and racial matters and the U.S. military. The Executive Order signed by President Truman ending segregation in the military in 1948 had a major impact in shaping a major national security instrument in response to domestic racial issues. Moreover, the reinstatement of the selective service after a short break immediately following World War II created a bridge between society and the military. The integration of the military and the selective service system, combined with a large number of World War II veterans in the population, provided an overarching context within which society, the military, domestic issues, and national security issues overlapped and intermingled.

Containment and Beyond

Americans were further drawn into national security issues with the containment policy. Triggered by fears of Soviet expansionism, the United States put into place a policy to preclude further expansion by the Soviet Union. The victory of the Chinese Communists heightened the concern over U.S. national interests and American security. A line was drawn around the Soviet Union and its satellites. Soviet adventures beyond this line were perceived as a direct threat to U.S. national interests. The Truman Doctrine, the North Atlantic Treaty Organization (NATO), the Southeast Asia Treaty Organization (SEATO), and a variety of other treaties and alliances were put into place to give substance to the containment policy. In addition, the United States embarked on a policy of deterrence, establishing a credible nuclear system to deter the Soviet Union from contemplating use of such weapons. Deterrence also included strengthening U.S. conventional forces in Europe to preclude use of Soviet forces in the European arena. The United States also worked through the newly created United Nations to respond to Soviet policies.

The Truman Administration expended much effort in educating the American people on the Soviet threat. National security became a legitimized call for support of a particular security or defense policy. Bipartisan foreign and national security policy was the clarion call for many in Congress. Following the Korean War, some distance appeared between domestic matters and national security with the relative comfort of the Eisenhower presidency. This was dispelled as McCarthyism, with its rampant anti-Communism, took on a circuslike spectacle on television. Nonetheless, the McCarthy period brought Americans face-to-face with the Soviet threat and Soviet efforts at subverting the United States, regardless of whether the threat was real or imagined.

The Kennedy Administration, while focusing on civil rights and the domestic agenda, became entangled in the Bay of Pigs, the Cuban Missile Crisis, and the Berlin Crisis, making it difficult to draw clear distinctions between domestic concerns and the external environment. Following the assassination of President Kennedy, President Lyndon Johnson initially was able to focus on domestic concerns, successfully pushing civil rights and welfare legislation through Congress.

President Johnson's Great Society program began on a note of high optimism with regard to reducing poverty in America and creating a just society; however, it became entangled in a major national security matter—the Vietnam War. The war forged an even closer relationship between domestic political, social, and economic matters and national security. The costs of the war in men and material combined with serious questions of morality divided the United States into warring groups and factions. The media's portrayal of the war and all its horrors had a major role in shaping domestic attitudes and caused the war issue to engulf virtually every domestic concern.[5] President Johnson's efforts to separate the Great Society from the war were to no avail. The war and American society virtually became one. In the end, President Johnson declined to be a candidate for a second term of office, in the main, as a consequence of the domestic impact of the Vietnam War.

Vietnam and Its Aftermath

The U.S. withdrawal from Vietnam and the signing of peace accords during the Nixon Administration set the stage for the defeat and the occupation of South Vietnam by the North Vietnamese and Viet Cong. America's withdrawal from Vietnam led to a quick return to the European landscape and the refocusing of the U.S. military accordingly.

With the burden of Vietnam lifted, regardless of what this did to the South Vietnamese allies, the notion of national security became more acceptable, and for many Americans, became a more comfortable perspective. The refocusing on the Soviet Union and Europe was a more predictable and orderly affair—a return to the American norm.

Yet the instruments of the national security establishment, including the military, seemed to languish under the Carter Administration. The notion of human rights that was part of the first years of the Carter Administration shaped national security as well as foreign policy, with mixed results. At the same time, the U.S. military's capability, now based on a volunteer system, eroded to a point where the then Chief of Staff of the U.S. Army called it a "hollow army." In the last year of the Carter presidency, policies were adopted to restore military effectiveness.

The Reagan Administration embarked on a policy aimed at increasing military strength, and with it came a reinvigorated national security effort. Most of this was aimed at the Soviet Union as the "Evil Empire." In the process, the military was seen as the mainstay of the national security effort. Survival of the American homeland and its way of life constantly linked domestic issues to the external world.

The national security strategy that was devised in the half-decade after World War II was simple and straightforward . . . defense of the U.S. homeland by deterrence of direct attack, and forward defense with allies against indirect attacks that could lead to defeat of the homeland over the long term. Although the details of our national security strategy have varied we have followed its basic outlines to this day.[6]

All of this began to change as President Ronald Reagan and Soviet President Mikhail Gorbachev found common ground. *Glasnost* and *perestroika* replaced the dogmatic Marxist-Leninist ideology—at least publicly—and the roots of Soviet dissolution were put into place.

To be sure, the linkage between domestic and national security agendas did not necessarily encompass all major areas of the domestic environment. Some matters had little, if any, relationship with national security issues. These had to do with bread-and-butter issues such as jobs and poverty. Such distinctions were put into an institutional format by one scholar who suggested two presidencies, one for foreign affairs and one for domestic affairs.[7] Nonetheless, the melding of domestic and national security issues was consistent throughout the Cold War period, even if at times it was obscured and latent.

In sum, from World War II until the dissolution of the Soviet Union, American national security and domestic agendas had clear points of contact and interaction. Moreover, separating the objectives of foreign policy from national security was difficult. The policies of containment and deterrence and East-West ideological confrontation provided the bridge between national security and domestic issues. The Communist victory in China, the Korean War, the Cuban Missile Crisis, Vietnam, a number of revolutions and unconventional conflicts, American covert operations, and a variety of peacekeeping efforts—all were shaped by the superpower confrontation and East-West ideological concepts, and all reached into the domestic arena with varying degrees of intensity.

The Post–Cold War Era

The last years of the Bush Administration coincided with the end of the Cold War, which ushered in a new world order and a changed strategic landscape. The Gorbachev-Yeltsin impact in the 1990s, the dissolution of the Soviet Union, and the unification of Germany marked the end of the Cold War and the superpower world. And with this development, the strategic map was redrawn, marked by the rise of domestic issues seemingly separate from external matters. Yet serious security issues surfaced in 1993, issues that intertwined domestic and national security agendas, albeit in a way different from that in the past. The rise of a new world order did not necessarily lead to a more peaceful world, but it did shift the focus of national security and raise questions about the relevancy of the Cold War national security establishment. Equally important, Americans turned inward, now that the possibility of major wars had diminished considerably.

For a number of Americans, economic power gained prominence as a major component of national security, while the use of the military seemed to be relegated to a distinctly secondary position. At the same time, the *National Military Strategy of the United States* planned a restructuring of the posture and orientation of U.S. military forces.[8] The overall impact of these developments and perspectives, combined with the focus of many Americans on domestic issues, suggested a clearer distinction between domestic and national security agendas. Although the changed world environment and the notion of a new world order had, on the one hand, reduced the fear of major wars, on the other hand, the changes seemed to unleash a variety of lesser conflicts. The new order also engendered movement towards regional trading organizations and regional power clusters. With this emerged an increasing recognition of the economic interdependence of the global system, and the concept of what some called the "global village."

This period also exhibited the beginnings of an economic transition in the United States into a high-tech information age combined with a restructuring of financial institutions and a shift of occupational roles to suit a more technical and computer-oriented workplace. The same forces drove the military into what one authority calls the "Third Wave." Frederic Brown writes,

For now, think of war as a combination of . . . three "waves"—primitive, industrial, and knowledge based. . . . Change accelerates in military requirements for national security, competing domestic needs, and the nature of war itself—Third Wave war. These are the "megatrends" that provide the backdrop for the future.[9]

In this new age, the interaction and linkage between domestic and national security agendas is complex and pervasive.

Conclusions

The conclusions from this overview can be summed up with four propositions. First, "In practice . . . national security policy in the 1970s and 1980s came to mean *foreign* policy in general and *military* policy in particular. Rarely, if ever, were domestic economic challenges seriously considered to be a significant part of the national security agenda."[10] Yet, always there were linkages.

Second, "national security has always been understood as having both external and domestic components, but these components have sometimes been seen as complementary, sometimes in competition with one another."[11]

Third, "as the United States identified its security with the security of other states, the American conception of security broadened to include the traditional interests of those states."[12]

Fourth, regardless of the periodic gaps between domestic and national security agendas that occurred during the past forty-five years, intimate points of contact between and intermingling of domestic and national security agendas existed.

The decade of the 1990s promises to usher in a new relationship between domestic and national security agendas. Yet a number of patterns from the Cold War continue, intermingled with a number of new issues. Such continuities are likely to be placed in a secondary position, however; containment policy is obsolete and fears of nuclear war have diminished considerably. While deterrence remains an important policy, its focus has dissipated as a number of threats have become global in scope and emanate from a variety of sources. The new strategic landscape does not appear to be seriously threatening to American national interests. Moreover, for many, the economic component became critical in national security. This easily translated into giving first priority to strengthening America's economic system and concern with the domestic arena.

But as David Jablonsky concludes, "Resultant tensions in national security affairs between domestic and foreign policies complicate the formulation of U.S. national strategy and pose severe problems for the American military establishment."[13]

These observations lead to four strategic guidelines as a framework for national security. *First*, national security policy has taken on a broader concept that envisions the use of a variety of instruments, with the military as a last resort, but often as the primary instrument in noncombat missions. *Second*, regional power clusters and international organizations have become major features of the new landscape, reflecting political and economic changes in the world environment. *Third*, changing notions of sovereignty and internal changes within a variety of states are likely to continue into the foreseeable future. *Fourth*, there is a visible intermingling and often a clash of strategic cultures. Thus, European-oriented scenarios based on Judeo-Christian perspectives may not necessarily be an appropriate overlay to conflicts outside of the European landscape.[14]

MILITARY AND SOCIETY

These political-military and strategic difficulties in dealing with the new strategic landscape are compounded by the changing relationship between the military and society. This relationship has two dimensions: the shape of the military with respect to the political-social expectations of society, and the role of the military in the political process or, more pointedly, civil-military relations. While these two dimensions are separate, they are closely related, and each is affected by the other.

Democratization?

In studying the linkage between the military and political-social expectations of society, the primary question is, To what degree does the military reflect society, or to what degree should the military reflect society? For some, this is seen as the degree of "democratization" of the military. More specifically, the military is struggling with establishing policies regarding homosexuals and the role of women in the military and trying to deal with the impact of demographic changes on the military system. Present minorities will, taken together, become a majority in the first decade of the new century, raising serious questions concerning multiculturalism. In turn, these concerns trigger a number of other issues, such as fairness of the military justice system, sexual harassment, and equality in career opportunities.

The most difficult domestic issue for the military is the nature of its response to "democratization." The storm of military outrage precipitated by the efforts of President Clinton immediately upon taking office to lift the ban on gays in the military underscored the divisiveness of such issues and signalled the difficult social issues facing the military. Earlier incidents such as the Tailhook Affair and debates over the role of women in the military reinforced what some in society saw as the need for the military to reform.[15]

Changing American demographics also linked domestic environment with instruments of national security. This not only had to do with military-age youth and qualifications for military service, but also with the changing face of America. The shift to a majority made up of minorities in the next century may also cause a reshaping of the Judeo-Christian heritage and the Anglo-Saxon orientation, as new interpretations of these legacies and heritage take hold in American society.

The concern about the impact of the changing face of America on the U.S. military is well expressed by one military author, who writes, "The societal trends indicate a fundamental change in national values. The country's primary value-influencing institutions are promoting altered values for future recruits. These altered values are significantly different than the Army's values."[16]

Over the course of the next several years, the U.S. military will need to reconcile its primary mission with the social developments spilling over from American society. Considering the political-social issues linking American society and the military combined with the need for strategic reorientation, new operational doctrines, and force restructuring, the military profession faces a difficult task in the immediate future in reshaping the military and strategic posture.

Civil-Military Relations

Another dimension of the relationship between military and society is civil-military relations. These relations produce a close link between the military and domestic politics. In turn, the education of military professionals and the resulting political-military posture are important components of civil-military relationships. Also, the military's response to social pressures affects the military's political role and its relationship with elected officials.

Military professionals historically have been suspicious of political leaders. For any number of military professionals, for example, the role of President Johnson and other officials in the conduct of the Vietnam War seemed to confirm their negative perceptions of politics and political leaders. The attempt to micromanage the war from the Oval Office and the contradictory political signals and confusing command structure did little to bolster the military professionals' view of the political leadership.

Looking back at Vietnam, General Norman Schwarzkopf, commander of coalition forces in the Gulf War, who served two tours of duty in Vietnam, wrote, "We in the military hadn't chosen the enemy or written the order— our elected leaders had. Nevertheless, we were taking much of the blame. . . . I couldn't shake the feeling that America had betrayed the South Vietnamese."[17]

Even though there are many who wish to put Vietnam behind us, the fact is that it is embedded in the American psyche and in military history. Almost twenty years after the war, the victory in the 1991 Gulf War was partly due to the fact that it was not Vietnam. This was made clear by General Schwarzkopf. The war was controlled from his headquarters in Saudi Arabia, not from the Oval Office.

But while the reality of Vietnam may recede in the background, the Vietnam Memorial will be a constant reminder to every generation of Americans. This memorial in Washington has become as visible and important as the Tomb of the Unknown Soldier. Moreover, because of the divisive nature of the war and the withdrawal of the United States from Vietnam, leaving its ally to face the enemy with little material backing from the United States, this war is likely to remain an enduring memory in the American military system.

The military professionals' bitterness about politics and political leaders in the Vietnam War was dissipated to a degree by President Reagan's labeling the U.S. involvement as a "noble cause." This was reinforced by the American success in the aftermath of the 1991 Gulf War. Indeed, the decade of the 1980s restored confidence within the military and created a degree of military confidence among the political leadership. In sum, in the 1980s and through the end of the Gulf War, civil-military relations were based on a relatively comfortable relationship between the military and society based on a strong degree of mutual trust.

The New Era

In the post–Cold War era, however, the civil-military equation is changing, partly as a consequence of the planned redeployment of most of the U.S. military to the continental United States and the sharp reduction of forces. This is further complicated by the view that the utility of military force has diminished in the national security arena, along with the belief that economic power has increasing importance. The Clinton Administration developed plans to reduce the military even further than that planned by the previous administration.[18]

At the same time, for any number of Americans the Clinton Administration represents a new generation of "baby boomers." Some in this generation reacted against the Vietnam War, and the activities of Bill Clinton during the latter part of the war, including his avoidance of military service and his participation in antiwar demonstrations, are illustrative of that reaction. Further, a new generation of elected officials will soon be the rule rather than the exception—a generation of the post–Vietnam era, few of whom may have had any military service and whose claim of leadership includes breaking from the "old" generation. This phenomenon has spilled over into the public realm already, creating a disconnect between the military and the Clinton Administration.[19]

A new generation of military leaders is also in the process of emerging. The Vietnam generation will soon have passed. This new military generation reflects the experience in the Gulf War and a variety of peacetime engagements, such as the mission in Somalia and hurricane assistance (for example, in the case of Hurricane Andrew in Florida). Equally important, this generation has been pushed more closely to social issues emanating from society, forcing a rethinking of the degree to which the military should reflect society and still maintain its combat effectiveness. Combined with the dynamics of domestic social issues, civil-military relations are likely to evolve into an equation reflecting the "fog of peace."

Organization: Command and Control

Changes in the Department of Defense structure, including the military command system, were being put into place in 1993. One of the first changes was instituted by Secretary of Defense Les Aspin, who began restructuring the department in early 1993. Among other positions, an Assistant Secretary of Defense for Democracy and Human Rights and an Assistant Secretary of Defense for Arms Proliferation have been established.[20] These changes seem to move in a political-diplomatic direction, prompting some to perceive a mini–Department of State emerging in the Department of Defense. It also appears that the Assistant Secretary of Defense for Special Operations and Low Intensity Conflict was deemphasized, based on Secretary Aspin's view that the post was a leftover from the Cold War, even though some argue that it was an innovative structure intended to last well beyond the Cold War. Also, General Colin Powell, then Chairman of the Joint Chiefs of Staff, announced a plan for consolidating some military activities, while avoiding more drastic restructuring within the military.[21] These plans included changing the Unified and Specified Commands and emphasizing joint systems. The Total Force policy—including the roles and missions of the Federal Reserves and the National Guard—is also undergoing change. Part of this is a result of the experience in the Gulf War and part is a consequence of the reduction of the U.S. military.

In 1993, however, it was not clear where these changes would lead or whether they would be the final changes. Congressional reaction to these changes has not crystallized. Moreover, assuming these changes are institutionalized, it is not clear whether the new structures will be able to respond more readily to issues of national security. Yet the reduction of military forces and the restructuring of the Department of Defense have clear implications for and linkages with the domestic environment.

NATURE OF CONFLICTS

The changed strategic landscape and the diminishing prospect of major wars between major powers has shifted attention to a variety of lesser wars and unconventional conflicts. While concerns remain regarding the final shape of Russia and the possibility of major conflict within the former Soviet Union, a great deal of attention is now turned to a variety of ethnic, religious, and nationalistic conflicts, such as those in the former Yugoslavia, and peacekeeping operations, such as that in Somalia. At the higher end of the conflict spectrum, the 1991 Gulf War represented a form of European scenario providing certain guidelines for the future.[22]

For the United States, the diminishing prospects of major wars pose a number of political-military problems. Plans are in progress to restructure the military to a more broadly based threat capability. In addition, the notion of peacetime engagements presumes a variety of capabilities covering four major categories: strategic deterrence, forward presence, crisis response, and reconstitution.[23] An important part of these plans is based on certain presumptions regarding the nature and character of future conflicts.

Much of the strategic orientation evolving from these considerations has to do with responding to lesser wars—operations short of war and unconventional conflicts, which are likely to characterize the conflict environment for the remainder of this decade and beyond. Such conflicts have characteristics that differ from conventional conflict patterns associated with a European scenario or the conflict pattern of the Gulf War. These range from unconventional conflicts such as revolution and counterrevolution to what have been called wars of conscience, such as the conflict that drew U.S. involvement in Somalia in 1992. Complicating the conflict landscape are conflicts associated with coalitions of drug cartels and revolutionary groups such as the Shining Path and drug cartel linkage in Peru.

The conflict environment makes it difficult to clearly identify adversaries and even more difficult to spell out political-military objectives. Indeed, in the aftermath of the Gulf War, some criticized the operation because it did not finish the job of deposing Saddam Hussein of Iraq, although this was clearly not the assigned mission. In any case, the likely conflict characteristics make developing the necessary support of the American people for military operations difficult. This is particularly true with respect to sustained, long-term operations. Low-visibility military operations may succeed for a time, but many see the use of military force as a blunt instrument not particularly relevant to the political-military problems likely to face the United States in the immediate future.

Placed in the context of changing U.S. demographics and a changing concept of national security, the conflict environment is becoming isolated from pressing U.S. concerns. To be sure, the potential for conflicts remains, particularly in the Middle East. But this has long been part of the conflict mosaic. During the Cold War period, such conflicts were particularly threatening because of the fear of Soviet involvement. Considering the ambiguous strategic landscape, in addition to the reduction of the U.S. military and the concern over deficits and economic issues in the United States, one can understand the resurfacing of the Weinberger Doctrine.[24]

This doctrine, spelled out by Secretary of Defense Caspar Weinberger in 1984, identified six criteria for committing U.S. armed forces.[25] In brief, these included the following:

1. The issue must be of vital interest to the United States.

2. U.S. combat troops should be committed wholeheartedly, with the intention of winning.

3. There must be clearly defined political and military objectives.

4. Relationships between forces and objectives must be continually reassessed and adjusted.

5. There must be reasonable assurance that U.S. involvement will have the support of the American people and Congress.

6. Commitment of U.S. forces should be a last resort.

What emerges from this is the inclination for some to advocate the use of alternate instruments and selective options to respond to and resolve conflicts or potential conflicts. While such alternatives and options have been historically available, they have been given increasing prominence in the post–Cold War era. The options include selective engagement, honest broker, and soft power, as spelled out by Zbigniew Bzrezinski, Paul Nitze, and Joseph Nye, respectively.[26] A close examination of these concepts leads one to conclude that they are sophisticated arguments rooted in the Weinberger Doctrine. These concepts make a distinction between the national security agenda and domestic issues by trying to clearly mark areas beyond U.S. concerns. At the same time, domestic and national security arenas are linked by basing external military efforts on support emanating from the domestic arena.

In the final analysis, conflicts in the new strategic landscape are likely to be less than major and less threatening to United States national interests (at least in the short run), and they are likely to fall into the full range of unconventional conflicts and a variety of peacekeeping missions—that is, peacekeeping, peacemaking, and peace enforcement. Humanitarian missions seem to be the latest popular view; examples are the military's role in Hurricane Andrew in Florida and the initial effort in Somalia. It has been demonstrated that the military can effectively perform humanitarian missions and a variety of other missions under the label "peacetime engagements."[27]

At this point in time, however, the capability and effectiveness of the military to respond to unconventional conflict, including the drug cartel–revolutionary coalition, remain questionable.

It is not clear that the American public, in general, and elected officials, in particular, fully understand the range of conflicts, their characteristics, and their impact on American domestic politics. As suggested by one analyst, the propensity for the new interventionism seems to focus on wars of conscience and missionary zeal. "The new interventionism has its roots in long-standing tendencies of American foreign policy—missionary zeal, bewilderment when the world refuses to conform to American expectations and a belief that for every problem there is a quick and easy solution."[28] Following such perspectives, involvement in military operations can easily lead to open-ended embroilment in an unconventional conflict environment, with all that this portends with respect to domestic political reaction and political-military complications.

NATIONAL SECURITY AS A CONCEPT

In the Cold War period, national security generally encompassed the following: the survival of the United States as a free and independent nation, with its fundamental values intact and its institutions and people secure; the promotion of the American way of life; the protection and growth of America's economic system; and a stable and secure world, where political and economic freedom, human rights, and democratic institutions flourish.[29]

While these have existed throughout the Cold War as the major national security interests and objectives, how these were interpreted and translated into specific policies and strategies varied depending on the state of international politics and the strategic landscape in any given period. For the greater part of the past fifty years, the primary focus of all of these interests and objectives was on the threat posed by the Soviet Union and the East-West ideological cleavage. And as S. J. Deitchman notes, "Throughout this period our primary national security concern was essentially military. Even our economic aid had military oriented overtones."[30] With the new world order, however, the interpretation and translation of these interests and objectives need to be redefined. In brief, national security in the post–Cold War period requires a different conceptualization.

As David Hendrickson writes, "We have reached a peculiar stage in the debate over American foreign policy. The customary antinomies that have long played a central role in America's self understanding . . . no longer seem an adequate guide to current circumstances."[31]

If this is the case, what then can be developed as an adequate guide in implementing U.S. national interests? Hendrickson states,

It is hard to speak, for instance, of the relative primacy of foreign and domestic policy without noting the immediate qualification that many domestic problems (such as economic competitiveness, financial indebtedness, environmental degradation, or migratory pressures stemming from explosive population growth in poor countries) have a vital international component. It seems obvious that solutions must be found for these problems on both the domestic and the foreign level, or they will not be found at all.[32]

This concept raises a host of questions, beginning with delineations between domestic and national security policy. If one accepts the view that the major issues of domestic policy cannot be separated from national security policy, then one is faced with the prospect that virtually all major issues of domestic policy can be easily translated into national security policy. Critics of such a perspective, however, argue that important distinctions must be made between domestic and national security policy. After all, they would argue, did not the American people elect Bill Clinton primarily on the promise of a better domestic economy? Foreign policy and national security were hardly issues in the 1992 presidential campaign.

As suggested earlier, the shape of the new world order is still unclear, but important signs indicate a changing political dimension, reshaping the notion of national security. The Gulf War seemed to establish a principle that aggression against another state's territorial integrity is a challenge to the entire world community, and therefore any state involved in such transgressions would face the wrath of the world community. A coalition of states would react to any such aggression. How effectively this principle will be followed in the future, however, remains to be seen.

In addition, a principle is emerging supporting humanitarian intervention based on the proposition that states unwilling or incapable of providing for their own people have given up absolute sovereignty. Accordingly, it is the duty of the international community to intervene in order to help the people in that particular state. "Sovereignty would no longer reside with states but with the people within them; self-determination would no longer refer to peoples, but to individuals."[33] Somalia is a case in point. In such circumstances, the United Nations takes on a particularly prominent role, even if it has yet to demonstrate its capability to quickly respond to international crises, presumed crises, or humanitarian issues.

Moreover, from the U.S. perspective, the various alliances and treaties established during the Cold War period now seem obsolete, at least in their original intent and substance. Further, a new set of relationships is developing with former adversaries, including Vietnam. Others point to the need to prepare a new policy with respect to Cuba. Equally important, the Pacific Basin is developing into an area for potential power projection and conflict as China and Japan vie for advantage in the area.

Traditional concepts of national security, along with the national security establishment created at the beginning of the Cold War, need to be revised to gain some relevancy in the new environment. This has led to at least two schools that advocate particular national security perspectives. First, the global village and interdependence school perceives national security as encompassing a number of nonmilitary issues, from the environment, demographics, and economics to humanitarian concerns. At the same time, these components are closely linked with major domestic policy issues and concerns of the American people. Those in this school tend to diminish the role of the military in carrying out national security policy, arguing that military force cannot effectively respond to the national security landscape that has changed so dramatically as a result of the end of the Cold War. Their view does not rule out the use of military force, but the military is conceived more as a peacekeeping and humanitarian force.

These arguments are summed up by Nye, who writes,

Traditionally, the test of a major power was its strength in war. Today the definition of power is losing its emphasis on military force. The factors of technology, education, and economic growth are becoming more significant in international power.... National security has become more complicated as threats shift from the military to the economic.[34]

Second, another school argues that the world remains a dangerous place. Those in this school point to a variety of conflicts in the world. While these do not necessarily threaten U.S. security in the short term, some may in the long term. Moreover, the argument proceeds, in light of weapons proliferation, the existence of stockpiles of strategic and tactical nuclear weapons, and the emergence of major powers in the Pacific as well as efforts by such countries as North Korea and Iran to become major regional powers, U.S. national security cannot simply disregard military capability in the name of budgetary considerations and humanitarian impulses. Those in this school also point out that the U.S. military has already taken significant budgetary cuts, plans are well on the way to reduce manpower and weaponry, and the Clinton Administration proposes even deeper cuts. And, the argument notes, nondefense spending in the United States continues to rise.

Both schools recognize that the strategic landscape has changed and that adjustments must be made. While the former stresses the nonmilitary components of national security, the latter cautions against precipitous cuts in the military and quick-fix solutions. In this context, a middle area which has yet to design a particular strategic posture may exist. Characterized by caution and pragmatism and trying to come to grips with national security and its points of contact with the domestic agenda, this middle area may well include many policymakers in both military and civilian circles. The hesitancy associated with this middle range reflects the uncertainty of the strategic landscape and how U.S. security interests are to be interpreted in specific policy objectives. Such uncertainty leads to attempts to delineate domestic and national security agendas more distinctly than in the past, as one step in trying to clarify the direction of U.S. national security.[35]

In any case, contrary to the inward perspective so clearly demonstrated during the 1992 presidential election campaign and in the early predilections of the Clinton Administration to give priority to domestic issues, the fact is that national security matters and the external landscape are not necessarily susceptible to the preferences of U.S. policymakers. Recognition of the intricate and intimate way in which domestic and national security agendas and policies are interrelated is also important.

In sum, national security encompasses components that range from economics and demographics to military force. At the same time, domestic politics and popular attitudes prefer to make clear delineations between domestic issues and national security, and this tendency is reinforced by the notion that major wars and real threats to the United States have diminished considerably. Further, changes within the Department of Defense and the national security establishment in general seem to reflect a more political-diplomatic perspective. Also, issues such as the international environment and ecology have become an increasingly important part of the total security equation, broadening the notion of national security beyond war and peace issues. In turn, nonmilitary instruments have become more favored in national security policy. The danger is that the placing of the military in a distinctly secondary posture may put the United States in a disadvantageous position in trying to deal with a variety of conflicts. This is particularly the case in so-called come-as-you-are wars. Thus, on the one hand, the United States cannot function as a "globo-cop," but on the other hand, it cannot withdraw into isolationism. The international political-military arena and global interdependence preclude such clear policy postures.

But the real issue has to do with the concept of national security and its translation into national security policy.

As James Schlesinger has written, "Our *permanent interests* are less clearly defined and more difficult to discern. In these radically changed and far more fluid conditions can the United States 'perservere in a fixed design' or 'await . . . consequences with patience'?"[36]

In the new strategic landscape, the concept of national security has taken on a paradoxical aspect. It encompasses everything from economics, the environment, and humanitarian considerations to concern over weapons proliferation and a variety of military operations short of war. But the focus of the Clinton Administration and many Americans is on the domestic arena, particularly on social and economic agendas. Thus, the scope of national security encompasses many important aspects of the domestic agenda. Yet, perceptions and attitudes try to clearly delineate between domestic and national security issues. In any case, one cannot deal with the domestic agenda without continual reference to defense spending and the national security landscape.

Regardless of whether one adopts the views of one or the other school, the fact is that the new world order has expanded issues of economic well-being, political survival, and security beyond any one nation-state. This is reinforced by the fact that the contemplated use of military force has expanded to cover a variety of operations other than war, linking the military instrument to a variety of domestic concerns that overlap into the external environment and national security. And to repeat Hendrickson, "It is hard to speak . . . of the relative primacy of foreign and domestic policy without noting the immediate qualification that many domestic problems . . . have a vital international component."[37]

CONCLUSIONS

The concept of national security and its operational guidelines have yet to be defined. While the fear of major wars reminiscent of the Cold War era has disappeared, it does not follow that America can rest easy by focusing primarily on domestic issues bereft of national security considerations. Indeed, both the global interdependence and fragmented world order perspectives cannot separate major domestic issues from national security. The broader concept of national security that encompasses, for example, economic and environmental factors, makes domestic and national security agendas inextricable. Due in part to an expanded role of the military in a variety of contingencies from war to operations short of war—socially relevant contingencies—the intimate and intricate linkage between domestic and national security agendas is likely to be strengthened, regardless of political rhetoric and popular perceptions to the contrary.

While it would seem that the best approach is to wait until clear directions evolve from the strategic landscape and from both national security and domestic agendas, the United States may not have the luxury of waiting for a better time. In such circumstances, changes within the national security establishment and its agenda and efforts to define critical components of national security must proceed with extreme caution amidst attempts to broaden the domestic agenda.

The United States cannot take on the role of "globo-cop." Not only does it have limited resources to undertake such a role, but such a policy is not likely to succeed in the emerging multipower world. But, the United States cannot retreat into isolationism or neo-isolationism, distancing itself from the political-military issues emerging in the new world order. Cautious pragmatism and selective engagement should be the basis of national strategy. But this requires that such options be clearly understood by the American public and its elected officials, and that these options be linked to American domestic well-being. In brief, successful American national security cannot be divorced from its relationship with the domestic agenda and the American people.

Distinctions exist between domestic and national security agendas in several important areas, such as job opportunities, education, and health issues.

But even in such instances, linkages remain between domestic and national security agendas. Without such distinctions, however, it is easy to argue that every domestic issue is also a national security issue. The policy and political turmoil emerging from such a concept will surely diffuse and denigrate national security policy to a meaningless exercise.

In this period of transition, it is clear that efforts must be undertaken by the military and national security establishment as well as by political leaders to develop and sustain a degree of awareness and sensitivity of the American people to the continuing dangers in the external world, to the reality that the end of the Cold War did not necessarily bring peace. Indeed, the "fog of peace" seems to have made it more difficult to design a strategic vision that clarifies U.S. national interests in the new world order. And in such circumstances it is important that the notion of national security not be so separated from domestic concerns that it becomes isolated along with the military instrument. Without such efforts, national will, political resolve, and staying power may be lacking in meeting serious threats that may emerge in the future. Without such efforts, sometime in the future the United States may be faced with a serious security threat that triggers a precipitous response and an open-ended commitment that leads to, yes, another Vietnam.

NOTES

1. David Jablonsky, *Why Is Strategy Difficult?* (Carlisle Barracks, PA: Strategic Studies Institute, June 1, 1992), p. 52.

2. John Chipman, "The Future of Strategic Studies," *Survival: The IISS Quarterly*, 34, no. 1 (Spring 1992), p. 112.

3. For a more detailed review see S. J. Deitchman, *Beyond the Thaw: A New National Strategy* (Boulder, CO: Westview Press, 1991), pp. 11–22.

4. "National (in) Security," *Courier* (The Stanley Foundation), no. 12 (Winter 1993), p. 9.

5. See Peter Braestrup, *Big Story: How the American Press and Television Reported and Interpreted the Crisis of Tet 1968 in Vietnam and Washington* (Boulder, CO: Westview Press, 1977).

6. Deitchman, p. 41.

7. Aaron Wildavsky, "The Two Presidencies," *Trans-Action*, no. 4 (December 1966), pp. 7–14.

8. *National Military Strategy of the United States* (Washington, DC: Government Printing Office, January 1992).

9. Lt. Gen. Frederic J. Brown, USA (Ret.), *The U.S. Army in Transition II: Landpower in the Information Age* (Washington, DC: Brassey's [U.S.], 1993), p. 7. See also General Gordon R. Sullivan and Lieutenant Colonel James Dubik, *Land Warfare in the 21st Century* (Carlisle Barracks, PA: Strategic Studies Institute, February 1993).

10. Peter G. Peterson with James K. Sebenius, "The Primacy of the Domestic Agenda," in Graham Allison and Gregory Treverton, eds., *Rethinking America's Security: Beyond Cold War to New World Order* (New York: Norton, 1992), p. 58.

11. Ernest R. May, "National Security in American History," in Allison and Treverton, p. 104.

12. May, p. 105.

13. Jablonsky, p. 52.

14. See Adda B. Bozeman, *Strategic Intelligence and Statecraft* (Washington, DC: Brassey's [U.S.], 1992).

15. See, for example, U.S. House of Representatives, Committee on Armed Services, *Women in the Military: The Tailhook Affair and the Problem of Sexual Harassment* (Washington, DC: U.S. House of Representatives, September 1992).

16. Lieutenant Colonel Robert L. Maginnis, "A Chasm of Values," in *Military Review*, 68, no. 2 (February 1993), p. 11.

17. General H. Norman Schwarzkopf with Peter Petre, *The Autobiography: It Doesn't Take a Hero* (New York: Linda Grey/Bantam Books, 1992), pp. 181 and 201. See also pp. 186–187.

18. See *FY 1994 Defense Budget Begins New Era* (News Release) (Washington, DC: Office of the Assistant Secretary of Defense [Public Relations], March 1993). See also Jim Tice, "Drawdown Accelerates," *Army Times*, April 12, 1993, p. 4.

19. See for example, "Clinton's Warrior Woes; Can a Man Who Avoided the Draft Ever Prove Himself as America's Commander in Chief?" *U.S. News & World Report*, March 15, 1993, pp. 22–24.

20. Michael R. Gordon, "Aspin Overhauls Pentagon to Bolster Policy Role," *The New York Times*, January 28, 1993, p. A17.

21. See, for example, William Matthews, "Powell Reports on Service Roles and Missions," *Army Times*, February 22, 1992, p. 4.

22. See, for example, Douglas W. Craft, *An Operational Analysis of the Persian Gulf War* (Carlisle Barracks, PA: Strategic Studies Institute, August 31, 1992).

23. See *National Military Strategy of the United States*.

24. For an examination of this doctrine see Alan Ned Sabrosky and Robert L. Sloane, eds., *The Recourse to War: An Analysis of the "Weinberger Doctrine"* (Carlisle Barracks, PA: Strategic Studies Institute, 1988).

25. Ibid, pp. 11–13.

26. Zbigniew Brzezinski, "Selective Global Commitment," *Foreign Affairs*, 70, no. 4 (Fall 1991), pp. 1–20; Paul H. Nitze, "America: An Honest Broker," *Foreign Affairs*, 69, no. 4 (Fall 1990), pp. 1–14; and Joseph S. Nye, Jr., "Soft Power," *Foreign Policy*, 80 (Fall 1990), pp. 151–171.

27. See President George Bush, "Reshaping Our Forces" (Speech delivered at the Aspen Institute, Aspen, Colorado, August 2, 1990). For a useful study, see Brian J. Ohlinger, *Peacetime Engagement: A Search for Relevance?* (Carlisle Barracks, PA: Strategic Studies Institute, October 15, 1992).

28. Stephen John Stedman, "The New Interventionists," *Foreign Affairs* (*America and the World 92/93*), 72, no. 1 (1993), p. 4.

29. For a more detailed elaboration of U.S. national interests see, for example, The White House, *National Security Strategy of the United States* (Washington, DC: Government Printing Office, January 1993).

30. Deitchman, p. 5.

31. David C. Hendrickson, "The End of American History: American Security, the National Purpose, and the New World Order," in Allison and Treverton, p. 403.

32. Ibid.

33. Stedman, p. 4.

34. Nye, pp. 155 and 157.

35. See Nye.

36. James Schlesinger, "Quest for a Post–Cold War Foreign Policy," *Foreign Affairs* (*America and the World* 92/93), 72, no. 1 (1993), p. 28.

37. Hendrickson, p. 403.

Part II

Domestic Issues: Shaping the National Security Agenda

2

War without Killing

Harvey M. Sapolsky

Americans do not want to die. By itself, this is not an especially distinguishing characteristic, but nearly alone among the peoples of the world, Americans are both rich enough and arrogant enough to try to do a lot about this very common desire. In attempting to avoid death by disease, war, and accident, Americans spend vastly more on medical care, the military, and risk reduction than do most other people. Our often professed religiosity notwithstanding, we seem distressed by the inevitability of dying.

We are becoming even more peculiar. Increasingly, we want our wars to be without killing of any sort. That we would not want Americans—civilian or military—killed in war is to be expected. There is nothing especially new or unusual here except perhaps how adamant we are about this. That we wish to avoid killing noncombatants, including enemy civilians, is also not unique, although the lengths to which we expect our military to go to ensure that noncombatants are not harmed surely is. But what are quite strange and new, as witnessed in our latest wars, are the growing qualms Americans apparently have about killing enemy soldiers.

This chapter explores the implications such qualms have for the planning and conduct of future wars. It seeks to understand the likely effects on America's willingness to fight, weapon development policy, military doctrine, and the reporting of war. It recognizes that the qualms are to a large extent a luxury of our current security, protected as we are from invasion by two big oceans, two docile neighbors, the demise of the Soviet Union, and our own fearsome military power. If a foreign army were to be slicing into, say, Oregon, I have no doubt that we would not only annihilate all the enemy military personnel but also attack the enemy's homeland, with little regard for the cost in noncombatant lives. It is precisely because our future wars are likely to be fought far from home and for national interest rather than national survival that the qualms about killing and similar worries about inflicting environmental and cultural damage become of interest.

The first portion of the chapter is devoted to examining civilian death rates in the United States. This is done not only to underline the great dislike Americans have for dying, but also to confront an apparent anomaly: the rapidly increasing civilian murder rate in the United States. If we are so willing to tolerate a high murder rate at home, why are we unwilling to kill others during wars, when killing is traditional? The tolerance of domestic violence and the squeamishness about the violence of war are, I believe, linked, and thus both need to be addressed here.

DEATH AT HOME

Although we are very reluctant to admit it, Americans are healthier and safer than we have ever been. The overall death rate, measuring the age-adjusted impact of disease and injury per 100,000 of the population, is in steady decline. Most of us can expect to live longer, healthier lives than our forebears. We even fare well in most international comparisons.

Accidental Deaths

Consider the leading causes of death in the United States: diseases of the heart, malignant neoplasms (cancer), accidents, and cerebrovascular diseases (strokes). Together they account for over 70 percent of the deaths. Heart disease has been in decline for at least forty years, with the current rate almost 50 percent lower than it was in 1950. Strokes are down even more, with the rate per 100,000 now a third of what it was in 1950. Accidental deaths are down by about 40 percent. Only the cancer death rate is up, but only slightly and selectively. The overall cancer increase during this period was about 7.5 percent. The colorectal and stomach cancer death rates are down, the breast cancer rate is unchanged, and the respiratory cancer rate is way up (more than tripling), the result, no doubt, of past cigarette smoking.[1]

But even here there is likely to be good news soon. With cigarette smoking in substantial decline since the Surgeon General's 1962 report, we should expect a substantial decline in lung cancers. At least some of the decrease in heart disease and stroke is attributable to the reduction in smoking, although the precise amount is in dispute. The cancer rate is thought to react more slowly. If it does not change soon, however, there will have to be much rethinking about the impact of cigarette smoking on health.

The experience with accidents is quite interesting. Although accidents account for only about 5 percent of total annual deaths (100,000 out of 2 million or so) in the United States, they are the major cause of loss of years of potential life before the age of 70, striking down the young much more often than the elderly. About half the accidents are motor vehicle related; the rest are primarily falls, fires, drownings, and occupational injury deaths. The motor vehicle rate can be measured in a variety of ways—per 100 million vehicle miles driven per capita, per 100,000 registered vehicles, for instance—and is affected by economic conditions, vehicle weight and construction, and traffic and safety regulations, among other factors. The general trend is down for motor vehicle deaths, but with variation according to the method of measuring, and the trend is substantially down only in terms of a post–World War II peak that occurred in the 1960s.

Almost all other accident rates are down consistently and sharply.[2] Fire deaths, for example, which have been falling since the turn of the century, are now on a per capita basis a fifth of what they were then. Some leveling off occurred in the 1950s and 1960s, but the downward trend has resumed more recently, aided surely by the widespread, often mandated, use of smoke detectors and sprinklers. The death toll for both civilians and fire fighters keeps falling. In 1990 it was 5,300; in 1991 it was 4,565.[3]

With good news on so many fronts, it is not surprising that life expectancy has increased in the United States. In 1900 life expectancy was just over 47 years; it's now just over 75 years. Most of the increase occurred early in the century, when improved urban sanitation eliminated the threat of many deadly diseases. But significant progress has occurred since 1960, when life expectancy was just under 70 years.

In these calculations, women fare better than men and whites fare better than blacks. Average life expectancy for a white woman today is nearly 80 years, not too far from what may be the biological limits of 85 and better than the average achieved for women in most industrialized nations.[4] White males were at the 72.1 year mark in 1989. That same year black women had a 74-year life expectancy, greater than that of white males, but less than the life expectancy for white women. Black males fare the least well of all, with a life expectancy of only 65.2. But there has been progress for blacks as well as whites. In 1900, when whites had a life expectancy of 47 years, blacks had an expectancy of only 33 years. Whites gained about five years since 1960, while blacks gained six years.[5] Most of these gains for blacks occurred during the 1970s; more recently blacks, especially black males, have been losing ground relatively and absolutely.[6]

Similar experience exists with infant mortality, another widely used indicator of national health status. Incredible progress has been made in reducing the infant death rate since the turn of the century for both blacks and whites. There exists, however, a gap between the races that sometimes narrows and sometimes expands, but never disappears.[7] It may be the persistence of this gap as well as the persistence of other inequities in our health care system that makes us so reluctant to revel in the success we have achieved to date in improving health status, but it is also likely that our reluctance comes at least in part from the recognition that we can only push back, not eliminate, mortality. As the head of the National Transportation Safety Board said in reporting the results for 1991—the best year ever in transportation safety and one that saw a 7 percent decline in deaths from the previous year—the death toll was "simply not acceptable."[8]

Murder in the Streets

But is there not one toll we accept quite easily—the large and now growing number of murders that occur in the United States each year? Over 22,000 Americans were murdered in 1988, the latest year for which complete figures are available.[9] In the preceding decade an incredible total of 217,578 Americans were homicide victims, approximately four times the number killed in the decade-plus-long Vietnam War, and more than two-thirds of the battle losses in the Second World War, our most costly conflict. The year 1980 had the highest murder rate ever recorded in the United States: 10.7 per 100,000. The rate declined somewhat by the mid–1980s to 8.3, but was back up to 9.0 in 1988. The homicide rate here that year was four to twenty times that of other industrialized nations.[10]

Murders are concentrated in particular segments of the population, with blacks much more at risk of being homicide victims than whites and males much more at risk than females. Although blacks constitute less than 13 percent of the population, they are nearly 50 percent of the murder victims. The homicide rate for whites declined throughout the 1980s, while that for blacks has increased since 1985. Murder is now the leading cause of death for black males between the ages of 15 and 34.[11] Largely because of black-against-black encounters, the firearm homicide rate alone for young black males in some urban counties exceeds 200 per 100,000.[12] It turns out that it is much, much safer for young black males to be serving in the American military than to be walking the streets in most American cities.[13]

Racism is the ready, if not the fully persuasive, answer to the question of why we tolerate such a dismal record. Most white Americans can remain isolated from the murder and mayhem of the inner cities, the argument goes, and thus do nothing about it. Television news reports the violence, but the violence has no impact on our lives beyond producing a pervasive fear of young black males and inner city neighborhoods.

However, the problem to address is, What would we do if we were motivated to intervene? Work, perhaps, on the underlying causes of poverty and discrimination? But the homicide rate in the United States increased most rapidly in the 1920s and again in the 1960s, when prosperity was expanding (see Figure 2.1). The 1960s and 1970s, a period of increased crime, was also a time in which many of the formal barriers to the full exercise of rights by minorities in the United States were removed. Although young adults commit most of the violent crimes, a growing youth population, according to the experts, only accounts for about half of the growth in violent

Figure 2.1
Homicide Rate in the United States, 1900–1990

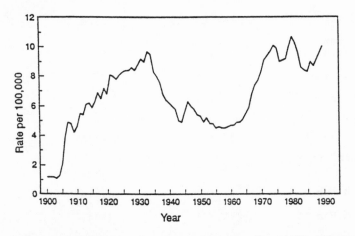

Source: Data from U.S. Public Health Service, "Homicide Surveillance, 1979–1988," *Morbidity and Mortality Weekly Report* (May 29, 1992), p. 29.
Note: 1933 was the first year all states reported.

crime.[14] Since the 1960s America has become a rougher, less restrained society, with cheap guns and cheap drugs easily available to the criminally minded.[15]

One important change in American society since the 1960s has been the significant restraints placed on the exercise of police authority. No longer can police conduct random searches, fail to inform detainees of their rights, beat the disrespectful, and so forth. Instead, officers must worry about public inquiries into the misuse of force, their own legal liability when making an arrest or questioning a suspect, and possible charges from citizen groups that they are harassing locals. These limits, imposed because of our concern about civil liberties, are still largely absent in Europe and Japan. As one acute observer recently put it, "If you get arrested abroad you will appreciate the constraints on the American police. The Swiss and the Swedes may strike you as civilized people, and they are, but I would not advise you to provoke the police in Geneva or Stockholm."[16] Although there is no certainty that tough security measures would reduce significantly the level of armed violence that exists in American cities to that of Europe, there is certainty that we will not impose them. We greatly prefer liberty—some would say license—to order. It is not surprising that we turn away from the cities where the problems are at least partially due to the breakdown of order. We have no acceptable answers.

I see a link between our unwillingness to permit random street searches and the shooting by police of fleeing suspected felons and our growing unease about the killing of enemy civilians or soldiers. We want the guilty, but not

Table 2.1

U.S. Military Losses in Major and Other Conflicts

Conflict	Combat Deaths	Other Deaths	Total
American Revolution	4,435		
War of 1812	2,260		
Mexican War	1,733		
Civil War (Union Only)	140,414	224,097	364,511
Spanish American War	385	2,061	2,446
World War I	53,402	63,114	116,516
World War II	291,557	113,842	405,399
Korean War	33,642	20,617	54,259
Vietnam War	47,312	10,691	58,003
Panama Intervention (1989-90)	23		
Gulf War	146	147	293

the innocent, to be punished. We want Noriega and Saddam to pay for their crimes, but we don't want to harm those who may have been coerced by poverty or threats to serve them or who just happen to be in the neighborhood when we come to get them.

Americans First

Of course our interest in saving lives in warfare focused first on saving American lives. The value placed on lives grew slowly. In the Civil War we lined up ranks of soldiers to march to battle across artillery-covered fields. In World War I our soldiers, just like British, French, and German soldiers, would clamber out of their trenches on command to charge into barbed wire and machine gun fire. But we learned eventually to do our fighting overseas, thus protecting our civilians from the ravages of war, and to increase our use of indirect fire in order to protect the troops who must close with the enemy.

In addition, significant gains occurred away from the battlefield. As Table 2.1 shows, a large portion of our early war loses were nonbattle deaths, the result of disease and accidents. Over time, American forces have become quite good at reducing this toll. Part of this success was due simply to the progress of modern medicine. But part was born of the recognition that our forces were likely to be stationed or do battle in strange places subject to strange diseases. Considerable effort was invested in learning about how to survive in the tropics, the arctic, and the desert.

As disease-caused deaths declined, accidental deaths have risen as a proportion of American nonbattle deaths. Our military's pioneering effort in aviation and its desire for realistic training have been costly in terms of lives. Preparing for war is very risky business. We lost 5,000 air crew members a year in aviation training accidents during World War II. We lost on average one aircraft and one pilot a day in the difficult transition to F–86s during the Korean War. But here, too, progress has been made. The Air Force's aviation fatality rate was 17 per 100,000 flying hours in 1947, 3.9 in 1967, and 1.7 in 1987. The Gulf War notwithstanding, 1991 was the Air Force's safest year ever, with the fatality rate falling to 1.1 per 100,000 flying hours.[17]

Even garrison life is becoming safer. The homicide rate is down within the military. There is always a campaign on to reduce the auto accident rate. Drinking and smoking are discouraged. And, as reported in a recent news item, the military even worries about small changes in the suicide rate among service personnel.[18]

Of course, the largest effort is expended to make the battlefield safer, because that is where the dangers are the greatest. No military can match our own in saving the lives of the wounded. We utilize medical evacuation helicopters, mobile army surgical hospital (MASH) units, hospital ships, and specialized ambulance aircraft for flights to regional and U.S. receiving hospitals. The salvage rate constantly improves from war to war, but the concern never lets up. Nearly 50,000 medical personnel, equal to almost one-tenth of the total assigned force, were sent to the Gulf.[19]

Saving the wounded is no longer enough, as the MIA/POW controversy demonstrates. In World War II there were 78,750 MIAs (personnel missing in action), military personnel whose remains were not recovered even though we eventually won the right to trample every inch of the fields of conflict. In Korea there were 8,170 who only now are being remembered. But the 2,273 MIAs from Vietnam remain very much a topic of public interest, even though most were air crew members certain to have died in the downing of their aircraft. Only one flag other than the American flag ever flies above the White House, and that is the MIA/POW (prisoner of war) flag. By state law at least one public building in every town and city in Massachusetts flies an MIA/POW flag. And every public school in liberal, antiwar Cambridge flies an MIA/POW flag. Our tolerance for casualties has diminished over time.

DEATHS IN WAR

The one sure way to keep American casualties down in war is to blast away at the enemy. We certainly have worked hard to increase the ferocity

Table 2.2
Manpower versus Firepower

	World War II	Korea	Vietnam
Millions of man-years	31.4	6.0	9.7
Casualties per 1000 man-years	30.7	22.8	19.9
Battle deaths per 1000 man-years	9.3	5.6	4.5
Wounds per 1000 man-years	21.4	17.2	15.2
Munitions expended tons/man-year	0.2	0.5	1.3
Combat exposure in million man-years	6.2	0.4	0.5
Tons of munitions per man-years of combat exposure	1/1	8/1	26/1

Source: William D. White, *U.S. Tactical Air Power* (Washington, DC: Brookings Institution, 1975), Tables 2.1 and 2.2, pp. 5 and 7.

and lethality of American forces. Our forces are, I am told, especially skilled in artillery and bombing—the best methods for delivering quickly very large amounts of ordnance on target. It is not at all safe to be the objective of an attacking American armor unit. War at that point is truly hell.

Table 2.2 describes the relationship between manpower and firepower in World War II, the Korean War, and the Vietnam War. What we have done is to substitute capital for labor, in essence throwing lead at the casualty problem. To cut our battle death rate in half, we have vastly increased the amount of munitions expended per combat-exposed soldier. We have also put fewer soldiers up front and more in the rear, no doubt to lug and inventory the munitions. We do not want American soldiers killed.

It is not surprising, then, that Americans have readily embraced the doctrine of strategic bombing, promising as it does victory without the gore of the trenches. The technological solution is the lure. Build the best machines, select the right targets, risk only a few men, and win the war, we are told.[20]

But what targets are the right targets? American bombing doctrine has usually emphasized military, industrial, and transportation targets over population targets, implicitly recognizing a disinclination to kill civilians. During

World War II, we certainly built the systems and sacrificed the air crews to follow this doctrine. Yet when the losses mounted without obvious result, inhibitions faded and civilian targets were attacked on a grand scale.[21] Official estimates are that we (jointly with the British) killed 300,000 German and 330,000 Japanese civilians (including those killed in the two atomic weapon attacks) in strategic bombing raids during the final phases of the war.[22] Tens of thousands more were the victims of our ground and tactical air attacks.

This was our one big experiment in killing civilians. Although we have periodically renewed our faith in strategic bombing, we have not wished to repeat the experience. The self-imposed restrictions against such killing, whether it be by air or ground assault, have grown in each succeeding war. Neither the failure to win clear victories nor accumulating personnel losses have tempted important deviations from the restrictions. On the contrary, our leaders have willingly absorbed the military's criticism of the minute management of the target selection process rather than risk attacks on politically sensitive targets, including, and most particularly, civilians.

The target constraints are indeed many, although they are not yet fully acknowledged or articulated. In addition to residential areas and medical facilities, we do not target crops, dams, irrigation systems, religious and cultural sites, markets, and other public gathering places. Most likely we have long ago sunk our last oil tanker and our last troop ship. All civilian casualties have to be unintentional. The attack on the air raid shelter in Baghdad, though arguably permissible by international rules because the shelter was thought to be empty of civilians and to house an active military communications facility, prompted closer supervision by Washington of the air war and nearly resulted in its early termination.[23]

THE LAST RESTRICTION

It seems we have begun to take the next and very last step in restrictions on the conduct of war. We now regret the killing of enemy soldiers. The regret started among the left during the Vietnam War with a sympathy for the peasant soldiers who were said to be fighting for their freedom against a force that was vastly advantaged in terms of the technologies of war. It then moved to a distaste for body counts, which were initially conceived as an objective measure of military progress, later viewed as a symbol of bureaucratic deceit, and finally seen as a bizarre goal of a failed strategy. In nearly every engagement since, we have had doubts about killing the opposing military. In Grenada, they were said to be only Cuban construction workers with rudimentary military training. In Panama, the Panama Defense Force (PDF) really was not the target of the operation. And in the Gulf War, we were supposedly shooting at vehicles, not people.

The Gulf War is especially instructive because of its scale and intensity. There was a very obvious reluctance on the part of our spokespersons to

Table 2.3
Estimates of Iraqi Casualties during the Gulf War

Source	Estimate
Defense Intelligence Agency 2/91	100,000 plus/minus 50,000
Greenpeace 5/91	52,500 to 83,000 in air war 20,000 to 35,000 in ground war 35,000 in civil war 70,000 to 90,000 after war
Newsweek 1/92	70,000 to 115,000 military 2,500 to 3,000 civilians
Washington Times 1/92	80,000 military 2,000 to 3,000 civilians
Gulf States estimate 1/92	50,000 total
U.S. Census Bureau 1/92	40,000 military 5,000 civilians 30,000 in civil war 70,000 after war
General Horner, USAF 2/92	10,000 killed or wounded military
U.S. News & World Report 2/92 (based on military experts)	8,000 to 20,000 military 3,000 civilian
Congressman Aspin 4/92	10,000 air campaign 20,000 ground campaign

discuss or provide estimates for the toll of Iraqi dead. When figures were given, they were vague, cited as uncertain, and not listed as official. Interestingly, the numbers shrink with time, reflecting perhaps more careful analysis, but also a growing recognition of the political consequences of high figures (see Table 2.3). First the number was 100,000 killed plus or minus 50,000, then it was 40,000 killed, and later it was 8,000 to 20,000 killed. General Charles Horner, the leader of the air war, suggested it could be as low as 10,000 killed and wounded for the air campaign. Only Les Aspin, then chairman of the House Armed Services Committee and protected by congressional immunity, and a Census Bureau analyst who was fired for her offense[24] offered higher estimates—in the case of the analyst, factoring in possible civilian deaths resulting from the destruction of Iraqi infrastructure.

The military's management of the news reflects this concern. Reporters were kept away from the battlefield, and no pictures of Iraqi dead were provided. When reporters were shown some gruesome gun camera film of Apache helicopter fire cutting down Iraqi soldiers, the film was quickly recalled. Boasting took the form of the flickering TV pictures of laser-guided weapons entering the air shafts of those ubiquitous command and control facilities and exploding. There were never people visible in these scenes.

Neither Saddam Hussein nor President Bush fully understand America's changing attitudes toward war. Saddam assumed that our unwillingness to suffer casualties would prevent us from employing force, that we would not risk the domestic political turmoil that a long conflict would likely generate, and that we would not bomb extensively because of our concern about inflicting civilian casualties. Our military doctrine, however, had adjusted to most of the constraints we have imposed upon ourselves. We employ overwhelming force to keep our losses low, seek a quick victory to prevent political chaos from developing at home, and utilize precision guided weapons to avoid what our military euphemistically refers to as collateral damage. Moreover, Saddam missed opportunities to gain the advantage that was his to have in the battle for American public opinion. He failed to reveal the full extent of the casualties his forces and the Iraqi people were suffering (Saddam actually claimed them to be low), and he did not provide pictures of the awful gore that cluster bombs and other weapons can inflict. Only after the war, when his brutal attacks on the Kurds and the Shiites and the environmental damage he caused in the Gulf region clouded the issue, did Saddam offer devastating pictures and high casualty estimates through neutral and antiwar sources.[25]

President Bush, of course, had a better grasp of American political realities than did Saddam. Although the President initially had trouble devising a saleable rationale for the application of force, he eventually made it clear that oil, nuclear weapons, and a Hitler equivalent were not a good mix for Americans. Moreover, he managed to wrap miles of yellow ribbon around the American troops, making it seem positively unpatriotic not to support them in their desert bivouac.

But President Bush did make mistakes, and especially at the war's end. He had no plan to deal with an Iraqi rout that was certain to come. Four days into the ground war, American pilots and tankers became increasingly reluctant to attack retreating Iraqi soldiers. Knowledge of the "Highway of Death" spread rapidly among the forces and the press. The war had to be terminated before significant portions of the Republican Guard could be destroyed in large part because of a reluctance to go on with the killing and a fear of the political reaction if reporters fully caught up with the story. As it was, pictures of the "Highway of Death" took much away from our joy of victory, though not the Kuwaitis'. Recently, President Bush said in defense of his decision to end the war that "we weren't in the business of slaughter."[26] The question, then, is: What business are we in when we make war?

THE FUTURE OF WAR

The American way of making war will have to change. We have long excelled at projecting power far from home, moving prodigious numbers of men and quantities of materials thousands of miles to meet an enemy. We have been superior at producing mass destruction and, more recently, of producing precise destruction. But all of this will do little to dissuade an antagonist who knows that we like neither to receive nor to give casualties, that we worry about killing innocents, including those who happen to wear uniforms, and that we believe war, most often for us, is a policy option, not a requirement.

Some of our favorite threats are beginning to lose all credibility with potential adversaries. We are not likely ever again to conduct an amphibious landing against a hostile beach (the last one occurred at Inchon, Korea, in 1950) or drop large numbers of paratroopers behind enemy lines (the last time was during World War II), as these are very risky enterprises. We are not likely to be torpedoing commercial ships because of danger to their crews and the potential for environmental damage from the spilled cargos.

More and more we will discover enemy military facilities colocated with civilian populations and at culturally or religiously valued sites. More and more we will worry about shooting too close to our own lines for fear of killing our own soldiers (the friendly fire problem). And more and more we will find American television reporters and camera crews witnessing the wails of the wounded and the horror of the dead after an American air strike or artillery barrage.

It is no wonder that the Department of Defense is beginning to explore, in a billion dollar program, nonlethal or minimally lethal weapons, things that will gum up motors, temporarily stun or disorient troops, shut off electricity, scramble computer programs, block bridges and roads, and disarm explosives.[27] Robots and drones also are gaining increased attention within the Defense Department.[28] There is even renewed interest in psychological warfare—ways to spread fear and doubts among enemy forces through propaganda, military demonstrations, or special effects.

Some of this is already part of the standard repertoire, for example, leafleting and B–52 raids. Some of this has appeared only in rare cameo roles, such as the boombox used against Noriega. But all of it will have to become central to American thinking about war. The need is for techniques that can creditably affect a state's or a military force's behavior without killing many (or any) people.

The problems are significant. It is technically difficult to develop nonlethal weapons that are both effective and not lethal to at least some people due to variations in physical conditions and health status. There is also the problem of proportionality. How do we match a nonlethal against a lethal attack? What is the comparative measure? And if most of the population is innocent, is it right that they suffer even nonlethally? Are we not driven to the capture or assassination of leaders as the just warfare solution?

Of course, leaders may be hard to apprehend and punish, may have lots of followers, and may seek to retaliate. There is a good analogy with our domestic violence situation. Murderers are difficult to apprehend, often have friends who protect them, and may take revenge. This is a police problem. For most of us, it is also an entirely avoidable problem. Unable to deal with domestic violence without doing violence to our principles, we have learned to turn away from the problem. The same will be true internationally. Like our urban policy, isolation will eventually be our answer.

NOTES

1. U.S. Department of Health and Human Services, *Health United States, 1989* (Washington, DC: Government Printing Office, 1990), Table 23, "Age-Adjusted Death rates for selected Causes of Death, according to Sex and Race: United States, Selected Years 1950–1987," pp. 121–122.

2. The best easily accessible source on accidents is Susan P. Baker, Brian O'Neill, Marvin J. Ginsberg, and Quohua Li, *The Injury Fact Book* (New York: Oxford University Press, 1992). On motor vehicle trends, see also Phil Gunby, "Traffic Death Toll May Be Declining, but Experts Not Ready to Celebrate," *Journal of the American Medical Association* 268, (July 15, 1992), pp. 301–312.

3. "News About Fires," (Press releases from National Fire Protection Association, Boston, Massachusetts, September 19, 1991, June 29, 1992, and August 3, 1992).

4. See James F. Fries and Lawrence M. Crapo, *Vitality and Aging* (San Francisco: Freeman, 1981), chap. 6.

5. U.S. Department of Commerce, *Statistical Abstract of the United States, 1991* (Washington, DC: Government Printing Office, 1991), Table 105, "Expectation of Life at Birth," p. 73.

6. U.S. Public Health Service, *Morbidity and Mortality Weekly Report*, February 21, 1992, pp. 121–125.

7. "U.S. Infant Mortality Rate Dropped to Low in 1991," *New York Times*, April 23, 1992, p. B5.

8. Quoted in "Transportation Deaths Decline 7% Last Year," *New York Times*, August 26, 1992, p. D2.

9. See U.S. Public Health Service, "Homicide Surveillance, 1979–1988," *Morbidity and Mortality Weekly Report*, May 29, 1992, pp. 1–34.

10. Lois A. Fingerhut and Joel C. Kleinman, "International and Interstate Comparisons of Homicide Among Young Males," *Journal of the American Medical Association*, 263, no. 24 (June 27, 1990), pp. 3292–3295.

11. *Morbidity and Mortality Weekly Report*, May 29, 1992.

12. Lois A. Fingerhut, Deborah D. Ingram, and Jacob J. Feldman, "Firearm Homicide Among Black Teenage Males in Metropolitan Counties," *Journal of the American Medical Association*, 267, no. 22 (June 10, 1992), pp. 3054–3058.

13. Ibid.

14. James Q. Wilson, *On Character* (Washington, DC: American Enterprise Institute, 1992), pp. 19–20, 25–40.

15. James Q. Wilson, "Contradictions of Capitalism," *Forbes*, September 14, 1992, pp. 110–118.

16. Ibid, p. 118. See also Christopher Jencks, "Is Violent Crime Increasing?" *American Prospect* No. 4, (Winter 1991), pp. 98–109; see especially p. 109 for a discussion linking declining authority with a rise in violence.

17. "Air Force Reports Safest Year Ever," *Defense Daily*, November 20, 1991, p. 294.

18. "18% Rise in Suicides in the Army Is Found between 1987 and 1991," *New York Times*, September 8, 1992, p. A14. So reads the headline, but it turns out that the combined rate for all the services was precisely equal to the national average.

19. "Another War . . . and More Lessons for Medicine to Ponder in Aftermath," *Journal of the American Medical Association*, 266, no. 5 (August 7, 1991), pp. 619–621.

20. See Williamson Murray, "The United States Air Force: The Past as Prologue," in M. Mandelbaum, ed., *America's Defense* (New York: Holmes & Meier, 1989), pp. 231–278. See also John L. Frisbee, ed., *Makers of the U.S. Air Force* (Washington, DC: Pergamon–Brassey's, 1989).

21. Ronald Schaffer, *Wings of Judgment: American Bombing in World War II* (New York: Oxford University Press, 1985).

22. United States Strategic Bombing Survey, *Summary Report* (Germany) (Washington, DC: Government Printing Office, 1946), p. 1; (Pacific), p. 20. Other estimates are usually higher. See, for example, *The Japanese Times Weekly International Edition*, August 24–30, 1992, p. 2, where 500,000 is cited as the Japanese government's estimate.

23. Lawrence Freedman and Efraim Karsh, "How Kuwait Was Won: Strategy in the Gulf War," *International Security*, 16, no. 2 (Fall 1991), p. 39.

24. Lawrence Jolidon, "War, Aftermath: 145,000 Iraqi Dead," *U.S.A. Today*, January 31, 1992, p. 1; Barton Gellman, "Census Worker who calculated '91 Iraqi Death Toll Is Told She Will Be Fired," *Washington Post*, March 6, 1992, p. 6. By April she was rehired. See "Agency Reinstates Tabulator of Iraqi War Deaths," *New York Times*, April 13, 1992.

25. "Gulf War Photo Book to Go on Sale," *The Japan Times Weekly International Edition*, March 9–15, 1992, p. 2.

26. President George Bush, "Address to the Veterans of Foreign Wars Convention," Indianapolis, August 17, 1992.

27. "DOD Urged to Adopt Nonlethal Warfare Strategy," *Defense Electronics* (March 1992), p. 2; "Pentagon Eyes Minimum-Lethality Weapons," *Aerospace Daily*, March 6, 1992, p. 377; David C. Morrison, "Bang! Bang! You've Been Inhibited," *National Journal*, March 28, 1992, pp. 758–759; Barbara Opall, "Pentagon Units Jostle Over Non-Lethal Initiative," *Defense News*, March 2, 1992, p. 6.

28. "Unmanned Ground Vehicle Office Will Study Emerging Technology," *Army*, November 1991, p. 49.

3

U.S. Conceptions of Democracy and Security in a World Environment of Culturally Alien Political Thought: Linkages and Contradictions

Adda B. Bozeman

The study of domestic and national security agendas must begin with a number of general propositions on the nature of political-social systems and strategic cultures. First, the inner order of a politically unified society is rooted in the belief systems, values, norms, and institutions around which generations have rallied in shared understandings of life's multiple demands. (In my language we are dealing here with the domain of culture, which has not ceased springing surprise developments even in our century when culture was harshly subdued in many places by totalitarian ideologies.)

Second, this inner order which is based on culture (and/or ideology) sustained by the governmental system is represented and protected in the outer world by foreign policies that include appropriate military programs.

Third, no politically organized society—be it a state or a nonstate entity— can survive intact unless its internal and external policies or agendas are closely linked in an overall commitment to preserve and defend the community's identity, integrity, and security.

Fourth, such a linkage is developed best when the state's vital interests at home and abroad are set out unequivocally in a comprehensive, long-range strategic doctrine or design.

Fifth, the basic requirements for conceptualizing and fashioning such a strategic master plan are knowledge of the national self, warts and all; an equally objective understanding of "other" in the world environment; and a disciplined commitment to think strategically about the interactions between internal and external affairs of state, thus avoiding contradictions.

The last axiom requires the following addendum:

Comparative studies indicate that meaningful understandings cannot be reached and strategic designs cannot be constructed, deciphered, or deconstructed unless one knows that each morally, culturally, or ideologically unified political society has its own religious or philosophical persuasion and artistic or aesthetic style as well as its own historical legacy, perception of geographic space, and worldview. Each can therefore be expected to have a mind-set of its own and to identify with its own prototype of political systems and its own modalities of political intelligence, diplomacy, warfare, and strategy.

In sum, strategists and policymakers can count on few if any international givens in world politics, except perhaps the following dual truths:

Unless the unifying cultural infrastructure of a political society is tended and defended carefully, the political system—be it the West's territorially bounded, law-based state, the Islamic sheikdom, caliphate, or "mulkh," black Africa's nuclear tribal chiefdom, or China's celestial or Maoist imperium—is likely to lose its identity and strength, perhaps even its capacity for survival.

Unless the cultural infrastructures of foreign political systems are carefully examined by intelligence analysts, policymakers will be critically hobbled in their efforts to think strategically and to shape successful foreign policies.

WHAT DOES AMERICA STAND FOR AT THE THRESHOLD OF ITS THIRD CENTURY?

The United States did not evolve a comprehensive strategic design in the twentieth century. It was not disposed to seek that dual knowledge of the "self" and the "other" upon which policy formation depends, and it was unable to link its domestic and its foreign agendas persuasively because it was as unsure of its outer security parameters as of its inner sustaining values. In brief, the nation finds itself in a serious identity crisis at the very end of the historically momentous twentieth century, when all processes of American policy-making ought to be issuing nearly automatically from a solid national consciousness of exactly what America stands for at home and abroad.

This perspective is shaped by two convictions. First, it is impossible to know what any country stands for in the world without knowing what it stands for within its boundaries. Second, a nation whose self-knowledge or self-image is askew or ambiguous at home will not be able to project itself successfully abroad.

America's Democracy Campaign: The Search for Identity

A recent conference of the Rockford Institute's Mainstreet Committee was asked to initiate a recovery of our nation's identity by mediating on the appropriateness of three different images: America as "fortress," as "empire," or as "beacon."

Reflections on these options show that it is not realistic to conceptualize the United States today either as a fortress or an empire. Although America still ranks as the major nuclear power in the world and although it was recognized throughout the last five decades as the leading power of the West—and by some as the "super" state of the world—it was *politically* defeated in all major conventional wars that it had chosen to fight—that is, World War II, the Vietnam War, and the Korean War. Further, it was unable to win the important unconventional wars and low-intensity conflicts—namely, those with Leninist and Maoist forces and their surrogates in northeast and southeast Asia; those in southern Africa (specifically Ethiopia, Angola, Mozambique, and South Africa); conflicts in neighboring Latin American states, notably Cuba, Nicaragua, and El Salvador; and those that pit the United States against its Islamic counterplayers in the Middle East. And finally, the prospects of becoming a fortress or an empire in the third century of its existence as a state are dimmed on the one hand by developments in continental Europe and the Eurasian realm of the former Soviet Union, and on the other, by the steady accumulation of evidence that our political and military intelligence continues to be inadequate for sustaining us in such roles.

But what about the third image option; can America be identified as a beacon for other nations?

The official answer has been a resounding affirmative in the last three administrations, most emphatically in those under Presidents Carter and Bush. The answer is unequivocal on the notion that America stands for the worldwide propagation and internationalism of its own norms of government, and on its own understandings of war, peace, international law, and a new world order.

Before discussing the merits and demerits of the present beacon image, it is necessary to recall not only that America was identified with much the same causes during the Roosevelt and Truman administrations, but also, and more important, that the United States was officially conceived by some of its founders as a beacon, a lesson, a service, and an asylum for the rest of mankind.

Two post-Revolutionary clubs, meeting together in Philadelphia on May 1, 1794, thus drank the following toast:

The Democratic and Republican Societies of the United States: May they preserve and disseminate their principles, undaunted by the frowns of power, uncontaminated by the Luxury of the Aristocracy, until the Rights of Man shall become the supreme law of every land, and their separate fraternities be absorbed in one great democratic society comprehending the human race.[1]

The beacon image, then, is powerful stuff.

And the thought occurs, isn't it likely that present-day Republicans and Democrats are also drinking this toast somewhere in a secret pleasant tavern of our land? True, their open disputations are decidedly fierce, but Republicans and Democrats indicate clearly that both parties are comfortably grounded today in Europe's eighteenth century, specifically in its *fin de siecle* excitement idiom whenever talk turns to the disorder of the wayward foreign world, and therewith to the tasks awaiting the "redeemer." "Let us democratize the world" is thus the beacon message now as it was then.

A Fateful Disjunction in the American Experience of History

In between the end of the eighteenth and the end of the twentieth centuries there was the nineteenth. It has dropped from the nation's consciousness, probably because beacon America spoke quite differently then. However, it's unlikely that America will ever clear up its identity crisis until it recalls what the nation stood for in its *first* full century.

The record is straightforward: America entered and left that century as a unified sovereign state and as a member of the European states system. Conscious of that dual identity, the United States had no difficulty accepting the basic principle of the European law of nations that states are free and independent in the choice of their forms of government. And as we have good cause to remember right now, the Wilson Administration went out of its way during and after World War I to propagate the twin concepts of national self-determination and statehood in conjunction with its determined war policy to break up the German, Austrian, and Ottoman empires.

In brief, the statehood image carries over the eighteenth-century beacon image. What should be noted, though, in the dense interplay of these two contending ideas, is the unobtrusive yet decisive presence of a sleeper-concept—namely, *culture.*

It is probably fair to say that Americans did not go out of their way affirming membership in Europe's civilization. Nonetheless, they belonged to it consciously, if only because most were of European extraction. Thus they knew full well (1) that their state was anchored in English and continental European conceptions of statehood and secular law—as were all European states, whether their forms of government were democratic or monarchical—and (2) that they could not ship all this to other nations, for example the Philippines. The commission charged with figuring out a suitable form of administration for those islands was therefore instructed by President Taft to accommodate native customs and institutions, even when these were patently not of the American kind.

America has greatly changed its identity in our times. In the first phase of this transposition, the United States was reconceived as a melting pot of diverse peoples. The European heritage was downgraded, and the general concept of culture disestablished in deference to the emotionally compelling eighteenth-century theory that all men on earth think, dream, and act alike and that they are therefore endowed with universally valid human rights, even though few of those listed in twentieth-century U.N. declarations and covenants are legally enforceable under Western (including American) systems of law.

In the second phase of this search for identity, the present one, the beacon modified its beam again. Now the United States is projected as a multicultural state, evidently because the country's non-Western inhabitants do not "melt" as foreseen by the eighteenth-century theorists. Far from shedding their native heritage, they tend to build it up and to abide by its norms and traditions while playing down their legal and political identities as citizens of the United States.

Governmental authorities did not methodically monitor or assess these nativist movements and activities. Nor did they subject immigration policies to searching reviews. This acquiescence helps explain why human relations could become rent by chronic hatreds and violent conflicts between different ethnic groups and why the nation could be dragged back to certain forms of segregation, this time chiefly under insistent pressures by spokesmen for black Americans who have come to view Africa, not America, as their true national home.

In sum, the United States will begin its third century as a state by standing for an apartheid system at home that is more incongruous than the one we go on punishing severely in the Republic of South Africa. Further, the United States is now a seriously conflicted, not a morally and politically unified, state, and as such it can no longer be viewed as a model for others. Also, since it has come pretty close to cutting its umbilical cord to Western civilization and its European base, it no longer qualifies as undisputed leader, and perhaps even as a bona fide member of the West's community of states.

In this vacuum of solid concepts of statecraft, beacon America had little to beam about. This was to change drastically when our zealous policymakers and image makers remembered the semantics and atmospherics of the bipartisan oath in 1794, and when beacon America was programmed to pledge over and over again that each country on earth would duly transform its government into a democracy under U.S. guidance and—as we have come to know—appropriate pressure.

AMERICA'S SEMANTIC AND CONCEPTUAL CONFUSIONS

Ideas have to be in good fighting shape when they are conscripted to do battle for a nation, and the same holds for the words chosen to carry the ideas. Is America on the right track in its search for identity at home and security abroad after having chosen democracy as (1) the key to understanding the United States on its own terms, and (2) the nation's emissary-plenipotentiary charged with the mission to tell all other governments and peoples just what America stands for morally and politically, at home and abroad, and what they too would be wise to identify with? The answer is no. Whether viewed as a comprehensive design linking domestic and foreign agendas or merely as an image-building gimmick, the democracy campaign seems an unfortunate aberration of political common sense and intelligence, one whose adverse effects on America's destiny will not be easily repaired.

The Anti-European Perspective

The reasons for this conclusion are well illustrated by the State Department's *Country Reports on Human Rights Practices for 1983.*[2] In this publication, which blots out Europe's civilization entirely, one finds not only explicit denials that democracy originated in classical Greece and Rome but also explicit assertions that in 1700 there were more extensive areas of democracy in black nonliterate Africa than in Europe, that Fiji, India, Costa Rica, and Japan (among scores of other listings) have long been "thriving" democracies. The work asserts that present-day American efforts to invigorate democracy in the rest of the world, including Europe, are "sustained by democracy's gradual expansion since the days of the American revolution."[3]

There's not a word in these governmental papers about the medieval Grutli Oath of the three cantons upon which democratic federal Switzerland continues to rest or about the establishment in the eleventh century A.D. of the Spanish *cortes.* Worst of all, there is no mention of the British House of Commons, where President Reagan had at just the time *Country Reports* was published given a historic address on the promise and problematics of democracy.

Europe, then, is obviously terra incognita for those in America's "nomenclatura" (bureaucratic decision makers and implementors) who run the Democracy Campaign. The linguistic, legal, philosophical, and historical roots of Western, that is, European, values and governmental institutions are thus studiously bypassed, even though there never could have been a United States of America without them. Readers of official policy statements are nowhere reminded that democracy has been a value in the West for 2,500 years because it is a form of government that is inextricably linked to two primary Western norms and values: the independent state and the rule of law—as concretized in Roman constitutional law, which continues to be the base of continental European state and international associations, and in English common law, which is often referred to as Great Britain's "constitution."

Since democracy is meaningless unless understood in this context, it is puzzling to find that the Democracy Campaign does not advance either of the two core concepts in its advisory admonitions to non-Americans. Several explanations of this neglect suggest themselves. Thus it is fair to say, I think, that World War II has reinforced the American disposition to think ideologically and spontaneously rather than realistically and historically about both, and domestic and academic elites have thus held fast to certain dream images that their precursors had culled from the Declaration of Independence while choosing not to reassess the records of the nineteenth century. In short, they slammed the door to all history that antedated the American experience of 1776, thus cutting the roots of constitutionalism and democracy while leaving wide open spaces for ideological improvizations.

The Predators

This vacuum of recorded European inventiveness and experience naturally attracted predators. Chief among them were Marxist-Leninist ideologues who had been programmed from about 1914 onward to dismantle Western civilization and conquer Europe by discrediting and decomposing the four-concept order upon which its culture rests: individualism, constitutionalism, Christianity, and the law-based state. Further, they had also been explicitly instructed by Leninist doctrine to use democracy as a chief tactical agent in the long-range strategic design to gain control of the West's state system. To foment insurgencies, agitate the electorates, deconstruct legislative assemblies, and disrupt elections with a view to establishing, in due course, communist dictatorships of the proletariat were thus Leninist agenda items throughout the last eighty years.

The United States never became a "captive nation." However, the public mind-set as represented particularly in the ranks of the country's communication and education elites was, to say the least, anesthetized by the nonstop onslaught of these Cold War offensives. Cut off from European legacies of norms and values that had traditionally hedged the integrity of democracy and basically ignorant of long-established non-Western and communist idea systems, Americans were incapable of defending the authentic meanings of democracy. The custodians of our language thus permitted this strategically vital concept to swing loose, convinced that the nation's founders had meant it to be an entitlement for all humanity, while our policymakers were not prepared to contest Leninist takeovers of traditionally democratic Western states. In short, the Marxist-Leninist idea system was allowed to settle comfortably in the American mind-set in deference precisely to the new identification of democracy as near total freedom in thought, political behavior, and government organization.

In the context of this chapter it is important to note that these particular transpositions of meanings were effected and legitimized under the academic auspices of cultural relativism and value-neutral social sciences that were at one in minimizing the uniqueness of Western civilization while maximizing the notion that all phenomena in world politics are essentially alike, and therefore were at one also in ruthlessly leveling whatever incongruities they could not help but admit.

Thus it goes without saying that the requirement to gain objective knowledge of the self and the other—which is here viewed as the prerequisite for good political intelligence and statecraft—is not just frustrated but canceled when reputable scholars admonish their government, their cocitizens, and their students to accept the Soviet Union as a near–identical twin of the United States,[4] or when the globe-spanning apparatus of the former Soviet Union's Communist party is officially recognized as just another nationally representative parliamentary party, or when the United States and the United Kingdom choose to abet rather than contest Soviet takeovers of continental European democracies as they did during World War II, in 1948, 1956, 1968, and at Helsinki in 1975. In brief, "constitutional democracy" was not a value in U.S. statecraft.

Democracy in the "Wilderness Language"[5]

Language guides thought in all speech communities, but when words originally coined to convey one distinct idea are allowed to shed that exclusive meaning and to acquire other, perhaps unrelated connotations, language ceases to be a reliable guide for thought. Mental processes get confused. Issues are not understood on their merits. Communication becomes either irrelevant or deceptive, and paralysis or impotence sets in when the occasion calls for clear-sighted decision making and purposeful action.

This is what happened to the West's classical vocabulary of law and politics when American custodians of that value language knew no better than to load the word "democracy" with new meanings and functions that seemed politically correct on the one hand for U.S. foreign policies in non-Western and Leninist provinces of the world, and on the other hand for domestic usage as "minority set-asides."[6] The concept of democracy thus degenerated into a mere camouflage of the gulag empires of the Soviet Union and Mainland China and an idea that lent cover of prestige to scores of non-Western states in which tradition and present-day considerations of security combined to favor less-than-democratic rule. However, it is certainly clear today, as we approach our third century, that we paid a heavy price for compromising the integrity of the democracy concept.

The evidence at home is that the United States does not really know itself as a nation-state today and that it lacks internal security and staying power because it is too divided ethnically and ideologically and because its general value system is too confounded.

Foreign Relations

On the level of foreign relations, meanwhile, America goes on registering policy and intelligence failures specifically in the non-Western world because we insist on being guided by our dream image of a unified humanity under America's moral guidance rather than by objective knowledge of the otherness of foreign nations. Beginning with the Carter Administration, Americans have thus gone on and on with verbal propagations of democracy and human rights without ever pausing to ask—and find out—whether this campaign had actually brought democracy or done some other good to Liberia, Kenya, Somalia, Sudan, Ethiopia, Angola, or any other country in black Africa, or to Haiti, Nicaragua, El Salvador, or Peru, or to Algeria, Iran, Iraq, Kuwait, or any other Islamic Middle Eastern state. Nor have Americans asked whether paying the price for this campaign in the coinage of compromising the authenticity of Western culture was really worth it in the context of furthering America's national interests in the world.

My answers to these questions are no in each case. To be sure, many friendly non-Western states comply with the technical requirements that we identified categorically as the very essence of democracy (see earlier sections of this chapter). But democracy did prove to be a "bitter pill to swallow," as the late General Mohammed Zia—a staunchly pro-American Pakistani president—had warned us several years ago. Too many friendly non-Western nations swallowed it at our behest but could not digest it and endure.

Conclusions

Should being a beacon unto others ever be the primary goal of any foreign policy? Specifically, should America's present "beaconhood" consist in inducing other friendly sovereign states to disclaim and decompose *their* cultural infrastructures of government in order to comply with our present, and in my view defective, version of democracy? Or, to put it differently, is it wise or good politics for a self-styled model state to invite identity crises in non-American societies by confusing their value systems, undermining their collective self-confidence, and thus impugning the very idea of the state—an idea which continues to be the cornerstone of the American-made world order? Indeed, isn't it a bit presumptuous for a society as unsure of its identity as ours is today to tamper with the identities of other, weaker, but older and more settled political systems?

In sum, beacon-America's democracy campaign should be suspended so that the United States can come to a realistic understanding of the present multicultural world society and of its own uniqueness.

INTO THE TWENTY-FIRST CENTURY

Ideally we should begin the nation's third century by repealing the eighteenth-century oath that bound Republicans and Democrats in a joint determination to democratize the earth. We should begin it by fashioning a new bipartisan oath that would obligate Americans to resolve contradictions in their value system and their view of the self, assess the new international environment objectively on its own terms, update their knowledge of others in world society, define the nation's security requirements, and come up with a strategically tenable comprehensive foreign policy design.

The chances for such a deliberate meeting of the minds are obviously slim in the 1990s. However, they can be improved, I think, by returning to the 1980s, when President Reagan succeeded, by dint of brilliant intelligence initiatives, in developing a "strategy for freedom" that proved instrumental in unraveling the ignominious Yalta deal and in liberating Poland from the Soviet stranglehold by returning it to its cultural roots in Roman constitutionalism and Christianity.[7]

We know today that the success of these secret and complex operations was indeed the beacon for the epochal anti-Communist German and East European revolutions in 1989–1990 that had the effect, eventually, of dissolving the Leninist imperium, restoring Western civilization, and revitalizing the concept of the independent law-based nation state. But too many among us forget that nothing of this historical magnitude would have happened had the Reagan Administration players—and they included the Pope, leading cardinals and archbishops, Lech Walesa and members of the Solidarity movement as well as William Casey, Vernon Walters, Alexander Haig, Richard Allen, and Richard Pipes—not understood the region's history, geography, cultural infrastructure, and, above all, the different, contending mind-sets and ideologies they were dealing with, and had they not turned off the self-propagating "beacon America" before deploying their clandestine masterplan in 1981–1982.

Since Americans were probably at one, regardless of party affiliation, in approving the outcome of the Reagan strategy as symbolized in the fall of the Berlin Wall and in deploring the bloody put-down of the democracy uprising in China's Approving (Tiananmen) Square, they would in all likelihood also be at one in underwriting an all-American strategic doctrine that is not egalitarian but discriminatory in its applicability to culturally different sectors of the international security environment.

Why Did Reagan's Clarion Call for Democracy Elicit Different Reactions in Continental Europe and Mainland China?

A comparison of the democracy drama as it played itself out in Approving Square and at the Berlin Wall in the epochal autumn of 1989 left me with the following conclusions:

"Democracy" could become a revolutionary codeword for law and freedom in East Germany because the core concept of constitutional law had in fact been at home there for over one millennium, and the Reagan group knew that or sensed it intuitively.

The East Germans—Leninized as they were—had the full backing of Europe's civilization in which their nation had evolved. They knew its history and the laws it had spawned; they lived each day surrounded by its legacies of religion, architecture, literature, art, and music. Therefore they could spell out the many interlocking norms and values that are merely implied in the term "democracy" as it is being heard and used today by freedom fighters elsewhere in the world. This kind of culture consciousness gave them the measure for judging Leninist rule and the self-confidence to reclaim what they knew was theirs. Further, but in the same context, they felt free to remind local German surrogates of Leninism that they too "belonged" and should therefore be ready to join in the task of reforming the governance of the state. Lately, culture consciousness gave the revolutionaries the courage to act resolutely yet serenely and spontaneously on behalf of freedom and democracy by joining in inspired but orderly demonstrations and staging a dramatic massive exodus into friendly neighboring lands on their side of the cultural frontier separating West from East.

The Chinese freedom fighters, by contrast, were all alone. They could not step back into the past looking for cultural sanctions of their daring undertaking. For one thing, their magnificent pre-Maoist civilization simply does not know the concept of democracy and has no equivalent for what the West understands as law.[8] For another, the Maoist engineers of thought control had spared no effort to purge the history books and anesthetize the human faculty for remembrance. In short, whereas the Communist revolution was compelled to let its German children go, it had no trouble devouring its Chinese progeny in the kind of bloodbath that has typified Leninist statecraft throughout the century.

The Standing American Failure to Understand Wars of Ideas

The significance of these two episodes for U.S. statecraft and intelligence may be briefly summarized as follows. Whether viewed as separate low-intensity conflicts or as connected battles in an ongoing transcultural war of ideas, they vividly illustrate certain flaws in the American approach to such contests.

Thus we relearned in 1989 what we had already learned in the course of World War II, in the Maoist takeover of China, and in the ill-fated German, Polish, Czech, and Hungarian uprisings against Soviet totalitarianism in the forties, fifties, and sixties, namely:

that the well-assembled records of European and Chinese culture histories—all "soft" sources—had not been studied

that relevant thought systems were not analyzed and could not therefore be compared

that reliable estimates of how Marxism-Leninism plays on the one hand in different sectors of Europe, and on the other in China, could not be formulated in the existing vacuum of knowledge and that American intelligence services were unable in such circumstances to keep track of shifting trends in the century's historically decisive war of ideas

Conjointly, these negatives explain why the United States has not had either comprehensive policy designs for its global democracy campaign or precise contingency plans for the unfolding of the democracy revolution in each of many separate regional theaters. Indeed, our foreign policy record in both Europe and China leaves the impression that we never knew whether, where, or in which circumstances it would be in our vital interests to render the kind of decisive support that would reassure success or at least forestall total failure.

For example, the Approving Square tragedy might not have occurred had we taken the pains to persuade the young Chinese activists during the formative stages of their revolutionary program to express their hatred of totalitarianism and their longing for freedom in the rich value language of Confucian China rather than in that of occidental democracy, and had we coupled this advice with the suggestion that they had a perfect model for their aspirations in the spectacular achievements of the Republic of China (Taiwan).

Such psychopolitical moves might have been forthcoming had the United States subscribed to James Forrestal's strategic vision of Taiwan as "the whole key to the future in the Pacific. He who controls Formosa can oversee the whole coast of continental Asia."[9]

This was not to be the thrust of U.S. policy in the ensuing decades, during which American scholars and policy planners were totally, and for the most part enthusiastically, absorbed in following the evolution of victorious Maoist China. The hope here was not that the totalitarian regime might be induced to democratize itself, but that it would condescend to strike a few reassuring diplomatic bargains with us. The Kuomintang thoughtways and values of the defeated Chinese, by contrast, have not merited serious assessment in American statecraft during the last half-century. The nation was therefore as unprepared for the phenomenal socioeconomic and political success of the Republic of China (ROC) as it was for the socioeconomic collapse and political betrayals of the People's Republic of China (PRC)—all symbolized by the events on Approving Square.

Cold Wars of Culture and Ideas Are Here to Stay

Several generations of Americans—and they include all of us and our contemporaries—have lived full-time since 1945 in a so-called Cold War against the Soviet Union. We declared this contest over in 1989–1990 when the Soviet imperium was dissolved by Eastern and Central European peoples. I am frankly dubious in regard to such a proposition. As noted earlier, the Marxist-Leninist idea system is comfortably ensconced in segments of our nation, as it is in those of other countries.

Further, it is significant that Democratic and Republican administrations have studiously excluded Leninist-Maoist China from the range of their Cold War speculations, and that their joint political intelligence has been mute and inactive when it comes to dealing with such strategically hostile nonstate players as the Communist party network in southern Africa, specifically, the African National Congress and the Communist party in the Republic of South Africa;[10] the Sandinista apparatus in Nicaragua, El Salvador, and other Latin American societies; the Incan-Maoist-Sendero-Luminoso forces in Peru; Pol Pot's Khmer Rouge faction in Cambodia—not to mention the established states of Cuba, Vietnam, and North Korea.

In sum, I am persuaded that the United States has not yet come to terms either with Leninist patterns of thought and ways of manipulating the thoughtways of Western and non-Western peoples or with the Cold War complex in general. I am convinced that we have so far been the losers in this kind of contest and that our intelligence capability needs updating and encouragement if we want to hold our own in international and intercultural conflicts short of all-out military war.

Since the view is obviously in counterpoint to the jubilant postmortems on the demise of the Cold War and America's victory that make the headlines, the following comments are in order.

Cold Wars of ideas do not and cannot end as automatically as strictly military wars because ideas do not perish as easily as the humans who had fashioned or upheld them, especially if they are deeply rooted in a culture or if they were carefully seeded in targeted national mind-sets as Leninist concepts were in Europe, specifically England, and in the United States. This proposition is borne out by post-1989 developments throughout the former U.S.S.R. as well as the East European nations that had been enslaved and brainwashed for half a century. It is also being illustrated in our times by the resumption of Islamic Cold War offensives against the Christian West, which had been stalled in 1492 when Spain succeeded, after eight hundred years of fighting the *guerra fria* (the term was coined by a thirteenth-century Spanish scholar), in ousting the Muslim conquerors from the Middle East and North Africa and reestablishing Spain as an independent, Christian, law-based state.[11]

These references relate to men, events, and centuries that do not fit readily into modern American perspectives on time. However, medieval Spain's enemies are readily identifiable in their thought structures as the ancestors of Saddam Hussein, Yasser Arafat, Muammar Qaddafi, Iran's diverse Shiite ayatollahs, and tens of thousands of fundamentalist, radicalized Muslims in the world at large who carry on "the jihad of the sword" as well as the "jihad of the spirit and the mind" against the selfsame West—this time represented not by Spain but by the United States of America.

In short, we have been and continue to be engaged in two transnational and transcultural wars—one against Leninism-Stalinism-Maoism, the other against Islam as interpreted and practiced by fundamentalist states and non-state regimes in the Middle East and North Africa.

Just how conscious are we of this particular dimension in our different regional conflicts involving Muslim personages? The term "Cold War" has to my knowledge never been applied in this context. Further, there's not even a hint in the records of our diplomatic and military dealings in the Middle East that American policymakers have thought of such things as kidnapping, hostage taking, terrorist assassinations, or anti-Western acts of war as aspects of a comprehensive, constant intercultural war. At any rate, no accommodation has been made for this type of unconventional warfare in the nation's worldview and global intelligence design.

This vacuum of political acumen probably explains why the United States still lacks the know-how to manage the Cold War relations with its Leninist and Islamic counterplayers and why it has been so deceived so often. The following misperceptions in particular deserve notice.

American Middle East experts do not know enough about the core concepts and values that together constitute Islam as both religion and political system. Specifically, they have not identified the complex meanings carried by the word "jihad" and the psychological dispositions normally triggered by this concept. The character structures of leading personalities are therefore enigmas to us. This may explain why the Bush Administration compared Saddam Hussein to Adolph Hitler (there are no affinities)[12] instead of linking him to one or all of the countless caliphs, sultans, kings, or ayatollahs in the Islamic tradition, and why the United States is insistent on personalizing its military and diplomatic offensives. America did win a military war, but according to a June 1992 National Intelligence Estimate, Hussein is stronger now than he was a year ago. The "jihad of the mind," then, has not been broken because we never understood the concept. In sum, present-day policymakers and advisors do not seem to know that "jihad" is a sacred concept for believers throughout the vast multiethnic Islamic world that sums up all foreign affairs as well as much of domestic statecraft, and that it is immune to our democracy and peace campaign.

The second significant misperception in this Cold War theater came to light when a renowned Soviet general told American television audiences after the U.S. victory in the Gulf War (and shortly before he committed suicide on the occasion of the coup against Gorbachev) of his role in Iraq. He stated that he had been very busy for decades building up and grooming Saddam Hussein's Republican Guard for its diverse assignments to take on the President's foreign and domestic enemies.

In sum, the Leninist and Arab-Islamic "Cold Wars cum violence" had been programmed to interlock, and the United States was not aware of that.

Shaping National Security for the Twenty-First Century

The records of the twentieth century support the proposition that international relations in a multicultural environment are bound to be conflicted and apt to find expression in critical clashes of rival or simply incongruent values and ideas that allow for the designation "Cold War." Put differently, this means that conflicts short of all-out war are here to stay after 2000 A.D. and that the United States should be well prepared and at ease when dealing with them.

As suggested earlier, the United States cannot attain this state of inner security and readiness unless its government and its citizenry reach greater depths in national unity and self-understanding than heretofore, and unless they are prepared to refashion or rethink several conceptual components of their domestic and national security agendas. And this revisionist stocktaking will proceed best if it is calibrated with a close examination of the international security environment in which our nation finds itself right now.

THE NEW WORLD ORDER AND NATIONAL SECURITY

The following "conceptual components" (to borrow a felicitous Sarkesian phrase) of the existing so-called world order should be the chief targets for reevaluation if America is seriously interested in exchanging its haunting dream of a unified mankind for an objective perception and understanding of the real world.

1. The states system has ceased to be what it used to be between the Groatian seventeenth century and our twentieth century.
2. Our understandings and definitions of "war" are hopelessly out of date, and the same holds, mutatis mutandis, for "peace."
3. The international law of war is basically irrelevant today, and I doubt it can become relevant again.
4. "National security" can no longer be calculated and rendered in terms of military preparedness and treaty provisions.

Since these themes interpenetrate in their respective substances as well as in practical world politics, they will do so also in my brief concluding comments.

The Western concept of the independent, territorially bounded, law-centered state is alien to Asian and African traditions of statecraft. Although the concept is officially installed everywhere today, it is being administered, as it were, under the trusteeship of locally dominant religions, philosophies, and customs.[13] The concept is openly refuted by Marxist-Leninist-Maoist theory and policy even as its semantic and tactical validity in "the class struggle" is stressed. In general, it is fair to say that Leninists concretize the idea of the state in the Communist party's power apparatus. This was represented in the Soviet Union by the KGB—hence John Dziak's apt definition of the Soviet Union as a "Counterintelligence State."[14]

In sum, twentieth-century states are hardly comparable or "equal." Not only is the concept "state" rendered in a bewildering array of images and meanings, but "the state" as reality is too multiform in our times to serve as an elementary norm for political organization and the maintenance of an international system of states.

In counterpoint to the nineteenth and early twentieth centuries, today there are no firm requirements, criteria, or standards to show cause why a group of people should or should not be called a state. States have thus been mushrooming, withering, dying, and reviving as if they were haphazard creations in botany or zoology. For example, no serious objection was raised when a vast imperium such as the Soviet Union was granted three statehood votes in the United Nations in 1945. Nor was any objection raised when the conquered states in Eastern and Central Europe that it had reduced to colonies, or, in U.N. parlance, non-self-governing territories, were nonetheless recognized in public diplomacy and the United Nations as sovereign states and voting members.

The 1989–1990 revolutions that conduced to the dissolution of the Soviet Empire returned some of these states, such as the Baltics, Poland, East Germany, Czechoslovakia and Hungary, safely not only to independence but also to their medieval roots as law-based nations. And much the same can be said of Russia proper and the Ukraine, which had received their early education in politics as well as law from Christian Byzantium. The prospects for other Soviet republics, particularly those in Asian and Islamic zones, are less certain, and so are the destinies of peoples in Southeast Europe and the Balkans, as the protracted disassembly of Yugoslavia suggests.

States have been falling apart also in the non-Western world, nowhere more so than in black Africa, where all governments must cope with inveterate tribal, ideological, and personal enmities and where few new states have avoided becoming battle zones.[15] In fact, developments in Africa suggest that the modern African state is indispensable only in the framework of world politics. In most of Africa it is being steadily eclipsed in efficacy of representation by the ruling regime of the day, and the same conclusion holds for the Arab domain in the Middle East, where the idea of the nation-state has no home either in Arabic culture or in the Islamic faith.[16]

The version of the Western-type state was bound to bring anarchy to international society because it was paralleled on one hand by the rise of assertive nonstate entities, chief among them the network of Communist parties, sects of Islamic militants, and a host of well-organized terrorist groups, all transterritorial in organization and operation, and on the other, by an equally strong movement, particularly evident now in the former

Soviet orbit, black Africa, and India, to escape the big multinational state and seek security in small, ethnically and culturally unified states. In brief, conflict, dissension, internal warfare, and secession mark intrastate life in many regions, thus accounting for the fact that the names, frontiers, and identities of many states have continued to be in flux.

How Should the U.S. Conceptualize International War in the New Global Security Environment?

As noted earlier, comparisons of non-Western and Communist thought systems show a striking convergence on the paramountcy of war and conflict in conceptualizing and conducting international relations and a corresponding absence of expressed commitments to peace. Further, surveys of present-day wars, revolutions, and violent or low-intensity conflicts as these are being fought, endured, resisted, or compromised in Asia, Africa, and parts of Latin America confirm the continuity of this legacy and the near-total eclipse of the classical Groatian or Westphalian state system that the "new" states had eagerly joined a few decades earlier.[17]

Should the "old" Euro-American group of states, and specifically today the United States, go on upholding the absolute validity of the Groatian maxims that (1) only states are subjects of international law, and (2) war and peace are antipodes in human existence, each endowed with its own rights? (Being a dedicated student of Grotius, I know that my mentor never thought of Fiji, Zaire, Tibet, Cuba, or the Soviet Union as members of his Christian concert of law-conscious peoples.) It is best that we keep his code as part of the constitutions of the European Community and NATO, but that we forget it when dealing with the rest of the world.

How Americans Should Deal with War

Next on the new security agenda for the twenty-first century is the question, How should we deal with war?[18] There is no uneasiness in the land when another full-fledged state violates the territorial sovereignty of the United States or one of its allies. Today, however, it is hardly ever possible to set interstate wars apart from internal wars, revolutions, insurgencies, counterinsurgencies, and the vast conglomerate of different species of guerrilla warfare or irregular warfare. Put differently, war is fluid and formless. It does not commence with an act of aggression that can be pinpointed in terms of time and space. Rather, most wars are nurtured in webs of covert action that are enacted within the state targeted for takeover. Other wars—among them some of black Africa's coup d'état wars and the scores of tragic subwars between power-seeking religious sects and separatist sovereign armies like the ones that finished off the state of Lebanon—are primarily private wars. Neither can be analyzed or controlled by reference to standing rules of international law of war, for these are addressed only to sovereign states. And the same conclusion holds for low-intensity conflicts and cold wars in which the participation of states and the incidence of violence is masked.

Now, these kinds of war were commonplace throughout time in Asia and Africa and highly developed in the context of Leninist statecraft, and they will in my estimation continue to mark human relations in the twenty-first century. Although they have been breaking up states, consuming scores of people in the world, and gravely affecting American national interests, we do not yet accept them officially as war for two reasons. First, they do not openly involve adversary states, and second, a strong emotion prevails in the nation to save our concept of peace from being swallowed by uncongenial concepts of war, an eventuality that would threaten the integrity of international law, which is anchored in the distinction between peace and war.

At any rate, claims on behalf of this particular case keep proliferating in our era. Indeed, as Americans distance themselves from the realities of war, they tend to assign the whole field of foreign relations, and therewith the nation's basic security interests, to the tender mercies of the rule of law, domestic as well as international. The dynamics of diplomacy and policy-making are thus locked out from realistic assessment by static legal or pseudolegal propositions that tell us as a matter of theory rather than good intelligence findings that war X should not be undertaken because the vocabulary of law does not provide for it; that covert action Y should be aborted because it actually *proves* to be covert and thus is liable to be judged illegal or criminal; that political or moral commitments to strict confidentiality or secrecy in human relations must be betrayed so that they may be accommodated in what present-day exponents of law have staked out as their exclusive intellectual preserve; or that psychopolitical operations and cold wars or ideas just make no legal sense, do not damage the nation, and can therefore be disregarded with impunity. Yet this nation surely is at risk today, and partly at least because events bear out Charles Dickens's dictum that law is or at least may become "a ass—a idiot."[19]

In sum, twentieth-century ways of warring have washed away the dams that Europe's law had built on earth, in water, and in air. Now is the time, therefore, for America to decide whether international peace really differs from what recent generations have experienced as international war. And if it does not, we must decide whether national security interests might not be served best by dropping the distinction between peace and war in the management of world affairs.

The case for this discriminatory approach was strengthened recently by Marcel Leroy of the Political Affairs Division of NATO, when he noted that the West is ill prepared to deal with serious problems that flare up in the Balkans, the Caucuses and the Middle East because we no longer confront states or treaty organizations but rather "many small," ethnically distinct but internationally influential, political organisms. "The CSCE and the

Council of Europe will therefore have to address conflict resolution at the sub-state level. This will lead to a whole new dimension to the concept of national sovereignty."[20]

Finally, the United States must develop a fitting security agenda in an international environment that may well be described as a welter of ambiguities. In my estimation, it goes without saying that the embattled security concept must be refashioned and rendered in military terms by military minds that are at ease clearing up the debris of ambiguities. However, security in the sense of collective self-assurance in the nation at large can be attained and utilized only when the citizenry in a democracy realizes that knowledge is a good adjunct shield when insecurity strikes.

In matters of statecraft, our private intelligence agendas should call for the acknowledgment that all human contests are in the final analysis mental and psychological and that they can be won or managed only by those who understand the mind-set of the counterplayer while being absolutely certain also of just who they are themselves and what they represent.

NOTES

1. Quoted in Eugene Perry Link, *Democratic-Republican Societies 1790–1800* (New York: Octagon Books, 1965), p. 109. This theme is discussed in Adda B. Bozeman, "The Roots of the American Commitment to the Rights of Man," in *Rights and Responsibilities: International, Social, and Individual Dimensions*, Proceedings of a Conference at the Annenberg School of Communications, University of Southern California, November 1978 (Los Angeles: University of Southern California Press, 1980; distributed by Transaction Books, Rutgers University), pp. 51–103; see in particular pp. 83ff.

2. Bureau of Human Rights and Humanitarian Affairs, Department of State, *Country Reports on Human Rights Practices for 1983* (Washington, D.C.: Department of State, February 1984), pp. 8 ff.

3. Ibid. See also Adda B. Bozeman, *Strategic Intelligence and Statecraft* (Washington, DC: Brassey's [U.S.], 1992), essay 7 on "American Policy and the Illusion of Congruent Values," and Bozeman, "U.S. Foreign Policy and the Prospects for Democracy, National Security, and World Peace," *Comparative Strategy and International Journal*, 5, no. 3 (1985), pp. 223–267.

4. For illustrations of truly ludicrous comparisons see Jerry F. Hough, *The Soviet Union and Social Science Theory* (Cambridge, MA: Harvard University Press, 1977) and Richard J. Barnet, *The Giants: Russia and America* (New York: Simon & Schuster, 1977). Both books are reviewed by Adda B. Bozeman in *Transaction*, November–December 1978, pp. 84–89. See also Michael Oksenberg and Robert B. Oxman, eds., *Dragon and Eagle: United States–China Relations: Past and Future* (New York: Basic Books, 1978), pp. 14, 17, 19, for the proposition that the United States stands for "liberty," (p. 14), the Soviet Union for the commitment to accelerate "economic growth," (p. 17), and Communist China for "economic equality and the capacity of the dispossessed to improve their lot through will and organization," (p. 19). Since

each of these values speaks to an important aspect of life, the United States is advised to seek adjustments along the following lines:

Can the ideas of Jefferson and Mao Tse-tung . . . coexist as we seek areas of cooperation? . . . If the terms of exchange between the two societies can become genuinely reciprocal, then we may discover that there is less tension between the values of our two revolutions than is currently believed (p. 14).

For a discussion of these and related shifts in American political thought, see Adda B. Bozeman, "Human Rights and National Security," *The Yale Journal of World Public Order*, 9, no. 40 (Fall 1982), pp. 40–77, particularly pp. 50ff.

5. "Wilderness language" is Caspar Weinberger's felicitous phrase.

6. See earlier sections of this chapter.

7. See Carl Bernstein, "The Holy Alliance," *Time*, February 24, 1992, pp. 28 ff., for an account of this policy initiative. It is important to note, however, that Secretary of State George P. Schultz never wavered in the beacon stance. He thus writes in "New Realities and New Ways of Thinking," (*Foreign Affairs*, 63, no. 4 [Spring 1985], pp. 705ff.) that we "have a duty" to transform the world environment in accordance with our primary goals, values, and ideals—these being peace, liberty, democracy and human rights; racial justice; economic and social progress; and the rule of law. Compare the approach of the State Department's Bureau of Human Rights and Humanitarian Affairs as discussed earlier in this chapter.

8. These themes are elaborated in Adda B. Bozeman, *The Future of Law in a Multicultural World* (Princeton, NJ: Princeton University Press, 1971) pp. 14ff.; and in Bozeman, *Strategic Intelligence and Statecraft* under the following headings: "International Order in a Multicultural World," "War and the Clash of Ideas," "The Traditional Roots of Political Warfare in Totalitarian Russia and China: A Comparative Study of Continuity and Change," and "Political Intelligence in Non-Western Societies: Suggestions for Comparative Research."

9. The reference is to a visit paid to Walter's staff during World War II while Forrestal was Secretary of Navy. See Vernon Walters, *Silent Missions*, (Garden City, NY: Doubleday, 1978), pp. 111ff. (quote from p.111). In light of our incessant reprimands of rights violations in places such as South Korea and other non-Communist Asian societies, it is interesting that we refrain from taking Mainland China seriously to task. For an analysis of the "rights" issue and U.S. policy-making in East Asia, see Bozeman, "Human Rights and National Security," pp. 64–77, and authorities there cited. See Richard C. Thornton, "John King Fairbank: A Critical Assessment," *Culture* (June 1992), pp. 591–609, for a most welcome, thoroughly researched, and footnoted assessment of Fairbank's writing on twentieth-century (specifically, Maoist) China and on desirable American policies in East Asia. Thornton's unassailable conclusion is to the effect that this leading American sinologist unabashedly pleaded the Chinese Communist cause throughout his professional life. To this he adds: "If our scholars fail to identify the proper questions to ask and instead insist upon perceiving the present as a reflection solely of an imperfectly understood past or pleading the cause of our adversaries, our chances of understanding the complexity of the present are nil" (Ibid., p. 609).

10. See James M. Roherty, *State Security in South Africa: Civil-Military Relations under P. W. Botha*, (Armonk, NY: M. E. Sharpe, 1992), for exceptionally lucid observations and findings in regard to this complex score.

11. For an account of this *guerra fria* see Bozeman, *Strategic Intelligence and Statecraft*, the concluding essay, "Strategic Intelligence in Cold Wars of Ideas."

12. Hitler seems to be the preferred standard or model for identifying particularly hateful twentieth-century counterplayers. More recently he served in that function again when the occasion called for "understanding" the chief Serbian culprit in savage interethnic war. Since Yugoslavia had been a thoroughly Stalinist state under Tito and his successors, and Serbs constituted the most radical Communist faction, the right analogy would have been Stalin. And the same holds, obviously, in the case of Saddam Hussein—at least when there's ignorance of Arab history.

13. For case studies leading to this conclusion see Bozeman, *Strategic Intelligence and Statecraft*, essay 5: "Statecraft and Intelligence in the Non-Western World"; essay 6: "Knowledge and Method in Comparative Intelligence, Studies of Non-Western Societies"; and Bozeman, "The Future of International Law in a Multicultural World," in Rene-Jean Dupuy, ed., *Proceedings*, Workshop on the Future of International Law (The Hague: Martinus Nijhoff, 1984).

14. John Dziak, *Chekisty: A History of the KGB* (Lexington, MA: Lexington Books, 1988). The entire book deals with the Soviet state as a counterintelligence state.

15. For an extensive examination of these themes, see Adda Bozeman, *Conflict in Africa: Concepts and Realities* (Princeton, NJ: Princeton University Press 1976).

16. The situation is altogether different in Egypt, Iran, and Turkey.

17. For a comparative analysis of the world's war ways see Bozeman, *Strategic Intelligence and Statecraft*, essay 2: "War and the Clash of Ideas."

18. For extended references and comments on this theme, see Bozeman, "The Impact of Modern Terrorism on American Conceptions of War and International Law" (unpublished paper).

19. Charles Dickens, *Oliver Twist* (London: Nonesuch Press, 1938), p. 51.

20. Quoted in Major General Evan L. Hultman, AUS (Ret.) ed., "ROA National Security Report," *The Officer* (July 1992), p. 46.

4

The American Economy, the Defense Budget, and National Security

Stephen Daggett

"[A] foreign policy," wrote Walter Lippmann in 1943, "consists in bringing into balance, with a comfortable surplus of power in reserve, the nation's commitments and the nation's power. The constant preoccupation of the true statesman is to achieve and maintain this balance."[1] Such a preoccupation has been at the center of debate over U.S. national security policy ever since. At times, the governing view of the balance between American power and commitments has been rather expansive—during the Kennedy years, for example, and through most of the first Reagan term. At other times, the nation's leaders have felt constrained to adjust policy to limited resources—in the Eisenhower era, for example, when the President feared that too heavy a military burden would weaken the economy, and, for different, political as well as economic, reasons, following the Vietnam War.

Occasionally, confidence in America's ability to lead the world has been a major issue in presidential campaigns; it may have been a factor in reshaping popular perceptions of the two political parties in 1960 and, especially, in 1980. Moreover, the balance between resources for commitments abroad and funding for domestic needs has often been a matter of intense debate both within Congress and between a Congress attuned to the needs of constituents at home and an Executive with greater constitutional responsibilities in foreign affairs. Samuel Huntington recognized the complexity of military policy-making. Writing more than thirty years ago, he concluded:

The most distinctive, the most fascinating, and the most troublesome aspect of military policy is its Janus-like quality. Indeed, military policy not only faces in two directions, it exists in two worlds. One is international politics, the world of the balance of power, wars and alliances, the subtle and the brutal uses of force and diplomacy to influence the behavior of other states. The principal currency of this world is actual or potential military strength. . . . The other world is domestic politics, the world of interest groups, political parties, social classes, with their conflicting interests and goals. The currency here is the resources of society.[2]

Today, the nation's ability to bear the costs of global leadership is once again a matter of widespread discussion and debate among academics, politicians, journalists, and other opinion leaders. This time, however, the issues are in many ways more tangled than in the past. The end of the Cold War has reduced the need for the United States to devote substantial resources to the military, but even much-reduced, long-term defense spending plans are proving difficult to sustain in the face of continuing disputes over the federal budget and tax policy. Budget politics have also limited measures to provide economic aid to Eastern Europe and the former Soviet Union. Moreover, given the state of the economy, the decline of defense spending is widely felt to be an economic burden rather than a boon. Perhaps most important, the issue is compounded by the prospect that the principal currency of international politics may be changing from battalions, weapons, and warships, as Samuel Huntington put it thirty years ago, to technology, education, and economic growth, as Joseph Nye, a Harvard colleague of Professor Huntington's, argued in 1990.[3] At a time when U.S. military preeminence is unchallenged, it appears that military power has been devalued as a basis for asserting global leadership.

Under these circumstances, the relationship between trends in the U.S. economy and the evolving debate over U.S. national security policy in the post–Cold War world is complex. There is widespread agreement in identifying the main challenges the U.S. economy faces over the next several years, but no consensus on how serious a threat these challenges pose to the relative strength of the United States in international economic, political, and military affairs. Moreover, there are substantial disagreements over means of solving the economic problems the country faces and over the extent to which solutions require changes in the U.S. global posture.

Even if one accepts a relatively optimistic view of the underlying strength of the U.S. economy and of America's stature in the world, the ability of U.S. policymakers to allocate resources to world affairs may nonetheless remain problematic. One reason is that the unresolved federal budget deadlock may make it difficult to stabilize defense and international affairs funding. A second is that persistent slow growth in the U.S. economy may engender a political climate in which competition for limited resources is fierce and popular support for international endeavors is grudging. A third is that strains caused by the ongoing internationalization of the U.S. economy may entail increasingly antagonistic public attitudes towards traditional American allies, with important implications for alliance relations and international burden sharing. None of these developments, of course, is preordained.

The discussion that follows begins by briefly reviewing trends in the economy that are especially important as reference points in debate over America's international stature. Next, the chapter analyzes some of the major political issues that follow from these economic developments. Finally, the chapter closes by very briefly discussing how varying perspectives on national and international economic matters shape differing views on national security policy.

TRENDS AND CHALLENGES IN THE U.S. ECONOMY

Several major problems are widely acknowledged across the political spectrum in assessing the health of the U.S. economy, including the following:

1. *A slowing rate of growth in labor productivity.* The Council of Economic Advisors has divided trends in labor productivity over the past century into three long epochs—"from 1889 to 1937, when productivity growth averaged 1.9 percent a year; from 1937 to 1973, when productivity grew 3.0 percent a year; and the period since 1973, when productivity growth averaged 0.9 percent a year."[4] Long-run advances in living standards depend on improvements in productivity; average output per hour will double every 23 years if productivity grows by 3.0 percent per year, but will take 77 years to double if growth averages only 0.9 percent per year. A rapid growth of productivity entails rapid growth in incomes and wealth; slower rates of growth in productivity imply that rapid progress for some can come only at the expense of others. Trends in real wages echo trends in productivity growth. Average hourly compensation grew by 2.9 percent per year from 1959 to 1973. Since 1973, real wages have grown by only 0.7 percent per year. The long-term effect is dramatic. Over the entire period from 1959 to 1990, wages grew by 69 percent. Between 1973 and 1990, however, cumulative growth amounts to only 11 percent.[5]

2. *A low rate of savings and investment.* Between 1950 and 1979, the United States had the lowest rate of growth of capital per worker among the seven leading industrial countries. Since 1979, the U.S. rate of investment has declined even further (see Figure 4.1).[6] One reason for low investment is a low savings rate. U.S. savings rates, already far below those of other major industrial countries, also declined in the 1980s.[7] A low rate of investment may be one reason for slow growth in labor productivity in recent years.

3. *Declining rates of investment in science and technology.* Overall U.S. public and private spending on research and development grew steadily from 1975 through the mid–1980s. Since then, the rate of growth has slowed, and, in 1990, research and development (R & D) spending actually declined in real terms.[8] At the same time, research spending by overseas economic competitors has continued to rise. According to recent estimates, today Japan devotes 3 percent of its gross national product (GNP) to civilian R & D, compared to a U.S. investment of 1.9 percent of GNP, and annual Japanese

Figure 4.1
U.S. Net Private Domestic Investment, 1961–1990 (five-year geometric mean % of GDP)

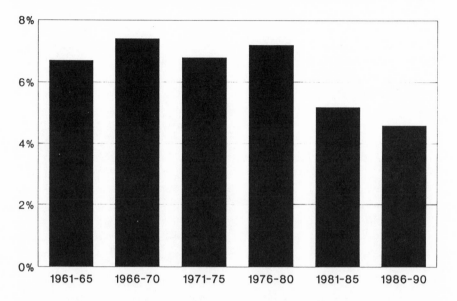

industrial R & D spending now exceeds the U.S. level.[9] Investment in civilian R & D affects both the long-term growth of labor productivity and U.S. ability to claim a share of international markets for new goods.

4. *Education and the quality of the labor force.* Labor productivity is determined as much by the quality of the labor force as by technology and capital investment. Moreover, in an era of rapidly changing technology, the adaptability of the work force is increasingly important. There is, however, a widespread sense that the U.S. educational system is failing at least a large part of the population and that the United States is losing the international skills race. By world standards, U.S. school dropout rates are high, and U.S. elementary and secondary school students score lower in science and math skills than students in other major industrial countries. While widespread access to high-quality college education makes up for these shortcomings for much of the population, many are left behind. Some, including President Clinton during his campaign, have argued that the United States makes little effort, compared to some competitors, to train non-college-bound students and should adopt apprenticeship programs and take other steps to help workers continually upgrade their skills.[10]

Other economic trends also profoundly influence the economy, though few see the effects as necessarily damaging. Of these other developments, the most important may be the internationalization of the U.S. economy. Over the past thirty years, exports and imports have doubled as a share of the overall economy (see Figure 4.2). Just as important, since exchange rates

Figure 4.2
Exports plus Imports as a Percentage of GDP, 1960–1990

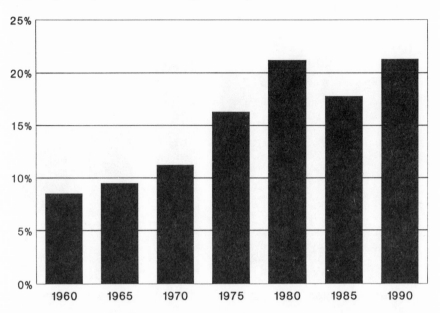

were freed twenty years ago, financial markets have become truly international. In many ways, the results are positive, with consumers especially benefiting. In international as well as domestic competition, however, there are economic losers as well as winners. Some parts of the U.S. labor movement, for example, whose members have been badly hurt, have effectively dropped out of the internationalist consensus that has governed U.S. trade policy since World War II. A widely troubling by-product of economic internationalization, moreover, is that economic and political developments not under the control of U.S. political and economic institutions directly and immediately affect the well-being of American citizens.

Imperial Overstretch

Along with broad agreement on some of the major challenges facing the economy, there is also a widespread consensus to the effect that certain developments do not threaten U.S. economic vitality. Among these is a so-called "imperial overstretch," which Professor Paul Kennedy and some others have postulated may, in the future, aggravate the nation's relative economic decline.[11] The Kennedy thesis stimulated a great deal of criticism and commentary, most of it holding that the notion does not apply very persuasively to the situation facing the United States. For one thing, it is hard to make a case that the military burden that the United States has borne in

Figure 4.3
U.S. Military Spending as a Share of GNP/GDP

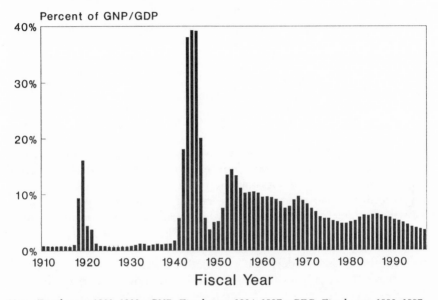

Percent of GNP/GDP

Fiscal Year

Note: Fiscal years 1910–1933 = GNP. Fiscal years 1934–1997 = GDP. Fiscal years 1993–1997: Bush Administration projection.

recent years and is likely to bear in the post–Cold War era could in itself be a significant drag on the economy. Even the Reagan-era peak of defense spending at 6.5 percent of GDP in 1986 is substantially below peacetime levels maintained in the late 1950s and early 1960s, when the economy was growing (see Figure 4.3). Current administration plans project a decline of defense spending to about 3.5 percent of GDP by 1997. Moreover, recent reviews of the impact of defense spending on the economy, even by onetime critics of U.S. defense policy, dismiss the argument that modestly greater levels of military spending can be correlated, either cross-nationally or over time, with slow productivity growth or other economic ills.[12]

To be sure, a premise of Kennedy's thesis is that growing foreign challenges to American preeminence may, in the future, lead the United States to spend much more on defense in a futile and self-defeating effort to remain "number one." If this turned out to be the case, then Kennedy's comparison of the United States with historical examples of overextended empires might be apt. Moreover, as this chapter will discuss later, Kennedy's classical "realism" about international affairs is widely shared and shapes perspectives on post–Cold War foreign policy among many leaders of the old guard of American foreign policy. Most of those who share a pessimistic view of international relations, however, also prescribe a more selective approach to U.S. international commitments, while those who have a mor ⌐ expansive view of the U.S. potential for global leadership tend to be op'imistic about prospects for international cooperation. Few share Kennedy's underlying proposition that a nasty turn in international politics and worsening relations with traditional allies will make the U.S. public more rather than less likely to support military activism abroad.

ALTERNATIVE ASSESSMENTS AND SOLUTIONS

Besides agreeing on some of the major challenges ahead, however, and rejecting a rigid version of the "relative decline" thesis, economists and political leaders are in accord on relatively little regarding major economic issues. The Bush Administration's Council of Economic Advisors, for example, tended largely, if not completely, to dismiss concern about the long-term decline of labor productivity, arguing that the post–World War II growth of productivity was unusual by historical standards, that all industrial economies have experienced a falling off of growth rates in the past two decades, and that worrisome trends, such as the low U.S. rate of savings and investment and the decline of civilian R & D spending, can be attributed to antigrowth tax policies that can be reversed with appropriate changes, including a capital gains tax cut, intended to reduce the cost of capital. By the same token, the council argued that the Bush Administration's initiatives to improve education were a key ingredient of long-term economic policy.[13]

Other economists and political leaders disputed such official optimism. One critical school of thought has tended to focus on the issue of technology policy—that is, on the presumed need for government to identify key long-term (critical) technologies, to assist private ventures in exploring these new technologies, and to reduce the cost and risk of doing so. Though most proponents of this view have backed away from advocating an explicit industrial policy, many still feel that the government can and should encourage the transfer of technology from government-funded research agencies to the private sector and should take the lead in developing advanced communications, transportation, and other technologies that might make up a post-industrial infrastructure.

Another school of thought might be called the "shared sacrifice" school. In this view, articulated most forcefully by Peter G. Peterson, growth in consumption in the 1980s was financed largely by borrowing, and much of the borrowing was done from abroad. The high interest rates needed to attract foreign capital, in turn, drove up the value of the dollar, which depressed U.S. exports and encouraged consumption of cheap imports. To reverse the trend will, in Peterson's view, require substantial sacrifices in domestic consumption, a medicine that American political leaders have been reluctant to prescribe and domestic interest groups have been even more unwilling to swallow.[14] Among political leaders, Paul Tsongas and Warren

Rudman have allied themselves with Peterson to promote federal deficit reduction and other measures to encourage savings and investment.

An important dimension of the debate on basic economic issues concerns U.S. international competitiveness and the related matter of overall trade policy. A major element of debate over technology policy has concerned government support for technologies that are important as bases for developing new products and winning civilian international markets in the future. American companies appear to be doing better in the international technology competition lately, but disputes with trading partners continue over troubling issues like supercomputer sales and efforts by competitors to break the U.S. lead in aerospace technology.

On trade policy more broadly, a major theme of Republican and Democratic candidates for office alike has been the need for American trade negotiators to get tougher in insisting that barriers to U.S. exports be lowered. The apparent resolution of the U.S. dispute with the European Community over agricultural subsidies may clear the path to agreement on new international trade rules. Moreover, with the decline of the dollar since the mid–1980s, exports have grown, easing protectionist pressures at home. A substantial trade deficit persists, however, and it is unclear how long America's major trading partners will continue to absorb increased U.S. imports.

CRITICAL DOMESTIC POLICY ISSUES

Bill Clinton's victory in the 1992 presidential election portends a shift towards a much more active government role in directing the economy and, to the extent international developments permit, a focus on domestic affairs. It does not, however, resolve all of these divergent views on basic economic issues. On the contrary, underlying differences even among leading Democrats on some fundamentals are apparent. Debate has already surfaced over the priority that should be accorded to reducing the federal budget deficit as opposed to measures designed to stimulate long-term economic growth by investing in infrastructure, education, defense conversion, and new technology development. The details of a long-term investment strategy, moreover, remain to be worked out. Finally, major aspects of trade policy may continue to be matters of bitter dispute.

Each of these unresolved issues is directly related to long-term U.S. national security policy. One question is obvious: how efforts to reduce the federal budget deficit will affect funding for defense and international affairs. A second set of issues is more difficult to define, but closely related—whether efforts to improve productivity and enhance economic growth will ease political conflict over the allocation of limited resources, and how the outcome will affect international policy. A third set of issues follows from the internationalization of the U.S. economy: how the country will adjust to the strains that necessarily accompany growing global interdependence. The discussion that follows reviews each of these sets of issues in turn.

The Federal Budget Deficit

From a defense planner's standpoint, the costs of failing to deal with the federal budget deficit are apparent. Neither the Bush Administration's defense plan, which called for spending $1.42 trillion on defense over the FY (Fiscal Year) 1993–1997 period, nor the marginally less expensive Clinton plan, which calls for spending $1.36 trillion, will prove sustainable if the budget deficit remains high. This is perhaps the major lesson of the late 1980s, when it became clear that the level of defense spending is directly dependent on political bargaining over the deficit, taxes, and nondefense spending. The end of the Reagan-era military buildup was written before Mikhail Gorbachev came to power in the Soviet Union when, in December 1984, then-Senator Goldwater, along with Senator Nunn, paid a visit to the White House to urge the President to agree to reduce projected increases in defense spending as part of a broader deficit reduction plan.

It is significant that the Goldwater visit came shortly after President Reagan had won a landslide election victory in which he had effectively criticized the Democrats for proposing to raise taxes. Later, during the 1985 budget debate, Republicans in control of the Senate initially proposed a deficit reduction plan that called for limited growth in defense spending and, most notably, a freeze on Social Security cost of living adjustments. The Republicans, in turn, were effectively assailed by Democrats for proposing to cut Social Security. Since then, neither political party has been willing to call either for more than marginal tax increases or for any cuts in Social Security benefits and other major individual entitlements. With these two avenues of deficit reduction closed off, the outcome, reflected in the terms of the Gramm-Rudman-Hollings deficit reduction act that was agreed to late in 1985, has been that both defense and nondefense discretionary spending have borne the brunt of annual deficit reduction exercises, with little real progress being made in reducing the structural shortfall in the federal budget.

The irony, as Figure 4.4 illustrates, is that neither defense spending nor domestic discretionary expenditures has been mainly responsible for the growth in federal spending over the past thirty years. On the contrary, federal spending has been driven higher largely by the growing cost of major entitlement programs and, in recent years, by the cost of interest on the debt. The growth of entitlement programs, in turn, is due to a number of factors. Only part of the growth of entitlements is due to conscious changes in government policy. Much of the growth is explained by long-term demographic and economic trends and by unexpected factors that increased the demand for and cost of government services.

Figure 4.4
Federal Outlays by Category, Fiscal Years 1965–1995

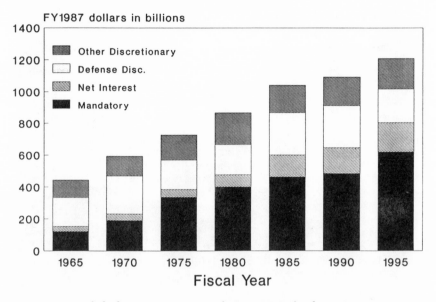

FY1987 dollars in billions

Legend:
- Other Discretionary
- Defense Disc.
- Net Interest
- Mandatory

Note: Figures exclude deposit insurance. Fiscal year 1995: Bush Administration projection.

Figure 4.5 shows the growth in major categories of mandatory spending (of which entitlements are the major component) since 1960. The largest growth has been in Social Security retirement benefits and in major medical programs. Much of the growth in Social Security and Medicare is due to simple demographics. In 1960 the number of Americans aged 65 and over totaled 16.7 million (9.2 percent of the population), and in 1987, 29.8 million (12.2 percent of the population). Moreover, the life expectancy for retirees has continued to grow. And since Social Security benefits (and federal pensions as well) are indexed to preretirement income, the long-term increase in average pay since the 1930s has also increased the cost of retirement programs. Costs of Medicare, Medicaid, and other health programs have also grown rapidly, first because of greater-than-expected utilization rates as the increased availability of care encouraged people to seek it, and second because the cost of health care in general has grown faster than the inflation rate.[15]

A major question in the deficit debate, therefore, is whether the Federal government can control the growth of entitlement costs. One reason to be optimistic is that some of the demographic trends that drove mandatory spending higher in the 1960s, 1970s, and 1980s are easing, at least until well after the turn of the century. Figure 4.6 shows a simple measure of the fiscal

Figure 4.5
Federal Outlays for Mandatory Programs, Fiscal Years 1965–1995

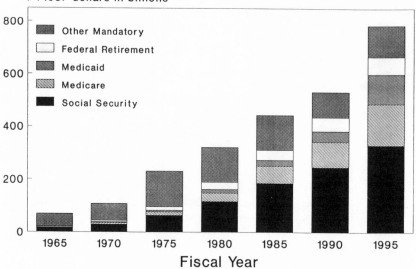

FY1987 dollars in billions

Note: Figures exclude deposit insurance. Fiscal Year 1995: Bush Administration projection.

burden of the retirement-age population.[16] Though many other factors also influence the cost of retirement programs, the leveling off of the retirement-age population relative to the working-age population should ease budget pressures over the next twenty years.

Projections of the cost of federal health care programs, in contrast, provide little reason for optimism. Figure 4.7 shows an actuarial estimate of total national spending on health care as a share of the economy.[17] The analysis projects a similar rate of growth of federal and other government health costs. Without control over the growth of health expenditures, therefore, the prospects for controlling the federal budget deficit are not very good.

Indeed, in the absence of controls over the growth of entitlement programs, projections of trends in the federal budget deficit are disheartening. According to an August 1992 study by the Congressional Budget Office, under the terms of the October 1990 budget compromise, annual federal budget deficits, excluding deposit insurance, may be expected to decline to $244 billion by FY 1995, which would equal about 3.4 percent of gross domestic product (GDP). Without new revenues or further reductions in spending, by the year 2002, deficits will exceed $500 billion per year and equal 5.3 percent of GDP. The main reason for the increase is the growth of entitlements, which will climb from 12.2 percent of GDP in FY 1995 to

Figure 4.6
Midrange Estimate of U.S. Old-Age Dependency Ratio, 1950–2070

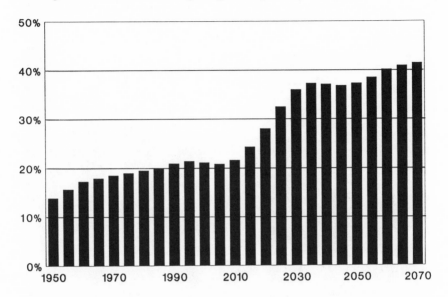

Note: Graph shows population over 65 as percentage of population aged 20–64.

14.1 percent by 2001, while the share for discretionary spending declines. Federal Medicare and Medicaid costs will grow from 4.0 percent of GDP to 6.1 percent, while the share for other mandatory spending declines.[18]

Significantly, control over entitlement spending and medical costs was at the center of the budget debate through much of 1992. In April, during consideration of the annual congressional budget resolution, Senator Pete Domenici, the ranking Republican on the Senate Budget Committee, and Senator Sam Nunn brought up an alternative long-term budget plan that called for phasing in a freeze on the growth of mandatory programs, allowing only sufficient increases to keep up with inflation and the growth of eligible population groups, plus 2 percent per year. The plan would have imposed automatic, across-the-board reductions in all entitlements, except for Social Security, if Congress and the President failed to take steps to reduce spending to meet the targets.

Opponents of the plan, led by Senate Majority Leader George Mitchell, complained that the Domenici/Nunn proposal represented an empty procedural approach to deficit reduction without explicitly addressing the hard choices that need to be made. In effect, opponents argued, it was a way of claiming to do something about the deficit in the present, while passing off to future Congresses the need to pay the real political price. Senator Mitch-

Figure 4.7
Projected U.S. Health Care Costs as a Percentage of GNP, 1965–2000

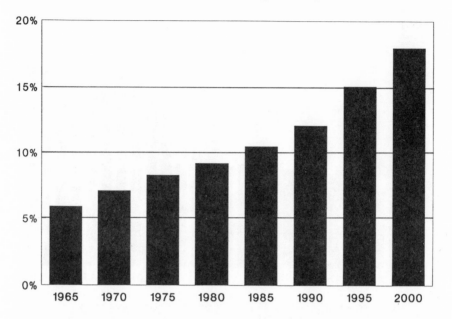

ell's allies in the Senate specifically argued that the rising costs of medical care explain almost all of the projected future growth of entitlement spending (beyond the growth caused by increases in the eligible population and inflation), so that the real task was to decide what to do about reforming the health care system. Moreover, they argued, it would be unfair to cut other programs that are not growing out of control to pay for a failure to control medical costs.

In any event, virtually all of the major organizations representing the elderly and other groups potentially affected by limits on entitlements strongly opposed the measure. Ultimately, Senator Mitchell made his point very effectively by proposing a long series of amendments that would exempt, one by one, major categories of entitlement spending from automatic cuts, and he resolved to force a role call vote on each amendment. Supporters of the Domenici/Nunn proposal, including Senator Rudman, decided to risk a test vote. The first amendment was to exempt veterans benefits from automatic reductions, and when it passed by a vote of 68 to 22, Domenici withdrew his proposal.[19]

Leaving aside any judgments about the merits of either the Domenici or the Mitchell position, the episode is important as an illustration of the current impasse in the budget debate. The root of the deficit problem is simply that the price of large, popular entitlement programs continues to grow while revenues are not keeping pace. Budget professionals in Washington, like

Senators Domenici and Mitchell, fully understand that the changes that need to be made will be politically very difficult and costly. Last April, Mitchell opposed the Domenici effort because it would have been a means of letting a Republican President off the hook, and he believed, for institutional as well as partisan reasons, that the President as well as Congress should be held accountable for making difficult choices.

It is significant from a national security standpoint that the alternative budget that Senator Domenici proposed incorporated long-term defense spending plans that Senator Nunn had worked out. These plans called for cutting defense through FY 1997 by close to the amount that President Clinton proposed during his campaign. Moreover, in late September, with considerable publicity, Senators Domenici and Nunn endorsed a yet more ambitious version of their April plan, this time issued as a report, *The Strengthening of America Commission*, sponsored by the Washington-based Center for Strategic and International Studies.[20] The new report extended the deficit reduction plan through FY 2002, added substantial revenue increases (many were surprised that Senator Domenici supported these measures in the heat of the presidential campaign), and, notably, included additional, substantial cuts in defense spending beyond FY 1997 (which some were surprised to see Senator Nunn endorse). The lesson is that further cuts in defense, beyond those currently planned, can be expected to accompany any compromise that is reached on the deficit, even assuming a compromise is possible. Until a long-term compromise is worked out, defense planners should not assume that funding plans will remain stable.

Redistributive Politics

The impasse over cuts in entitlement spending may also illustrate a more general point—political decisions in Washington, and perhaps allocative decisions more broadly, are increasingly being shaped by an environment of scarcity rather than growth. It wasn't always this way. To use one example, in the early years of the Kennedy Administration and well into the Johnson years, economists and political leaders assumed that a growing economy, together with a progressive tax code, would generate ever larger government surpluses that had to be disposed of in order to avoid creating a drag on the economy. As Walter Heller, the chairman of President Kennedy's Council of Economic Advisors, explained in 1966,

[I]n a growth context, the great revenue-raising power of our Federal tax system produces a built-in average increase of $7 to $8 billion a year in Federal revenues. . . . Unless it is offset by such "fiscal dividends" as tax cuts or expansion of Federal programs, this automatic rise in revenues will become a "fiscal drag" siphoning too much of the economic substance out of the private economy and thereby choking expansion.[21]

One result of these expectations of a perpetual "growth dividend" was that the federal government was willing to undertake commitments to new programs, including Medicare and Medicaid, on the premise that growing costs in the future could be paid for by the natural expansion of the economy. Political scientists have described the result as "distributive politics," in which interest groups can each claim a share of a growing pie. Scarcity, however, ultimately engenders a kind of "redistributive politics" in which gains by one group can come only at the expense of others.[22]

Expectations of growth in the past also contributed to the notion that the country could afford both guns and butter. In a curious fashion, Ronald Reagan was able to resurrect the sentiment and some of the substance of the old politics of growth with a direct effect on his approach to national security.[23] Joseph Nye has neatly summarized a point made by the historian John Lewis Gaddis as follows:

In surveying postwar strategies of containment, . . . Gaddis noted that the Democrats (Harry Truman, John Kennedy, and Lyndon Johnson) were fiscal liberals willing to tax and spend. They tended to take a broader view of containment because they were optimistic about the means of U.S. power. Republican fiscal conservatives (Eisenhower, Richard Nixon, Gerald Ford) were more reluctant to tax and spend and thus chose more selective goals and methods of containment. Not only did Reagan take an expansive view of containment, but his supply-side fiscal unorthodoxy broke the postwar partisan pattern. On security issues, he spent like a Democrat but taxed like a Republican.[24]

Notwithstanding the obligatory economic optimism that President Bush and Governor Clinton articulated throughout the presidential campaign, a kind of redistributive politics has in recent years held sway in debates over security policy. Early in 1992, for example, the Bush Administration was unwilling to ask Congress to approve a package of assistance to the former Soviet Union for fear that the President would prove vulnerable to criticism that he was putting foreign aid ahead of domestic needs. The package was announced only after the White House learned that Governor Clinton planned to endorse the aid in a major speech. Even with support from both presidential candidates, the assistance package faced tough opposition from both sides of the aisle in Congress, with conservative House Republicans opposed to "giveaway Democrat foreign aid" programs, and some liberal Democrats determined to tie the aid to assistance to Los Angeles and other urban areas. While the aid program was ultimately approved, there appears to be relatively little enthusiasm in Congress for a more ambitious assistance effort along the lines of the "grand bargain" that Harvard's Graham Allison and others have advocated.[25]

For its part, the Clinton Administration appears committed to pursue an essentially internationalist foreign policy, with the United States continuing to play a leading role in global affairs. Public expectations about the prospects for long-term growth of the U.S. economy, however, are, at best uncertain. Meanwhile, senior Clinton economic advisors are trying to limit expectations, arguing that it will take time to reinvigorate the economy. Under the circumstances, it seems unlikely that foreign policy and national security programs can, for the foreseeable future, escape contentious domestic debates over the allocation of limited resources.

International Economic Relations

A third broad set of issues that may affect national security policy concerns the effects of the internationalization of the U.S. economy on public attitudes about the U.S. role in the world. Global interdependence unavoidably creates strains both domestically and between the United States and other nations that may be both allies and economic competitors. Domestically, the strains have appeared recently in debates over trade policy between groups that have lost jobs to international competition, largely in the "rust belt," and groups that have benefitted from imports and exports, especially on the two coasts. Earlier there were bitter disputes over U.S. international energy policy between energy-consuming states in the North and energy producers in the South. These internal political strains merely illustrate the intensity of feeling that could result if relations with major economic partners were to deteriorate over any number of issues.

Even if extreme conflicts, like the Arab oil embargo in 1973 or the Organization of Petroleum Exporting Countries (OPEC) price increases of 1978, do not arise in the future, the vulnerability of the U.S. economy to the economic policies of other nations has certainly affected public attitudes in the United States towards international relations. Moreover, even assuming that the federal deficit problem is resolved in the near future and that policies designed to promote domestic economic growth succeed to a substantial degree, the integration of the United States into the international economy may be expected to shape public perceptions of the U.S. role in the world. With the development of a more or less equal balance of economic power among the United States, Japan, and Western Europe, sentiment inevitably has grown to the effect that allies should more equitably share the burden of ensuring international security. At the same time, Americans clearly still like to feel that the United States is in a position to lead the world. These conflicting sentiments may entail real difficulties in reshaping NATO and other alliances and in negotiating cost sharing arrangements with allies where the United States maintains troops overseas, and responsibility sharing with allies in future international crises.

PERSPECTIVES ON NATIONAL SECURITY

The academic debate over theories of relative decline, the end of the Cold War, and the U.S.-led triumph in the Persian Gulf War have generated a remarkable array of articles, books, and papers on fundamental matters of strategy and the U.S. role in the world. While this is not the place to review this literature at any great length, it may be worthwhile to consider how different underlying assumptions about national and international economics may shape perspectives on international security issues. One can identify at least four different schools of thought on the relationships between economics and security.

One school of thought argues that the U.S. international role has imposed a heavy economic burden on the domestic economy and concludes that the United States should separate itself from entangling alliances abroad and either focus inward or, alternatively, follow a strategy abroad that carefully and selectively advances U.S. interests without pretending to enforce global order. Defined broadly, this category covers a wide range of analysts, from libertarians like Ted Carpenter, to advocates of an interest-based foreign policy like Alan Tonelson, to proponents of devolving international responsibilities to the allies, like David Calleo.[26] Calleo's views deserve a separate note; he argues that U.S. allies, and not only the United States, have paid a price for supporting the U.S. role in the world. The allies, he argues, have increasingly been expected to prop up a declining U.S. economy and therefore have an interest in developing an independent security policy of their own.

A second school of thought begins from the premise that U.S. and allied economic interests will increasingly diverge unless the United States gets its economic house in order. Starting from this premise, Peter Peterson warns that economic conflict with major U.S. allies can be avoided only if the United States focuses inward on improving the domestic economy by making necessary sacrifices. He draws few direct conclusions about U.S. national security strategy and foreign policy, but implicitly he seems to suggest that global military leadership is relatively unimportant compared to the need to address U.S. economic ills. A similar premise underlies Fred Bergsten's thinking, but, interestingly, Bergsten argues that the United States should continue to play a major international security role. Indeed, he hints, without offering many specifics, that a leading security role should provide the United States with leverage on international economic matters.[27]

A third school of thought holds that international economic and political interdependence should unite, rather than divide, major nations in seeking to establish and maintain world order. The most comprehensive presentation of this point of view has been offered by Joseph Nye.[28] Nye has argued that international politics is becoming less polarized but also more complex, that shifting coalitions of nations will develop based on common interests on different international issues, and, most important, that common perceptions of shared interests are the key to international order and that the United States should be in a position to shape perceptions of shared interests. Nye is optimistic, therefore, about America's ability to play a leading international role, provided the nation is led effectively. A similar optimistic perspective may be seen among political leaders, including Senator Joseph Biden, who have advocated multilateral approaches to international security issues.[29]

A fourth school of thought disputes the premises underlying a multilateralist view and holds that U.S. perspectives on international affairs will increasingly diverge from those of other global powers, and that the United States should play an active but selective role in world affairs in accordance with a clear vision of its national interests. A forceful proponent of this view is Henry Kissinger, who has argued that six major world economic and military power centers will evolve—"the United States, Europe, China, Japan, whatever emerges in the Soviet Union and probably India." He argues, "For America, reconciling somewhat different values and very different historical experiences among countries of more or less equal strength will be a novel experience and a major departure from either its isolation of the last century or practical hegemony during the Cold War."[30] Kissinger shares the view that economic strength, as an element of national power, will become increasingly important, but he believes that international economics will tend to divide rather than unite major powers.

These differing perspectives have important implications for many aspects of U.S. foreign policy. In the short term, perhaps the most profound issue concerns the future of U.S. alliances. Many analysts appear to believe that NATO, especially, as the major U.S. Cold War alliance, will inevitably become less relevant in global affairs, and that U.S. interests will increasingly diverge from those of its old allies to the extent that economics replaces security as the central element in international affairs. Others appear to believe that alliances should be expanded to incorporate new members and new responsibilities or, alternatively, that new multilateral means of cooperation should evolve. From a popular perspective, the key issue may be whether alliances, which have been seen as an entangling drain on U.S. resources, will instead be seen as a way of sharing responsibilities and reducing burdens on the United States. In short, the immediate practical matter at issue in much of the current discussion of the economy and national security concerns U.S. policy on the evolution of major alliances in the post–Cold War era.

NOTES

The analysis and conclusions reflect the author's views and do not represent the views or findings of the Congressional Research Service.

1. Walter Lippmann, *U.S. Foreign Policy: Shield of the Republic* (Boston: Little, Brown, 1943), pp. 9–10.

2. Samuel P. Huntington, *The Common Defense* (New York: Columbia University Press, 1961).

3. Joseph S. Nye, Jr., "Soft Power," *Foreign Policy*, 80 (Fall 1990), p. 154.

Huntington makes a similar point in "America's Changing Strategic Interests," *Survival*, 33, no. 1 (January/February 1991), p. 5.

4. Council of Economic Advisors, *The Annual Report of the Council of Economic Advisors* (Washington, DC: Government Printing Office, February 1992), p. 91.

5. Ibid., p. 95.

6. Ibid., pp. 93, 306, 314.

7. Ibid., p. 328. See also, Peter G. Peterson, "The Morning After," *Atlantic Monthly*, 260 (October 1987), p. 48.

8. William J. Broad, "Research Spending Is Declining in U.S. as It Rises Abroad," *New York Times*, Feb. 21, 1992, pp. A1, A16.

9. National Science Board, *Science and Engineering Indicators, 1991* (Washington, DC: Government Printing Office, 1991), p. 342. Genevieve J. Knezo, "American Science at a Critical Crossroads," Congressional Research Service Issue Brief IB92016, updated May 26, 1992, pp. 2–3.

10. For the Bush Administration view on educational shortcomings and the economy, see Council of Economic Advisors, *Annual Report*, pp. 94, 97–99; for a broader discussion, see Debra L. Miller, "A Domestic Agenda to Strengthen America," *Washington Quarterly*, 15, no. 2 (Spring 1992), pp. 205, 217–221; for the Clinton view see Governor Bill Clinton, "Putting People First: A National Economic Strategy for America," mimeo, June 1992, p. 12.

11. Paul Kennedy, *The Rise and Fall of the Great Powers: Economic Change and Military Conflict from 1500 to 2000* (New York: Random House, 1987). See also Robert Gilpin, *The Political Economy of International Relations* (Princeton, NJ: Princeton University Press, 1990) for a view that focuses less on military power and more on what might be called "financial overstretch."

12. See, for example, David Gold and Gordon Adams, *Defense Spending and the Economy: Does the Defense Dollar Make a Difference?* (Washington, DC: Defense Budget Project, 1987). See also Congressional Budget Office (CBO), *The Economic Effects of Reduced Defense Spending* (Washington, DC: CBO, February 1992).

13. Council of Economic Advisors, *Annual Report*, pp. 91–97.

14. Peter G. Peterson, "The Morning After," *Atlantic Monthly*, 260 (October 1987), pp. 43f.

15. For a discussion of these and other factors, see Gene Falk and Richard Rimkunas, *1991 Budget Perspectives: Federal Spending for the Human Resources Programs*," *CRS Report For Congress*, 90–259 EPW (Washington, DC: Congressional Research Service, June 13, 1990).

16. Data are from: Board of Trustees of the Federal Old-Age and Survivors Insurance and Disability Insurance Trust Funds, *1992 Annual Report* (Washington, DC: OASDI, April 2, 1992), pp. 149–150.

17. Sally T. Sonnefeld et al., "Projections of National Health Expenditures through the Year 2000," *Health Care Financing Review*, 13, no. 1 (Fall 1991), pp. 1–54, esp. p. 16, for 1965–1980; Congressional Budget Office, *Projections of National Health Care Expenditures* (Washington, DC: CBO, October 1992), p. xi, for 1985–2000.

18. Congressional Budget Office, *The Economic and Budget Outlook: An Update* (Washington, DC: CBO, August 1992), pp. 38–39.

19. *Congressional Record*, 102d Congress, Second Session, April 10, 1992, pp. S5421–5464.

20. Senators Sam Nunn and Pete Domenici, cochairs, *The Strengthening of Amer-*

ica Commission: First Report (Washington, DC: Center for Strategic and International Studies, 1992).

21. Walter W. Heller, *New Dimensions of Political Economy* (Cambridge, MA: Harvard University Press, 1966), p. 65.

22. Theodor J. Lowi, *The End of Liberalism* (New York: Norton, 1969, 1979); the first edition (1969) emphasized the distinction between distributive and redistributive politics in what is essentially a conservative critique of "interest-group liberalism."

23. One provocative view from the left, however, holds that slow growth in the U.S. economy since 1973 has engendered a fundamental shift in American political life that Ronald Reagan reflected. See Joel Krieger, *Reagan, Thatcher, and the Politics of Decline* (New York: Oxford University Press, 1986).

24. Joseph S. Nye, "Understating U.S. Strength," *Foreign Policy*, 72 (Fall 1988), p. 111, citing John Lewis Gaddis, "Containment and the Logic of Strategy," *National Interest*, 10 (Winter 1987–88), pp. 27–38.

25. See the testimony of Professor Graham Allison in U.S. Congress, House Committee on Armed Services, Defense Policy Panel, "The Grand Bargain—Should the West Bankroll Soviet Transformation to a Free Market Economy?" Hearing, HASC No. 102–26, 102nd Cong., 1st sess., July 30, 31, and Aug. 1, 1991. (Washington, DC: Government Printing Office, 1992), pp. 2–87.

26. See Ted Galan Carpenter, "Uncle Sam as the World's Policeman: Time for a Change?" *U.S.A. Today Magazine*, January 1991, pp. 21–22; Alan Tonelson, "What Is the National Interest?," *Atlantic Monthly*, 268 (July 1991), pp. 35ff.; David O. Calleo, *Beyond American Hegemony: The Future of the Western Alliance* (New York: Basic Books, 1990).

27. Peterson, "The Morning After," and C. Fred Bergsten, "The Primacy of Economics," *Foreign Policy*, 87 (Summer 1992), pp. 3–24. For a view similar to Bergsten's, see a statement by Senator Joseph Lieberman, *Congressional Record*, 102d Congress, Second Session, Sept. 18, 1992, p. S13997.

28. See esp. Nye, "Soft Power," pp. 153–171.

29. See a series of speeches on the Senate floor by Senator Joseph Biden on June 29, June 30, and July 1, 1992; *Congressional Record*, 102d Congress, Second Session, June 29, 1992, pp. S9098–9102; June 30, 1992, pp. S9173–S9179; July 1, 1992, pp. S9496–9502.

30. Henry Kissinger, "What Kind of New World Order?" *Washington Post*, December 3, 1991, p. A21.

5

Demographics and the American Military at the End of the Twentieth Century

Mark J. Eitelberg and Stephen L. Mehay

For almost twenty years the United States has been able to sustain a 3-million-member military, two-thirds in active-duty status, without the aid of compulsory service. This is a remarkable accomplishment by any measure, but it has not come easily or cheaply. Indeed, in 1976 Congress decided to take away GI Bill benefits for new recruits at a time when military pay was eroding, the civilian job market for young men was improving, and the enlistment propensity of prospective volunteers was falling. By 1979, the combined effect of these and other influences had placed the all-volunteer force on the brink of disaster: recruiters missed their goals, personnel attrition seemed uncontrollable, troop morale waned along with public confidence in the military, reports of disciplinary problems and substandard performance were widespread, and there were repeated charges that the force was hollow. Around the same time, it was learned that the military's method for scoring the enlistment test had been seriously flawed since 1976—and, as a result, the test scores of Army recruits had bottomed out, descending even lower than the scores of men examined during the period of heavy mobilization for World War II.[1] This situation prompted Congress to set ceilings on the proportion of lower-aptitude recruits, spurred the creation of several government advisory panels and independent study groups, and inspired numerous recommendations to restore the draft.

The greatest fear of defense officials at the time centered on the projected demographic depression, or the declining population of military-age youth, which was forecasted to fall by 25 percent by the mid–1990s (see Table 5.1). If recruiting for the armed services suffered when the supply of available manpower peaked in 1979, many asked, what would happen when the supply began to wither away? The answer to this question, as it turned out, was that recruiting improved with each passing year, and measures of personnel quality soared from an all-time low to unprecedented heights.

Table 5.1
U.S. Population of 18–24-Year-Olds, 1960–2010 (numbers in thousands)

	Gender			Change in total from previous period	
Year	Male	Female	Total	Number	Percent
Actual					
1960	8,093	8,034	16,168	-	-
1970	12,451	12,261	24,712	8,544	+52.8
1975	-	-	28,005	3,293	+13.3
1980	15,327	15,022	30,350	2,345	+8.3
1985	14,529	14,219	28,749	−1,601	−5.2
1990	13,216	12,924	26,140	−2,609	−9.0
Projected*					
1995	12,290	11,991	24,281	−1,859	−7.1
2000	12,770	12,461	25,231	950	+3.9
2005	13,628	13,290	26,918	1,687	+6.6
2010	13,752	13,402	27,155	237	+0.8

Source: U.S. Bureau of Census, *Statistical Abstract of the United States, 1991* (Washington, DC: Government Printing Office, 1991).
*Projections are based on "middle series" assumptions concerning fertility rates (number of births per woman), average life expectancy, and number of immigrants entering annually.

The reasons for the "recruiting renaissance" of the 1980s—in the face of a birth-dearth population and the impending return of conscription—reveal a great deal about the relationship between military staffing and demographic trends. The armed services, in achieving their manpower successes, were forced to respond to the projected changes in the demographic environment. In the process, an important lesson was learned about the steps needed to sustain that success throughout the twentieth century and beyond.

This chapter briefly examines the lessons of the military's all-volunteer era and proceeds to explore the decade ahead. Some basic demographic trends are described and evaluated with respect to military manpower management and national security during the post–Cold War period. The discussion focuses on domestic trends and issues, even though there are also some important changes in global demographics that could influence the direction of U.S. military policy in the coming years.[2]

RISING FROM THE ASHES: THE LESSONS OF DEMOGRAPHICS AND MANPOWER FROM THE 1980s

Ancient Egyptian legend tells of a bird, the phoenix, that was consumed in fire by its own act and then rose in youthful freshness from the ashes. The story of the phoenix is a good allegory for the all-volunteer military of the late 1970s and early 1980s. Just when it seemed as though a return to the draft was inevitable, recruiting rebounded with a vengeance.

The military's eventual success in staffing its ranks—despite worsening demographic conditions—was attributed to "vigorous recruiting efforts, additional recruiting resources provided by Congress, increased military pay and compensation, and higher youth unemployment."[3] Some observers likewise credited a "surge of national pride, a reawakening of patriotism, or a similar shift in the mood of the country and public attitudes toward the military." However, the best explanation simply relates to the fact that the armed forces eventually became more experienced and more adept, along with Congress and the manpower research and development complex, at operating in an all-volunteer environment. Through several years of trial and error, coming after three decades of compulsory service, the nation's leaders finally learned how to fill the military with able recruits and careerists.

The learning experience of the early years was multifaceted. It taught the manpower community many important lessons about (1) the effect of various changes in the economy and the youth labor force on the military's ability to recruit and retain highly qualified personnel; (2) the importance of pay and benefits, especially educational assistance, as recruiting and retention incentives; (3) the importance of having accurate and current information as well as a set of plans and management procedures to counteract manpower shortfalls; (4) the importance of adequate recruiting and advertising resources; (5) how to gauge youth attitudes and propensities and then adopt appropriate policies to attract recruits; (6) how to identify alternative market segments and sell the military's product; (7) how to better manage occupational assignments, the Delayed Entry Program, and personnel attrition; (8) how to better select, assign, and train new recruits; and the list goes on.[4]

The most fundamental lesson, perhaps, was that recruiting and retention programs can be successful—despite environmental changes such as demographic fluctuations or shifts in the economy—if there are informed policies in the right areas. Thus, if recruiting begins to falter, one can calculate the required response from accumulated research and, say, raise pay incentives, increase recruiting or advertising resources, modify admission standards, tap into alternative markets, reduce the accession requirement for recruiting by allowing increased retention, or take any of several other actions. The point is, manpower problems are *manageable*. They may wind up costing somewhat more—as did the recruiting renaissance of the 1980s (along with a twofold increase in the annual defense budget over a five-year period)—but the all-volunteer system can be managed to succeed.[5]

A key element in the equation for success, in addition to adequate resources, is the ability to anticipate problems and to take necessary action before these problems become intractable. Preparing for demographic changes should be fairly easy, since data on the American population are collected regularly, projections can be made with a fair degree of certainty, and the effects of demographic changes are generally felt only gradually over a long period of time. However, the full dimensions of demographic effects are typically difficult to forecast, and they can easily be overstated or miscalculated. One reason for this is that other, more important cyclical or long-term influences frequently intervene to offset or overwhelm the effects of population changes.

For example, in the early 1980s, when manpower analysts were busy studying the possible consequences of the demographic depression on military recruiting, there were several predictions that the shrinking supply of young workers would increase youth wages.[6] It was therefore concluded that substantial increases in military pay would be necessary to maintain recruitment levels throughout the 1980s and early 1990s. We now know that the real wages of civilian youth did not rise as previously predicted; in fact, these wages declined in real terms throughout the 1980s. The unanticipated drop in youth wages is attributed to equally unexpected occurrences that caused a major restructuring of the American economy.[7]

Changes in the size, distribution, and characteristics of the population must certainly be considered by the military's manpower planners in setting a course for the future. Indeed, demographic data on the future attributes of the military's human resources are continuously available for analysis: at any point in time, one can say that the military's recruits for the next eighteen or nineteen years have already been born. But demographic factors interact with other environmental trends that are often less predictable and more powerful in their effect on the armed forces. Predictions based on demographic trends are thus subject to failure if they do not consider economic, social, or political conditions that may either counteract or reinforce the expected effects on the military of changes in the population.

The remaining sections of the chapter briefly examine several demographic trends and their possible implications for staffing the U.S. military in the years ahead. The trends include changes in the racial or ethnic composition of the population, the "greying" of America, shifting patterns of participation in the labor force, the emergence of new family forms, and an apparent decline in the abilities of entry-level workers. This is followed by a concluding observation on the military's changing environment.[8]

THE RACIAL AND ETHNIC COMPOSITION OF THE UNITED STATES

The current downsizing of the U.S. military makes the demographic depression (portrayed in Table 5.1) seem fairly unimportant for manpower planning, given the drastically reduced requirements for reenlistees and new recruits. Based on the President's 1993 budget request, the armed services expect to enlist about 211,000 new recruits for the active-duty force

Table 5.2

Distribution of Population by Race and Hispanic Origin, 1960–1990, and
Projections to 2010 (in percentages)

	White	Black	Other Races	Hispanic Origin*
		Actual		
1960	88.6	10.6	0.9	NA
1965	88.1	10.8	1.0	NA
1970	87.6	11.1	1.3	NA
1975	86.9	11.5	1.7	NA
1980	85.9	11.8	2.3	6.0
1985	84.9	12.1	3.0	7.0
1990	83.9	12.3	3.8	9.0
		Projections		
1995	82.8	12.6	4.6	10.1
2000	81.7	12.9	5.4	11.1
2005	80.7	13.2	6.1	12.2
2010	79.6	13.6	6.8	13.2

Source: Actual figures are from: U.S. Bureau of Census, *Statistical Abstract of the United States, 1991* (Washington, DC: Government Printing Office, 1991). Projections are taken from: U.S. Bureau of the Census, "Population Projections of the United States, by Age, Sex, and Race: 1992 to 2050," *Current Population Reports*, Series P–25, No. 1092 (Washington, DC: Government Printing Office, 1991).
*Persons of Hispanic origin may be of any race.

by the end of fiscal 1992, increasing to 223,000 in fiscal 1993, then dropping to 181,000 in fiscal 1994.[9] By comparison, almost 420,000 were recruited in fiscal 1975, 312,000 in fiscal 1978, almost 360,000 in fiscal 1980, 327,000 in fiscal 1981, and just over 300,000 in fiscal 1989.[10] Many knowledgeable observers believe that the military's need for new recruits will be cut even more than currently scheduled. For example, the Army expects to reduce its enlisted strength from 482,000 in fiscal year 1993 to 432,000 in fiscal year 1995.[11] "The Army's recruiting goal for 1994 will be 75,000. . . . Before the drawdown began, recruiters were enlisting up to 120,000 annually. As recently as 1990, the target mission was 89,500."[12]

Nevertheless, the demography of the nation is changing in many other ways that have both a direct and an indirect bearing on the military. One change involves the increasing proportion of racial or ethnic minorities in the population, commonly called "the browning of America." As shown in Table 5.2, the 1990 racial and ethnic minorities constituted one-fourth of the population. By the year 2020, some projections indicate that the number of U.S. residents who are minorities will more than double (to 115 million), while the white population will barely expand.[13]

The rate of increase is most rapid for Hispanics, who will become the

Table 5.3
Minorities as a Percentage of Children under Age 18 for the Whole United
States and Selected Large States, 1990, 2000, and 2010

Year	U.S.	California	Florida	New York	Texas
1990	30.7	46.6	46.4	39.9	47.1
2000	34.0	51.4	48.6	45.8	51.9
2010	38.2	56.9	53.4	52.8	56.9

Source: Adapted from *American Demographics*, May 1989, pp. 36–37, Table 5.3.

nation's largest minority group within the next twenty years, accounting for
up to half of U.S. population growth.

Changes in the racial or ethnic composition of the population are occurring
sooner in the younger age groups and in certain regions of the country. For
example, in New York State, about 40 percent of all elementary and high
school students were racial or ethnic minorities as of 1992, and in California,
Hispanics accounted for one of every three children enrolled in public
schools, African-Americans constituted 9 percent, and persons of Asian or
"other" descent represented 16 percent—thus making white, non-Hispanic
children a minority as well. Table 5.3 shows the proportion of racial or ethnic
minorities in the school-age population (within the total for the U.S. and for
four states) as of 1990 and projections for the years 2000 and 2010. As seen
in the table, by the year 2010, nonwhites and Hispanics will constitute a
majority of all children under the age of 18 in four of the nation's largest
states: California, Florida, New York, and Texas.

These changes in the population mix are driven largely by high immigration rates. Immigration also plays a major role in the growth of the total
population. In the 1980s, legal immigration accounted for 27 percent of the
increase in the U.S. population. When illegal entrants are included, immigration was responsible for 38 percent of population growth. With slow
rates of natural population increase and public policy continuing to favor
immigration, it is expected that these population growth trends will continue
in the years ahead.

The changing racial and ethnic composition of the nation means that the
military's manpower pool will contain a greater percentage of minorities and
recent immigrants, with significant regional variations, in the years ahead.
This suggests that the composition of the military may likewise change to
the extent that admission standards permit, and immigrants will constitute
an even greater share of U.S. armed forces. This conditional factor is offered
because the military's enlistment standards have become considerably more
selective over the past few years. At the same time, the high school dropout
rate for Hispanic-Americans is 28 percent—a level that has not varied much
in the past fifteen years and is considerably higher than the rate for either

non-Hispanic whites (15 percent) or blacks (22 percent).[14] Hispanic-Americans also have been underrepresented in the military since information on ethnic origin has been available for study; and the reasons for the underrepresentation of persons in this ethnic group may be deeply rooted in some Hispanic cultures.

Furthermore, research concerning the effects of aptitude and education standards on the enlistment eligibility of the youth population shows that substantial differences exist between the nation's principal racial/ethnic groups. For example, roughly 83 percent of white men between the ages of 18 and 23 would be expected to qualify for enlistment in the Army. In contrast, just under half (49 percent) of all Hispanic men and about one-third (35 percent) of black men in the same age group would be expected to meet the Army's basic enlistment criteria.[15] This disparity between the qualification rates of racial/ethnic groups is even greater in the other services. In addition, relative differences between the projected qualification rates for whites and minorities widen as higher aptitude standards are applied— and standards are considerably more selective for the military's highly technical occupations. Just 3 percent of black young men, for instance, would be expected to qualify for assignment to training as a satellite communications repairer in the Army; this compares with 9 percent of Hispanics and about 30 percent of whites.[16]

As the proportion of whites declines, so too does the proportion of the youth population considered eligible for military enlistment or for training in many technical jobs. At first glance, this does not appear to pose a problem for the armed forces, which are expected to actually raise enlistment and reenlistment standards even more under the downsizing. Because of the trends outlined above, raised standards will cut more deeply into the pool of blacks and Hispanics than of whites. Moreover, raised standards could affect the skill-training prospects of minorities who are still able to qualify for basic enlistment but unable to compete for the military's most desirable jobs. In fiscal 1989 and 1990, blacks accounted for 22 percent and 21 percent, respectively, of all new recruits; but, by fiscal 1991 blacks represented less than 17 percent of recruits, the smallest proportion since the end of the draft.

It is estimated that, spread over the 1990s, hundreds of thousands of minorities who may have otherwise joined a larger military force will be turned away.[17] This will result in a "trickle-down effect" within the civilian labor force, where minorities who once may have qualified for military service (as high school graduates with relatively high aptitude test scores for their demographic group) displace other minorities standing somewhat lower on the socioeconomic ladder. Oddly enough, when combat jobs are opened to women and more women decide to apply for these positions, minorities may well become losers once again. There are over 9 million more women than black men 18–23 years old who are at least minimally qualified for military enlistment. Thus, the removal of a long-standing barrier for women—when the military is reducing its force and maintaining or raising its admission standards—may act to reinforce a familiar obstacle for minority men.

It is difficult to speculate about the implications of declining participation in the military by minorities, even as we watch the minority segment of the general population grow. The American military runs the largest training and education establishment in the world, each year taking a multitude of raw recruits, mostly teenagers without job experience, and training them in occupations as diverse as cook and cryptoanalyst. The military experience also socializes young people and teaches them obedience, respect for authority, discipline, citizenship values, how to work as a small cog in a large organization, how to deal with adversity, how to build self-confidence, and how to lead as well as follow, among other things. Now, under the downsizing, the opportunity for a young person to serve in the military has diminished substantially. One must then ask, Will this training or socialization or "bridging environment" (as some have called the military experience) be replaced within the civilian sector? And if not, will the loss of this contribution to society by the military become an issue of national security? Certainly, poverty, joblessness, and a sense of "going nowhere" among many young people can foment discontent, social disaffection or the urge to "fight back" in the form of crime and violence.

These problems may be exacerbated by two important economic trends in the United States: falling real wages for youth, especially for lower-skilled and less-educated workers, and an apparent growing inequality in overall earnings in recent years.[18] These trends have been attributed to a major restructuring of the domestic economy, brought on by a shift in employment from manufacturing to the services sector, growing international competition, and falling worker productivity. These changes have also resulted in an increased financial return to college graduates relative to high school graduates, further separating the "haves" from the "have-nots." At a time when growing numbers of American youth could be turning to the armed forces for stable employment, good pay, and marketable training, the military's welcome mat may be gone.

THE GRAYING OF THE POPULATION AND BUDGETARY PRESSURE

The aging of the U.S. population is arguably the nation's most important demographic trend. As seen in Table 5.4, the proportion of the population aged 65 and older has grown by approximately one-third over the last three decades, and will nearly double in the coming three decades. By the year 2010, the number of persons over the age of 65 will likely exceed 40 million, constituting 14 percent of the population.[19] At the same time, the median

Table 5.4
Age Characteristics of the U.S. Population, 1960–2030

	65 Years or Older (Percent)	85 Years or Older (Percent)	Median Age
Estimates			
1960	9.2	0.5	29.4
1970	9.8	0.7	27.9
1980	11.3	1.0	30.0
1990	12.7	1.3	33.0
Projections*			
1995	13.1	1.5	34.7
2000	13.1	1.7	36.4
2010	14.1	2.0	38.9
2020	18.2	2.0	40.2
2030	22.9	2.4	41.8

Source: U.S. Bureau of the Census, *Current Population Reports Series P–25, No. 1018*, "Projections of the Population of the United States by Age, Sex, and Race: 1988 to 2080," 1989.
*Projections are based on "middle series" assumptions concerning the fertility rate (number of births per woman), average life expectancy, and number of immigrants entering annually.

age of the population will rise from 33 years in 1990 to almost 39 years in 2010, when the oldest "baby boomers" are preparing to celebrate their 65th birthday. The possible effects of the aging population on the military are not altogether evident. After all, the youngest members of the baby-boom generation (born in 1964) will start retiring from the military as early as the year 2001. The main effect for the defense establishment will be indirect—in the form of increasing pressure to trim the defense budget in favor of spending in social areas.

The largest growth in federal spending has occurred in Social Security retirement benefits and major medical programs. These expenditures have increased due to rapidly rising health care costs, as well as the aging of the population. Health care costs have grown faster than the rate of inflation and most projections indicate they will continue to do so. It is not clear how all of this will be affected by major health care reform adopted by Congress. Thus, the future will find a swelling population of elderly Americans depending on programs and services that already consume a substantial part of federal spending. The generation of baby boomers—able to extend their life expectancy through advances in medicine and increased attention to diet and exercise—will be a healthy population of senior citizens, to be sure, but one that will still rely heavily on the medical-care industry.[20]

The longer-term problems of the elderly are signaled by present difficulties in meeting the needs of this group and by the often heard warnings about the collapse of retirement programs for grey-haired baby boomers. The post–

Cold War scramble for federal funds will probably find the military at the bottom of the heap. Many defense programs will become increasingly difficult to justify as the numerically powerful, aging population demands attention and America's unfinished wars—on drugs, crime, inner-city decay, unemployment, illiteracy, homelessness, poverty, and environmental pollution—continue to rage.

The military is widely viewed as having received preferential treatment during the 1980s, when the rapid defense buildup strained the federal budget. This may help to explain why, with the collapse of Soviet Communism, the American people tend to favor cuts in defense spending as the preferred means of reducing the federal deficit and why there is a concurrent expectation that the defense drawdown should yield a "peace dividend." Historically, it should be no surprise: increases in defense spending have come to some extent at the expense of social programs, and emphasis on domestic concerns usually means less for defense. This traditional "guns versus butter" trade-off will take on added urgency as social programs cry for attention and the budget deficit constrains policymakers at every turn.

LABOR FORCE CHANGES

Population trends represent one of two major factors shaping the size and composition of the future work force; the other is the labor force participation rate for various groups.[21] Both factors have worked to create significant changes in the projected size, growth, and composition of the labor force. The Bureau of Labor Statistics makes work-force projections for the 15-year period from 1990 to 2005, and then compares the projected figures to actual patterns in the previous 15-year period (1975–1990).

As shown in Table 5.5, the U.S. labor force will grow more slowly in the future, expanding by just 21 percent in the next 15 years, compared to a growth rate of 33 percent in the previous 15 years. The aging population is the primary cause of this change in the number of workers. It can also be seen in Table 5.5 that the composition of the labor force will change considerably during the forecast period. Consistent with the overall "greying" of the U.S. population, the labor force itself will mature, as the number of workers aged 55 and over increases at twice the rate of growth of the total labor force. The number of women in the labor work force will expand by about 26 percent, exceeding the growth of the total labor force but falling far short of their 51 percent increase during the previous 15-year period. Despite this slower growth, the percentage of women who work is expected to rise from 58 percent in 1991 to 63 percent in 2005. The heightened participation of minorities in the labor force will also exceed the degree of growth in the overall labor force. For example, the proportion of workers

Table 5.5
Civilian Labor Force (16 Years and Older) Growth Rates and Percent
Distribution, by Gender, Age, Race, and Hispanic Origin, 1975 and 1990, and
Growth Projections to 2005

Demogaphic Category	Percent Change 1975–1990	1990–2005	Percent Distribution 1975	1990	2005
Total	33.1	20.8	100.0	100.0	100.00
Men	21.2	16.3	60.0	54.7	52.6
Women	50.9	26.2	40.0	45.3	47.4
Ages 16–24	−6.0	13.2	24.1	17.0	16.0
White	29.4	17.4	88.3	85.9	83.4
Black	45.7	31.7	9.9	10.8	11.8
Asian and Other	144.9	74.4	1.8	3.3	4.8
Hispanic Origin*	NA	75.3	NA	7.7	11.1

Source: Bureau of Labor Statistics, *Monthly Labor Review*, November 1991.
*Persons of Hispanic origin may be of any race.

Table 5.6
Projected Changes in the U.S. Labor Force, by Racial/Ethnic Group, 1991–2005

Racial/Ethnic Group	Entrants (Percent)	Leavers (Percent)
White, Non-Hispanic	65.3	81.9
Black	13.0	10.5
Hispanic Origin	15.7	5.2
Asian and Other	6.0	2.4

Source: Bureau of Labor Statistics, "Outlook 1990–2005," *Monthly Labor Review*, November
   1991.

who are black is projected to increase by 32 percent, those who are Asian
and others by 74 percent, and those of Hispanic origin by 75 percent. The
proportion of whites in the labor force, on the other hand, will increase at
a rate that is slower than the growth rate for the labor force as a whole.

The dynamic changes in the labor force can be seen in Table 5.6. New
entrants to the labor force over the next 15 years will be disproportionately
represented by Hispanics, blacks, and Asians and others, while those who
leave will be disproportionately white. As a result, by the year 2005, the
relative proportions of each group in the labor force will have changed
considerably. The share of whites in the labor force will have dropped to 83
percent (see Table 5.5), but the share of non-Hispanic whites will have
dropped from 78.5 percent to only 73 percent. The proportion of blacks will
grow to 12.4 percent, while the shares of Hispanics and Asians and others
will rise to 11.1 percent and 5.0 percent, respectively. Consequently, minorities will account for over 27 percent of all working people in the United

States by the year 2005. In some regions of the country this figure will exceed 50 percent.

Labor force statistics provide a more accurate picture of the people who form the military's manpower pool—although it should be noted that there are greater age constraints on the military's work force than in the labor force as a whole. (In fiscal 1990, about half of the enlisted force was between 17 and 24 years old, with the other half between 25 and 44 years of age. The average age of the enlisted force was 26.7 years; and the average age of the officer corps was 33.6 years.) Nevertheless, it is likely, judging from the combination of information on the labor force and on the population, that the traditional profile of a military applicant or prospective recruit will be changing along with changes in the labor force. There is no guarantee that the military work force will reflect the nation's labor force; indeed, the armed services of the all-volunteer era can hardly be called a microcosm of the general community. However, there is a feeling among many that the American military should be representative of the nation's population, and pressure from the public and Congress has often tried to make it so.

The removal of laws and regulations barring women from combat-related occupations is considered by many as inevitable (signaled by Congress in 1991 when it repealed a decades-old law keeping female pilots out of combat aircraft).[22] The future will consequently witness greater efforts on the part of the military, as it is pushed by external influences in the post–Cold War, peacetime setting, to overcome problems that impede the participation of women. Women currently constitute about 11 percent of active-duty personnel, a level that is far below their proportion of the civilian workforce (about 46 percent). The proportion of women in the military is likely to grow substantially throughout the next decade, as women continue to gain expanded opportunities for service.

THE EMERGENCE OF NEW FAMILY FORMS

In the 1950s, men constituted 70 percent of the labor force and were generally the sole support of their families, divorce was the exception, and few workers retired before the age of 65. Today, men represent just over half of all workers, the majority of families have two careers, divorce rates have doubled, and most workers retire before the age of 61.[23]

A lot of the changes in the labor force and the behavioral patterns of workers can be traced to changes in the American family. It is estimated that by the year 2000, less than 4 percent of all families will reflect the traditional model of American folklore—that is, a working husband, a homemaker wife, and two children. Families are increasingly characterized by more frequent divorce, middle-aged singles, cohabiting singles, unmarried mothers, remarried parents with step families, and young adults living with parents. Family patterns are now so complex that generalities are difficult to apply, and diverse family forms will become even more prevalent in the future.[24]

One aspect of the rapidly changing family is the rising number of single-parent families and the declining number of two-parent households. In March 1990, only 26 percent of all households consisted of married-couple families with children under 18 years of age. This figure is down from 31 percent in 1980 and 40 percent in 1970. For whites, the primary reason for the growth of single-parent families is divorce. It is estimated that 40 percent of white children reach age 17 without two biological parents in the household; and for black children it is twice that proportion. For blacks and Hispanics, the growth of single-parent families can often be traced to an unwed mother. By the end of the twentieth century, it is predicted that 42 percent of black children and 17 percent of Hispanic children will be living with a mother who has never married.[25]

A related family trend is that the number of female-headed households rose to 17 percent of the total in 1990, compared with 15 percent in 1980 and only 11 percent in 1970. Women alone headed 13 percent of white families, 44 percent of black families, and 23 percent of Hispanic families in 1990.[26]

Moreover, the U.S. is becoming a nation of small families. In the last two decades, the number of households with only one child increased by more than half, while those with three or more children declined by over a third. During the same period, one-person households increased from 17 to 25 percent of the total, and households with five or more persons dropped from 21 to 10 percent of the total.

Of all the changes in the American family, the military's personnel planners are perhaps most concerned about the growth of two-income couples, who are expected to represent three-quarters of all married couples by the year 2000. This particular trend has been accompanied by a more equitable sharing of parental responsibilities between men and women—which, along with certain demographic changes, has forced employers to take greater interest in developing "responsive workplace policies." In fact, more U.S. companies are attempting to create a so-called family-friendly environment for their employees, recognizing that by helping people balance job and family responsibilities, recruitment can be strengthened and valued workers can be retained. Consequently, more civilian employers are implementing flexible work schedules and job-sharing plans, offering expanding opportunities for people to work at home, placing greater emphasis on participative management, and introducing new compensation programs tailored to the needs of individual workers.

The military has made great strides since the end of the draft in creating stable communities for service members and elevating the quality of family life. A good example is in the area of child care; available spaces almost tripled (from 53,000 to 150,000) between 1981 and 1991.[27] Other programs, such as family advocacy (for parenting support and assistance), have been developed under a broadening effort to provide family support services. These actions stemmed largely from a fundamental principle of military manpower management: the armed forces enlist individuals but they *reenlist* families. As a result—with the added help of pay hikes and other economic factors—personnel retention programs enjoyed considerable success during the defense buildup of the 1980s. Obviously, times have changed; and the military is devoting as much or more effort to releasing people as to keeping them. Nevertheless, the need to retain valued personnel has not ended, and there are indications that some trouble may lie ahead.

This speculation comes from the understanding that both the military and the family are "greedy" institutions in the sense that each places great demands on individuals regarding commitments, loyalty, time, and energy.[28] Moreover, the military is highly unusual in the pattern of demands it requires of its members and their families, including personal risk, 24-hour availability, emergency deployment, geographic mobility, periodic separations and isolation, foreign residence, normative pressures, and related obligations of service life.[29] The two greedy institutions clashed during Operations Desert Shield and Desert Storm, when 17,000 single parents (including 7,200 with children below the age of five) and 3,200 dual-service couples (6,400 military husbands and wives, over half of whom had children) were deployed to the Middle East.[30] These people constituted a small fraction of the nearly 570,000 U.S. military personnel sent to the Persian Gulf between August 1990 and February 1991, but their presence and their problems received widespread attention in the national news media and in Congress.[31]

A more pressing issue for the military concerns the long-term struggle to recruit good people, keep them (and their families) content, and retain them for a full career. Some worry that in a tight budgetary climate, family-related programs and support services may be given much lower priority than at present. The trend in civilian industry is toward developing family-friendly environments, flexible work schedules, and flexible compensation systems for employees.[32] This trend could affect the military's competitive position in the job marketplace and make it increasingly difficult to attract and retain family-minded members, since most military jobs are less adaptable to environmental change and the organization itself is generally less flexible. Added to this is the possibility—based on the projected operating tempo—that a downsized force may be asked to exceed its functional capabilities and that those still in the force may have to work longer and harder to make up for personnel shortages.[33]

The idea of homesteading or home-basing military personnel, that is, having them stay in a single location for multiple consecutive assignments, has captured the interest of many officials because it would make service life less burdensome for military families and would also save a lot in travel costs. In the Army, it has been estimated that a soldier could eventually expect to have just one or two overseas tours during a full career; and the standard stateside tour would be seven years (as opposed to four).[34] It would thus be possible for a typical soldier to complete an entire career at one U.S. base with just one excursion out. The consequences of home-basing have not been fully explored, but analysts have noted at least as many potential problems as expected benefits.[35]

THE ABILITIES OF ENTRY-LEVEL WORKERS

A great deal of attention has been devoted to the influence of emerging technology on the military's requirements for highly capable and well-trained personnel.[36] Indeed, in the mid–1980s some observers suggested that the Army's weapons systems of the future might well be beyond the abilities of its manpower.[37] Several indicators of ability levels in the youth population have fueled this concern.

The performance of young people on a number of standardized tests is comparatively lower than in years past. However, average scores for a population will vary according to the test instrument as well as the characteristics of test takers, suggesting that these performance measures may be somewhat unreliable as indicators of population ability over time. More disturbing are the results of tests designed to measure national trends in student achievement through the past two decades; they show little or no improvement in tasks involving moderately complex operations. For example, evidence indicates that young people lack certain higher-order skills and abilities that are needed in the working environment. Additionally, over two-thirds of employers consulted in a recent survey reported problems in finding qualified candidates for entry-level jobs, citing deficiencies in information processing, technological knowledge, communications, problem solving, and interpersonal relations as well as basic skills in reading, writing, and mathematics.[38]

Some analysts have also claimed that the education, training and basic skills of entry-level workers in the years ahead may not be adequate to meet the requirements of civilian jobs expected to grow most rapidly within the next 15 years.[39] This has been termed a "skills mismatch." Furthermore, although young adults have completed more years of education over the past several years—and high school dropout rates have been declining (especially among blacks)—increases in educational attainment have been small since 1975. Other information suggests a general decline in U.S. education, reflected in many ways.[40]

All of this suggests increasing competition for highly capable young people in entry-level occupations, especially those in technical fields. The military should likewise expect rising competition from postsecondary institutions (a continuing trend), as colleges and universities confront a serious drop in enrollments. Businesses and colleges will also continue to draw upon the military's most successful strategies in luring and recruiting new members. These recruiting strategies may draw away many of the military's best and brightest people, who would have otherwise remained in service for a full career. Another source of competition may come from a national youth training (or apprenticeship) program, which has been proposed in Congress and is now gaining increasing support. The downsizing of the military and wider participation of women will probably lessen the potential difficulty in meeting certain manpower requirements; however, the perception that a career in the shrinking military is uncertain or threatened or unappreciated could alternatively harm efforts to recruit and retain highly capable people.

CONCLUSIONS

The end of the Cold War and disintegration of the Soviet Union have caused the United States to reexamine the very purpose of its military forces and to redefine the role of the nation as the world's sole superpower. At the same time, as the United States plans for drastic cuts in defense—reducing active and reserve forces, consolidating and closing military installations, laying off government employees, eliminating weapons systems, canceling defense contracts, pulling troops from foreign bases—the environment for staffing the military is quickly changing.[41]

Environmental change can be found in a population that holds the military in highest regard yet questions the need to pay for it; in educational indicators, test results, and other measures showing that American teenagers lack certain higher-order skills and abilities; in a civilian labor force where new entrants are more likely to be women, blacks, Hispanics, and Asians as the competition for talented young people heightens; in an economy with a falling standard of living and level of productivity among workers; in a society with rising numbers of two-income couples, more diverse family forms, shifting spousal responsibilities, and a swelling need for family-friendly conditions; in a peacetime force whose mission is being reformulated both at home and abroad; and, most directly, in a military that may be expected to do the same or even more with fewer people and resources.

Meanwhile, the competition for scarce federal money is building as a result of several demographic trends, such as the growing numbers of elderly citizens, immigrants, racial or ethnic minorities, and single parents, which can be expected to place added burdens on health care, public education, and many other social services. Furthermore, studies indicate that the economic gap between the rich and the poor in America has grown over the past several decades. This gap between the "haves" and the "have-nots" also exists on an international scale, and the United States will be called upon to provide economic (and military) aid to the have-nots as a favored means of promoting national security.

With a shrinking supply of talented young people and a growing dependence on high-tech workers, the military may have to struggle harder to get its quota of high-quality recruits, even in a downsized force. With a spreading interest in family-oriented services and flexible workplace policies by rising numbers of single parents and dual-income couples (who may also be parents), the military may also have a difficult time preventing its best members from shucking their uniforms for civilian life. Once again, adequate resources will be a key factor in the military's continuing effort to recruit good people, keep them content, and retain them for a full career.

The American armed forces face an uncertain future, to be sure, and one that will see its fair share of problems. Still, times of great change are also opportunities to move ahead and grow in new directions, a worthy goal for the post–Cold War military that survived the twentieth century.

NOTES

1. Mark J. Eitelberg, *Manpower for Military Occupations* (Washington, DC: Office of the Assistant Secretary of Defense [Force Management and Personnel], April 1988), p. 74.

2. See Mark J. Eitelberg and Stephen L. Mehay, *The Shape of Things to Come: A Compilation of Trends and Projections Expected to Affect Army Recruiting and Manpower Policy in the 21st Century* (Monterey, CA: Naval Postgraduate School, March 1992).

3. U.S. Department of Defense, *Profile of American Youth* (Washington, DC: Office of the Assistant Secretary of Defense [Manpower, Reserve Affairs, and Logistics], March 1982), p. 21.

4. See Curtis Gilroy, Robert Phillips, and John Blair, "The All-Volunteer Army: Fifteen Years Later," *Armed Forces and Society*, 16 (Spring 1990); and William Bowman, Roger Little, and G. Thomas Sicilia, eds., *The All-Volunteer Force after a Decade* (Elmsford, NY: Pergamon-Brassey's, 1986). See also Martin Binkin, "Manning the American Military in the Twenty-First Century: Demographics and National Security," in Lindsey Grant, ed., *Elephants in the Volkswagen* (New York: W. H. Freeman, 1992).

5. There is no reason, then, to expect that all-volunteer recruiting will collapse—even in the face of significant demographic shifts—unless the military's leaders and Congress allow it to do so. This is not to say that a draft may never again be needed. The American people could decide that a system of compulsory service (or national service) would be good for the country even though it might not be necessary to meet manpower requirements. Certainly a global conflict or catastrophe could trigger a mobilization of the youth population. Or the nation could be forced into resurrecting the draft by an unlikely combination of events: a sustained and unpopular conflict with heavy casualties, a substantial plunge in the relative value of military pay and benefits, a vastly improved economy and swelling job opportunities for military-age youth, a serious drop in public opinion of the military, and the occurrence of an otherwise "inconceivable" event.

6. Hong Tan and Michael Ward, *Forecasting the Wages of Young Men: The Effects of Cohort Size* (Santa Monica, CA: Rand, 1984), p. 7.

7. See, for example, Jacob Klerman and Lynn Karoly, "Trends and Future Directions in Youth Labor Markets: Implications for Army Recruiting" in Mark J. Eitelberg and Stephen L. Mehay, eds., *Marching Toward the 21st Century* (Westport, CT: Greenwood Press, forthcoming).

8. The discussion of trends and projections draws from Eitelberg and Mehay, "The Shape of Things to Come." This source, in turn, is based on a collection of material from the Army Futures project, a major study of various trends that are likely to affect the manpower and recruiting policies of the Army and other services in the years ahead. A two-day conference was held in January 1992 in Arlington, Virginia, as part of the Army Futures project. The conference was titled "Marching Toward the Twenty-First Century" and featured over twenty speakers, including U.S. Army and Department of Defense officials, academics, and subject-area experts from several government agencies. Papers from the conference can be found in Eitelberg and Mehay, eds., *Marching Toward the 21st Century*.

9. See Secretary of Defense, *Annual Report to the President and Congress* (Washington, DC: Government Printing Office, February 1992), p. 47.

10. Gary R. Nelson, "The Supply and Quality of First-Term Enlistees under the All-Volunteer Force," in Bowman, Little, and Sicilia, eds., *The All-Volunteer Force*, p. 27.

11. Jim Tice, "Enlisteds: Drawdown Takes Shape," *Army Times*, July 19, 1993, p. 13.

12. Ibid., p. 14.

13. William A. Henry III, "Beyond the Melting Pot," *Time*, April 9, 1991, pp. 28–31.

14. Department of Education, *Educational Research Bulletin*, Fall/Winter 1989–90.

15. Eitelberg, *Manpower*, p. 122.

16. Ibid.

17. Janice H. Laurence, "Implications of the Defense Drawdown for Minorities" (Paper Presented at the Biennial Conference of the Inter-University Seminar on Armed Forces and Society, Baltimore, Maryland, October 1991).

18. These trends have been documented in a number of studies: Paul Ryscavage and Peter Henle, "Earnings Inequality Accelerates in the 1980s," *Monthly Labor Review*, December 1990, pp. 3–16; Gary Burtless, ed., *A Future of Lousy Jobs?* (Washington, DC: Brookings Institution, 1990).

19. Eitelberg and Mehay, "The Shape of Things to Come," p. 22.

20. See Stephen Daggett, "The American Economy, the Defense Budget, and National Security," chap. 4 of this volume.

21. This section draws from Eitelberg and Mehay, "The Shape of Things to Come," pp. 31–35.

22. See Mark J. Eitelberg, "Military Manpower and the Future Force," in Joseph Kruzel, ed., *American Defense Annual 1993*, 8th edition (New York: Free Press, 1993).

23. Eitelberg and Mehay, "The Shape of Things to Come," p. 50.

24. D. Olson and M. Hanson, *2001: Preparing Families for the Future* (Washington, DC: National Council on Family Relations, 1990).

25. U.S. Bureau of the Census, *Household and Family Characteristics: 1990 and*

1989, Current Population Report Series P–20, No. 447 (Washington, DC: Government Printing Office, 1990).

26. Ibid.

27. Secretary of Defense, *Annual Report*, p. 45.

28. Mady W. Segal, "The Military and the Family as Greedy Institutions," *Armed Forces and Society*, 13 (Fall 1986), p. 9.

29. Ibid, pp. 15–23; and Jane Gross, "Needs of Family and Country: Missions on a Collision Course," *New York Times*, December 9, 1990.

30. The figures do not include reservists to the Gulf. See Mark J. Eitelberg, "Population Representation in Operations Desert Shield and Desert Storm: A Preliminary Assessment," appearing as Appendix D in U.S. Department of Defense, *Population Representation in the Military Services, FY 1990* (Washington, DC: Government Printing Office, July 1991).

31. See, for example, cover story on "Mom Goes to War" in *People*, September 10, 1990. The article is titled "A Mother's Duty" and appears on pp. 42–49. See also Barbara Kantrowitz and Mike Mason, "The Soldier-Parent Dilemma," *Newsweek*, November 12, 1990, p. 84; Bill McAllister, "Cheney Urged to Support Exemption for Parents," *Washington Post*, February 14, 1991, p. A36; Adam Clymer, "Senate Rejects Call to Exempt Parents from Service in Gulf," *New York Times*, February 21, 1991, p. 18; and Katherine Seelye, "Bill Would Extend Birth Leave," *Philadelphia Inquirer*, March 31, 1991, p. 13.

32. See "Compensation Trends in the 21st Century," *Monthly Labor Review*, February 1990.

33. Operating tempo, or OPTEMPO—measured in ground vehicle miles, ship steaming days, and aircraft flying hours—is expected to remain fairly constant (at a minimum) as the force shrinks. In fact, as the Department of Defense observes, "[I]n some areas, such as joint and combined operations, increased OPTEMPO may be required." See Secretary of Defense, *Annual Report*, p. 48.

34. Lt. Gen. William H. Reno, "The Future as I See It" (Transcript of Address at "Marching Toward the 21st Century: A Conference on Manpower and Recruiting Issues for the Future," Arlington, Virginia, January 30, 1992). Reported in Jim Tice, "A New Army Order," *Army Times*, February 17, 1992, pp. 3, 61.

35. See Eitelberg, "Military Manpower," p. 24.

36. See, for example, Martin Binkin, *Military Technology and Defense Manpower* (Washington, DC: Brookings Institution, 1986).

37. Martin Binkin and Mark J. Eitelberg, "Women and Minorities in the All-Volunteer Force," in Bowman, Little, and Sicilia, eds., *The All-Volunteer Force*, p. 92.

38. U.S. Departments of Labor, Education, and Commerce, *Building a Quality Workforce* (Washington, DC: Government Printing Office, July 1988).

39. Forecasts of occupational growth by education level are available in Bureau of Labor Statistics, *Monthly Labor Review*, November 1991.

40. See, for example, Eitelberg and Mehay, "The Shape of Things to Come," p. 19.

41. See Eitelberg, "Military Manpower," for an expanded discussion of this topic.

Part III

The Domestic and International Security Landscapes: Contradictions and Complexities

6

U.S. National Security Agenda and U.S. National Security Policy: Realities and Dilemmas

William J. Taylor and Don M. Snider

Framing national security policy options that will find a bipartisan consensus at home and international consensus among our allies, as well as among our counterparts in the U.N. Security Council, is now extraordinarily complex. The United States as well as the rest of the industrialized world is experiencing a post–Cold War period during which the world order is undergoing momentous change. It is simply unknown how long this period of change will extend between the essentially bipolar order of the Cold War and whatever order ultimately replaces it. History teaches, if the era after World War II is predictive, that it may take half a decade or more, a major war, and at least one set of national elections before America can again chart a recognizable, consensual course in world affairs. Perhaps the new military strategy that began to take shape in the early 1990s will produce the functional equivalent of the containment strategy that began to take shape in the latter 1940s. Perhaps the Persian Gulf War of 1990–1991 was the modern-day equivalent of the Korean War, which produced NSC 68. And perhaps the nation has the leadership requisite to a new national security strategy needed for a new world order.

Let us summarize those factors in this transitional environment that are broadly apparent to policymakers and that are strongly influencing future U.S. national security policy. These factors are transitional guideposts to policy formulation. They do not determine its exact content, but policymakers seeking effective foreign policy must consider how these factors, both foreign and domestic, are now shaping the security environment. Let us also frame for analysis the evident challenges U.S. national security policy must address as the nation moves through the 1990s, and conclude by sketching some of the main themes in the emerging policy.

Even the current guideposts, however, are rapidly changing from those previously used. In the recent past one common guidepost for most all national security policy considerations was the "threat," in all its different manifestations and dynamics. Now, as the Director of Central Intelligence testified in early 1992, that threat has receded, and in its place are myriad "destabilizing, dangerous, and, in many cases, unexpected challenges, such as the appearance of fifteen new countries in the place of a single, familiar [Soviet] empire."[1] This fading threat has caused decision makers within the National Security Council to reformulate foreign policy, particularly its defense component, with uncertainty about challenges or opportunities that lay ahead. As Joint Chiefs of Staff (JCS) Chairman Colin Powell noted:

The decline of the Soviet threat has fundamentally changed the concept of threat analysis as a basis for force structure planning. We can still plausibly identify some specific threats—North Korea, a weakened Iraq, perhaps even a hostile Iran. But the real threat is the unknown, the uncertain. In a very real sense, the primary threat to our security is instability and being unprepared to handle a crisis or war that no one expected or predicted.[2]

Policymakers must, however, continue with their analysis and decision making regardless of how many guideposts are changing or how uncertain and murky the environments, both external and internal. American interests and our political system demand no less, nor should they. What follows, therefore, is our best estimate of those factors now guiding the development of U.S. national security policy.

THE CHANGING INTERNATIONAL ENVIRONMENT

Without doubt the current and future security environment of the United States is radically altered from that of the past forty years. Many have found it difficult to acknowledge the extent of change and its implications, even more so because U.S. foreign policy has been so successful in bringing the Cold War to a close without a catastrophic nuclear exchange. As former Secretary of Defense James R. Schlesinger noted, "We are tempted to rest on our laurels; rather than seriously to reconstruct our foreign policy, we are tempted to believe that a few modest adjustments will suffice."[3] What are the major changes in the international environment that should serve as guideposts to the future? At a minimum, three stand out: the end of the Cold War, a shift in U.S. policy from global to regional strategy, and certain changing elements of national power.

The End of the Cold War and Its Bipolar, Competitive Superpower Relationship

Most fundamentally, the demise of the Soviet empire means that our nation's security now needs redefinition, and the role of the United States as Iran and Iraq in the Middle East. In fact, just as President Bush was announcing in the now-famous Aspen speech of August 2, 1990, that the demise of the Soviet Union and the reunification of Germany—the end of the Cold War—would allow a 25 percent reduction in U.S. military forces, Saddam Hussein's forces were invading Kuwait.[6]

Thus began the first major war of the post–Cold War era, a limited, regional war fought by a remarkable coalition of Western nations and their Arab allies under United Nations auspices against a rival Arab power. At stake were both vital U.S. economic interests (access to oil) and important political interests (the rule of law and the peaceful settlement of disputes). Also at stake was U.S. leadership, as President Bush created the unique, ad hoc coalition that successfully prosecuted the Persian Gulf War under the auspices of the United Nations. The successes of the war will be debated for years, though most observers agree on several very clear lessons for future U.S. foreign policy.

First, the world is still a very dangerous place, awash in a vast pool of armaments left over from decades of production during the Cold War. Second, the United States has a unique leadership role to play in world affairs as the residual superpower of the Cold War. By the end of 1992 that role was not well defined, nor was there any political consensus in the United States as to exactly what it should be. But there was general agreement after the Gulf War that only the United States had the political legitimacy and influence necessary to lead the world community, through the structure of the United Nations, to a multilateral response to Iraq's aggression.

Third, and in contrast, most agreed that in the early 1990s, while U.S. leadership may be necessary, it is insufficient by itself, since America is financially dependent on its allies for costly undertakings.[7] Fourth, the cost of the war was a reflection of the new technology of conventional warfare, a form of war so lethal that it holds potential to change the way policymakers will view the military instrument of power in the future. And fifth, most could agree that, notwithstanding their lethality, U.S. military forces were dependent on the logistical support of our allies to successfully execute the war, particularly for airlift, sealift, and in-theater transportation.[8] This created some very real constraints on the yet-undefined leadership role the United States could assume in the future.

Thus the political-military guideposts for future foreign policy established by the Gulf War seemed clear. A focus at the regional level was accepted, as was the necessity for U.S. political leadership.[9] Also accepted were the real limitations to that leadership, and therein resided the dilemma of just what role in the world the U.S. should assume, a dilemma that will take some years to resolve.

Taken together, these first two changes mean that the central paradigm of Cold War foreign policy is hopelessly outdated. Stated simply, it had three elements: (1) contain Soviet expansion, defeating it if the Cold War became in world affairs to provide for that security, however redefined, needs com plete rethinking. One could hardly note more radical change. Gone for th foreseeable future is the need for the United States to lead Western de mocracies in a global effort to protect the Eurasian landmass from hostile domination. Not only is there no longer a political threat to our values, there is no longer a military threat to our physical security.[4]

The immediate implications of this change are striking, to say the least. The vast military capabilities of the United States, particularly the nuclear components, seem remarkably in excess. In 1991 President Bush moved well ahead of the laborious arms control processes of the Cold War and unilaterally eliminated all tactical nuclear weapons from the U.S. Army and the surface forces of the U.S. Navy. Our foreign policy planning for Europe can now expect the Europeans, in the face of lesser threats, to establish more of their own security identity, and to bear fully the economic burden for it. And our relations with the Third World need not be seen any longer through the prism of the Cold War, wherein the two superpowers competed for influence and prestige and were often played off against each other by the developing nations.

Thus the demise of the Soviet Union means that the well-understood organizing principles of U.S. foreign policy and the resulting patterns of relationships are gone. The world is now a much less dangerous place, but not necessarily a more stable community. How we will define our interests in this new international order and seek to pursue them in relation to other members of the community of nations is the central challenge.

A Focal Shift from Global to Regional Strategy for U.S. Foreign Policy

From the end of World War II to 1989, U.S. foreign policy had a global focus, an inherent aspect of George Kennan's formulation of the strategy of containment.[5] While the main line of defense was across a divided Europe, countervailing pressure to Soviet expansionism was to be applied around the periphery of that empire wherever it attempted to extend its influence.

In contrast, the end of that bipolar confrontation now allows U.S. foreign policy to be focused individually on each region of the world in which we have interests. This focus also responds, as it must, to trends in international economic relationships, particularly the creation of regional economic arrangements to foster free and open trade on a regional basis as well as to enhance various regions' competitive stature in global markets, for example, the European Community, the North American Free Trade Area, and the Asian Pacific Trade Council.

Other factors also have influenced the move toward a regional policy focus factors such as the rise of states with extensive military power aspiring to be dominant regional powers threaten U.S. allies or interests, states such hot; (2) promote an open, global economic system; and (3) provide the U.S. leadership requisite to moving the free world to accomplish the first two goals. This paradigm embodied ideological conflict, was global and heavily focused on defense and arms-control issues, and employed the theoretical, abstract, often arcane literature of nuclear deterrence theory and related fields.

While no new paradigm has yet emerged, it is clear that only the last two elements of the earlier version remain applicable. Further, the new model will have a regional focus and will be much more contextual at that level, focusing on promoting regional stability and economic growth, using the disciplines of history, language, ethnic and religious studies, and economics.

The Changing Elements of National Power

This third major change in the external security environment is found in the evolving structure of the post–Cold War international political system. It is not only much more fragmented, but at the same time more interdependent. The fragmentation comes from the demise of the major bipolar blocs of the Cold War, as well as the corresponding alignments of Third World nations within that structure. Nation after nation, and even some subnational groups, are now relatively free to pursue independently their interests among the community of nations. Obviously this means a high degree of instability and potential for conflict in many regions of the world.

But at the same time, the ability of these nations as well as that of the United States to pursue their interests will be channeled and constrained by growing patterns of national interdependence. These patterns are caused by the continued growth in global economic and financial trading systems; by growth in nonstate actors such as transnational corporations and international interest groups for transnational issues, for example, the global environment; and by the pervasive flow of ideas and information via global communications systems.

What this structural change means for U.S. national security policy is really quite important. In the new structure, national power is much more diffuse, making the exertion of influence by any nation over any other nation much more difficult. With global diffusion of power, national security policy also becomes less fungible, less coercive, and less tangible, and the challenge becomes to use successfully the traditional military forms of power to leverage economic and diplomatic issues. Soft forms of power, such as the ability to manipulate interdependencies, become more important, as does the long-term economic strength of the nation, which is the base for both hard and soft forms of power.[10]

The obvious question this raises for US. foreign policy is whether America has, or is developing for the future, the right mix among the elements of national power. Specifically, is U.S. economic power, eroded by massive internal debts and negative international financial flows, too weak relative to the military? And, in terms of implementing U.S. policies, are the policy instruments available to implement U.S. foreign policy—informational, diplomatic, economic, and military—sufficient to the tasks ahead? Since we can no longer exert power and influence by exporting national security in the form of extended nuclear deterrence, does America have other instruments of effective influence and persuasion? At least some observers are doubtful, one noting that Washington "must now strive for multiple channels of influence without, in many cases, the assurance either of a continuing commanding role or of easy policy coordination—to do this with grace will be hard, to do it effectively, still harder."[11]

THE DOMESTIC ENVIRONMENT

As we all know, U.S. national security policy decision making is a shared responsibility between the Executive and the Congress, thus ensuring that the domestic influence on U.S. policy is large indeed. Even the judiciary has a valid, if lesser, role. Traditionally these shared roles have left the Executive in the position of proposing the policy initiatives, such as treaties or agreements; and the Congress, particularly the Senate, in the role of disposing, by such actions as ratifying treaties or approving foreign aid budgets and the appointment of ambassadors.[12] A reversal of these roles has occurred on occasion, for example, in the case of the Nicaraguan peace initiative by House Speaker Jim Wright in 1987, which sparked intensely heated, partisan controversy on the American political scene.

As that instance demonstrated, there have been, and doubtless will continue to be, deep differences over both policy and process between these two institutions, which share the responsibility for making U.S. foreign policy.[13] This is largely due to the fact that the members of these institutions represent different constituencies and thus tend to see the same issue from different perspectives. The President can view a matter of foreign trade policy, such as the North American Free Trade Agreement, from the perspective of the nation as a whole, and how that policy will influence overall macroeconomic performance. Individual members of Congress, however, tend to view the same issue from the perspective of its impact on their particular constituents, seemingly regardless of the overall impact.[14]

A number of major changes in the U.S. domestic environment serve to heighten these institutional differences and to make more difficult the coordination and cooperation necessary for the formulation of coherent, consensual foreign policy. As we view U.S. national security policy for the rest of the 1990s, these domestic changes and their influences on both policy and process need to be highlighted, because they also serve as guideposts to future policy formulation.

The Rise of a "Choiceless" Society and the Primacy of the Domestic Agenda

There are many explanations for why the U.S. government has not made choices in the recent past on domestic issues of acknowledged strategic importance to the nation. Part of the reason is obviously economic; a federal government spending more than one billion dollars each day in excess of its revenues (the U.S. federal deficit for 1992 alone exceeded 380 billion dollars) has no easy choices to make. Therefore, our government does not address the difficult choices. Part of the reason is also lack of domestic consensus, with deep, but roughly equal, divisions within the electorate on many value-laden domestic issues. Thus our society remains "choiceless" in several major areas: energy policy, social and health care policies, federal deficits, federal entitlements, and education policy, to mention but a few.[15]

Now, after four decades of the Cold War and with no certain military threat, many feel that these are really issues of national security. The failure to invest in productive capacity, research and development, and infrastructure; the crisis in American education; the exploding underclass; the pervasive drug culture; and other domestic problems may well have a greater direct impact on our future national security than any foreign military threat.[16]

What this means for future U.S. foreign policy is straightforward, at least in some areas. In the near term it means the primacy of the domestic agenda over the foreign policy agenda. This does not necessarily mean a more isolationist foreign policy, but it does mean that the nation's traditional foreign policy and national security focus must broaden considerably to consider much more fully the domestic dimensions of national security. For the institutions of our government, this means, given expected resource constraints, more frequent and visible trade-offs between pursuit of foreign versus domestic policy goals. Just such a choice is being faced in the early 1990s between U.S. foreign aid for Russia (the Freedom Support Act of 1992) versus assistance to U.S. cities in crisis.

In contrast, and at a more specific level, it is not clear what it means for future U.S. foreign policy when these "more visible and frequent" trade-offs have to be made. The implications for foreign policy of focusing on strengthening America in the 1990s need urgent clarification. World events and relationships simply do not wait for any particular nation to decide whether it is interested in emerging issues, particularly a nation aspiring in some manner to a leadership role.

The Impact of Divided Government on Foreign Policy Making

Since the early 1980s, political science literature has increasingly documented the impacts of divided government—the fact that the major institutions of the U.S. government—the Congress, and the presidency—each have been dominated by one party. In twenty of the past twenty-four years, the Republican party occupying the White House did not have a majority in Congress, usually not even in one house of Congress. The result of ticket-splitting voting behavior, the electorate during the 1970s and 1980s preferred not to give one party "the chance to govern."[17]

However, when combined with the Congressional reforms of the 1970s, which weakened the role of parties and decentralized decision making within the institution, the result of divided government has been a form of gridlock in which many issues of critical concern to the nation, both domestic and foreign, cannot be resolved for lack of an effective political consensus.[18] Even more problematic than the lack of consensus was the evident lack of trust and comity with which the two parties and the two institutions viewed each other, as first one institution and then the other attempted to assert primacy over foreign policy-making during the late 1970s and the 1980s.[19] One participant of the process noted in 1989:

We are witnessing government by procedural improvisation: crucial foreign policy decisions are being shaped in Washington today by awkward parliamentary gimmicks. Controversies are resolved on the basis of last-minute presidential letters, nongermane legislative amendments, and executive orders waiving statutory requirements. Whether the issue is aiding the Nicaraguan rebels or arming Middle East belligerents, prosecuting war or concluding a peace, process has become almost as important as policy. Many of the toughest issues are ducked again and again. . . . In the midst of such parliamentary confusion it is virtually impossible to build a governing consensus.[20]

With the November 3, 1992, election of Democrat Bill Clinton and the retention of a Congress with a majority of Democrats, there is a reasonable chance of eliminating the prevailing gridlock. But in case this institutional struggle continues into the 1990s, it is necessary to understand the evolving implications. As the conflict from the late 1970s continues unabated over the *formulation* of foreign policy, that is, the setting of national objectives, it has also spread in the 1980s to policy *implementation*. This has occurred, under the auspices of legislative oversight, in the form of congressional micromanagement. While many in the executive branch lament the burden caused by such intrusions into executive-department administration, recent studies document improved implementation when Congress imposes effective oversight.[21]

If this costly interbranch conflict continues, it will cause the Executive to maneuver the gauntlet of legislative procedures that allow Congress to influence strongly both the direction and implementation of future U.S. foreign policy. Such issues as foreign economic and developmental assistance, the sale of U.S. arms broad, the control of security-related technology and investment, and particularly the stationing and use of U.S. military forces will remain very contentious issues, often impeding the effective execution of U.S. national security policy.

The Reduction and Restructuring of U.S. Military Capabilities after the Cold War

It is more than a little ironic that the invasion of Kuwait that started the Persian Gulf War occurred on the same day that President Bush was announcing to the American people a gradual 25 percent reduction in U.S. military forces, thereby creating a small "peace dividend" at the end of the Cold War. This was the first announcement of a rather detailed plan to reduce and restructure U.S. military capabilities for the post–Cold War era, a plan that was not fully presented to Congress until early 1991.

When fully presented, the plan had two major components—a new military strategy and a military base force that the administration believed to be the minimum necessary for executing the new strategy in the uncertain future. This post–Cold War military strategy contained four central concepts:

• strategic nuclear deterrence and defense

• forward presence

• response to regional crises

• reconstitution (of more military capabilities, if needed)

The last two elements, new to this strategy, were designed in response to the foreign factors already discussed, a focus at the regional level as well as the recognition that smaller threats could be countered with fewer standing forces because longer warning time allowed a reconstitution period if greater forces were needed.[22]

Accompanying the new strategy was a base force that the administration intended to result from a planned build-down during FY (Fiscal Year) 1991 through FY 1997. Measured in active-duty forces, it would contain about .5 million fewer military personnel, 12 Army divisions as opposed to 16, 15 tactical fighter wings instead of 22, and 82 fewer battle force ships than in 1991.[23] In terms of dollar resources, the administration requested budgets for the Department of Defense for Fiscal Years 1992–1997 that represented a real reduction in defense outlays of 20 percent between 1991 and 1997. By 1997 outlays were to be reduced to a level of about 3.6 percent of gross national product, compared with 5.5 percent in 1990 and 6.4 percent in 1987. Further, with military procurement overall sharply reduced and over 100 programs canceled outright, about 1.1 million defense-related jobs were expected to be eliminated by 1995.[24]

The failure of the August 1991 coup in the Soviet Union and the subsequent dissolution of the U.S.S.R., as well as pressing needs in the United

States, led many in Congress and the larger policy community to believe that even larger reductions could be made.[25] And ultimately that may happen, but the lingering recession throughout 1991 and well into 1992 led Congress, at least through FY 1993, to reduce only at the schedule preferred by the White House. The FY 1993 defense budget was $274.3 billion, or 4.3 percent of gross domestic product (GDP). But even then, by 1997 the amount of resources allocated to defense will be at the lowest level since before Pearl Harbor.

The importance of the defense build-down for future U.S. foreign policy derives from the fact that dollars do strongly influence future defense policy and capabilities. As one authority noted, "The defense budget is the linchpin of U.S. defense policy. Planning is irrelevant and operations impossible if the budget process does not result in the correct mix of manpower and material."[26]

Not only is the right mix important, but so are the locations of the forces. Under the new military strategy of the early 1990s, the role of forward-presence forces is particularly important if U.S. military capabilities are to leverage our diplomatic and economic relationships, as they will have to do to foster stability in regions of U.S. national interest. However, given the planned reductions, particularly in those forces stationed overseas, the capability is problematic. Before the Persian Gulf War, America had no forward-presence forces in or near Kuwait. As one diplomat put it, "If we had an effective forward presence, we could have brilliantly deterred the Gulf War, rather than having to fight to brilliantly win it."[27] The point is, future U.S. military power, as one of the major instruments of our foreign policy, is also undergoing a very turbulent transition, the outcome of which will be quite consequential to our ability to implement future policies.

U.S. FORCE STRUCTURE: BACK TO BASICS

The fact of the matter is that the United States will not be able to effectively meet the changing threats to U.S. security interests unless we conduct a fundamental review of what have long been referred to as U.S. military "roles and missions." The case of the challenges presented by the 1992 crisis in the former Yugoslavia is highly instructive.

The public outcry for Western governments to "do something" about the grisly civil war in Yugoslavia sounded like a call to arms. But what sort of arms could prevail in a country that is a tactical quagmire and a strategic nightmare—the military equivalent of another Vietnam or Beirut, or both simultaneously?

Some advocated using air strikes on the guns of Sarajevo to lift the siege of the Bosnian capital. Others foresaw the need for ground forces to guarantee humanitarian relief throughout the strife-torn region. Still others warned that an intervention could lead to a commitment of Western troops to Yugoslav soil for decades to come.

These painful realities continue to raise urgent questions about the roles and missions of the United States forces in the post–Cold War era. Indeed, in 1992, Gen. Colin Powell, chairman of the Joint Chiefs of Staff, summoned all ten regional and force commanders-in-chief from around the world for a conference to discuss the challenges of what may become a deadly new age of little wars and how the "roles and missions" might be better divided to deal with them.

It is the right moment to ask some difficult questions: What unique strengths do our forces bring to such conflicts? Does America have the right kind of military forces for this type of international disorder?

The uncomfortable truth is that the United States (as well as other Western nations) is much better at fighting war, when the necessity and political will exist to do so, than it is at "waging peace." This is especially so in a setting such as Yugoslavia, which demands war-fighting capabilities, as well as Somalia, where peacekeeping forces may be needed to provide local security for humanitarian relief personnel among warring clans or tribes.

Despite the urgent need for change, efforts since World War II at reshaping U.S. military forces have failed to integrate military capabilities of the separate services to effectively wage peace.

The first—and perhaps most important—step is to overcome the refusal of all the services to prepare for peacekeeping operations. Where are the forces—specially selected, organized, equipped, and trained—to conduct such difficult and sensitive military operations? We don't have them. Indeed, does America have the range of nonlethal as well as lethal capabilities needed, deployable on a moment's call? What forces will fulfill those roles, and how will they be coordinated among the services?

The claims of service leaders that such missions are "nonmilitary" or that they taint the "warrior ethic" are pure foolishness and ignore the needs of the nation.

If America's military capabilities are to be reshaped correctly, leaders must accept the realities of the new security environment as well as the emerging military-technical revolution. These new factors provide, respectively, the strategic context for new military missions and the organizing principle around which review and necessary reshaping of all of our defense establishment should occur. The roles and missions review, submitted to Congress in the fall of 1992, made some contributions to this debate—but that review needs to be broadened to include both these areas. If the debate become fixated on cost reductions or on hammering the services for duplications in capabilities, a great opportunity at redefining our military will be lost.

SPECIFIC CHALLENGES FOR U.S. NATIONAL SECURITY POLICY

U.S. policymakers during the 1990s will have to focus on several key aspects of our foreign policy as it is redefined to fit the changing environment just described. Since not all aspects fit in the category of key ones (even such important aspects as immigration policy), let us examine here those few one might judge to fit that category:

1. *Adapting and bolstering the U.S. relationships with Germany and Japan.* In many ways U.S. relations with its former World War II adversaries will now, some five decades later, be pivotal to the formulation of our new policies. These are key democratic and economic powers, whose influence in their respective regions is immense, both for good and, in the eyes of some, potentially for bad. The challenge will be to manage these relationships to reassure all nations that the economic power centers of the free world are like-minded on the central issues. The United States, Germany, and Japan will be redefining their roles in the world during this uncertain period, heightening the importance of these relationships and the formulation of a collective approach to national security policy that respects the sovereignty of each nation.

2. *Fostering a "democratic peace" with states of the former Soviet Union and Eastern Europe.* Simply stated, the crown jewels of the Cold War will not be secured until the experiments in democratic and economic freedom underway throughout Eastern Europe and the former Soviet Union are successfully completed. Speaking on behalf of the Freedom Support Act of 1992, President Bush stated the challenge concisely:

Today I want to talk to you all about the most important foreign policy opportunity of our time—an opportunity that will affect the security and the future of every American, young and old, throughout this entire decade. The democratic revolutions underway in Russia, in Armenia, Ukraine, and the other new nations of the old Soviet empire represent the best hope for real peace in my lifetime. . . . The Cold War is over. The specter of nuclear Armageddon has receded, and Soviet communism has collapsed. In its wake, we find ourselves on the threshold of a new world of opportunity of peace. But with the passing of the Cold War, a new order has yet to take its place. The opportunities are tremendous, but so, too, are the dangers. So we stand at history's hinge point—a new world beckons, while the ghost of history stands in the shadows.[28]

But there is immense confusion in Washington about how to move beyond this rhetoric to formulate policies and affordable programs to develop infrastructures for democracy in these countries.

3. *Strengthening an open economic order and U.S. competitiveness within that emerging order.* Unproductive General Agreement on Tariffs and Trade (GATT) negotiations (over four years) have been but one major indication of a global economic order struggling to keep national markets unfettered. The rise of regional trade cooperation, within North America and elsewhere, is a healthy sign, but should not occur if it causes trade diversions and protectionism among other regions, thereby lowering world trade and openness. The challenge to the United States is to get in order its own economic house, particularly federal deficits, so that the United States can lead credibly

and effectively, influencing others toward more economic freedoms. Until then, and even after, much of this economic policy will have to be pursued multilaterally, particularly through those institutions working toward macroeconomic stabilization in the emerging democracies.

4. *Containing arms proliferation and regional disorder.* Everyone from the Director of Central Intelligence to leading members of Congress and the Executive agreed in the early 1990s that the largest U.S. security challenge foreseen—global or regional—was the proliferation of weapons of mass destruction and their potential impacts on regional instabilities. But consensus on a challenge does not necessarily make it more tractable. In this case, unique solutions must be pursued within each region, while global safeguards are strengthened under a number of regimes, most notably the Nuclear Non-Proliferation Treaty (NPT), the Missile Technology Control Regime (MTCR), and the suppliers' cartel emerging from the Gulf War.[29] Obviously, pursuing such arrangements will cause difficult trade-offs for U.S. policymakers. One example is the continued testing of nuclear weapons versus global leadership under the NPT. Congress has attempted to resolve this issue by favoring the curtailment of nuclear tests. Another example is the future direction of U.S.-Chinese bilateral relations, given that China has become a major exporter of intermediate-range missiles and their production technology to the developing world.

5. *Promoting democratic institutions amidst the explosion of global populism.* This last challenge is a relatively new one, developing because there are so many countries around the world in which the spark of democratic freedom is continuing to ignite progress toward human rights. One example is the spark that ignited in Thailand in May 1992, forcing a repressive regime from power by a sharp display of nonviolent, but adamant, national protest.

Not surprisingly, American national security policy through the decade will have to tread a fine line between those ideals and values underlying U.S. policy and the realism with which they are applied in particular circumstances. One need only to examine the multiple crises in the former Yugoslavia and the U.S. response to them to make the point. But the goal will be clear: to create broadly the institutions of democracy in as many countries as want and need our assistance—institutions that will help make permanent the existence of democratic and economic freedoms for those peoples. The challenge will be to harness the formidable capabilities of both the American public and the American private sectors since the range of institutions, from legal to judicial, military to civil, and urban to rural, will need expertise far beyond the capability of our government alone.

HEADING FOR THE TWENTY-FIRST CENTURY

The foregoing discussion should have made clear the four elements minimally necessary for a successful national security policy for the United States in the 1990s:

- U.S. leadership role defined
- Coalition building for collective engagement as the norm for conflict management and resolution
- Restructured U.S. security policy institutions, both executive and congressional
- Restructured U.S. forces to meet new challenges
- Economic renewal at home

Easy to say, yet the tasks ahead are daunting. However, even in our increasingly interdependent world, the vast majority of the tasks are at home and are within our power to achieve. The realist school of international politics suggests that international politics, like all politics, is a struggle for power. That may well be true, but the outcomes of struggles for power are, more often than not, decided by leadership. President Eisenhower once defined leadership as "the ability to get someone to do something you want done because they want to do it."[30] He was talking primarily about persuading and motivating people to believe that a preferred course of action is more valid, just, and effective than any other alternative. Properly motivated, the people of America and their allies have enormous capabilities that can be harnessed to promote international peace and stability. Given a bipartisan national consensus on a vision for the future, Americans have proven repeatedly that they can arise to almost any challenge. As this chapter has tried to suggest, the challenges to American national security are many and varied, and many tough choices must be made. But with the right kind of leadership at home under the Clinton Administration working in tandem with a Democratic Congress, the United States can not only put its own house in order but also provide the leadership the world expects and requires.

NOTES

1. Robert Gates, "Statement of the Director of Central Intelligence before the Senate Armed Services Committee," January 22, 1992, mimeo., p. 1.

2. Gen. Colin Powell, "Testimony before the House Committee on Foreign Affairs," March 4, 1992, mimeo., p. 3.

3. James R. Schlesinger, "Statement before the House Committee on Foreign Affairs," May 6, 1992, mimeo., p. 2.

4. Gates, "Statement," p. 4.

5. See John Lewis Gaddis, *Strategies of Containment: A Critical Appraisal of Postwar American National Security Policy* (New York: Oxford University Press, 1982), chapters 2 and 3.

6. President George Bush, "Address to the Aspen Institute Symposium," August 2, 1990, White House Press Release, mimeo., p. 2.

7. Eugene J. McAllister, "Testimony before the House Ways and Means Committee," July 31, 1991, Department of State *Dispatch* (August 5, 1991), p. 590.

8. See Jim Blackwell, Michael Mazarr, and Don Snider, *The Gulf War: Military Lessons Learned* (Washington, DC: Center for Strategic and International Studies, July 1991), pp. 5–10 (chap. 2).

9. The White House, *National Security Strategy of the United States* (Washington, DC: Government Printing Office, August 1991), p. v.

10. See Joseph S. Nye, Jr., "American Power and a Post–Cold War World," in the Aspen Institute Strategy Group, ed., *Facing the Future: American Strategy in the 1990s* (Lanham, MD: Aspen Institute and University Press of America, 1991), pp. 33 and 54.

11. Catherine McArdle Kelleher, "U.S. Foreign Policy and Europe, 1990–2000," *Brookings Review*, 8, no. 4 (Fall 1990), p. 9.

12. See, for example, Edward S. Corwin, *The President: Office and Powers, 1787–1957* (New York: New York University Press, 1957), or Cecil V. Crabb and Pat M. Holt, *Invitation to Struggle: Congress, the President, and Foreign Policy* (Washington, DC: CQ Press, 1989).

13. Roger H. Davidson and Walter J. Oleszek, *Congress and Its Members* 3rd ed. (Washington, DC: CQ Press, 1990), p. 394.

14. See I. M. Destler, *American Trade Politics: System under Stress* (Washington, DC: Institute for International Economics, 1986), chaps. 4 and 5.

15. Peter G. Peterson and James K. Sebenius, "The Primacy of the Domestic Agenda," in Graham Allison and Gregory Treverton, eds., *Rethinking America's Security: Beyond the Cold War to New World Order* (New York: Norton, 1992), pp. 85–93.

16. For examples, see Samuel Huntington, "America's Changing Strategic Interests," *Survival*, 33 (January/February 1991), pp. 3–17; and Robert Hormats, "The Roots of American Power" *Foreign Affairs*, 70 (Summer 1991), pp. 132–149.

17. David Broder, "Bob Michel's Challenge: The Only Real Way to Ensure Accountability Is to End Divided Government," *Washington Post*, May 27, 1992, p. A12.

18. For a compelling review of the impact of gridlock on federal budgeting, including foreign aid assistance, see Allen Schick, *The Capacity to Budget* (Washington, DC: Urban Institute, 1990).

19. The National Academy of Public Administration (NAPA), *Beyond Distrust: Building Bridges between Congress and the Executive* (Washington, DC: NAPA, January 1992), pp. 20–23.

20. Gerald Warburg, *Conflict and Consensus: The Struggle between Congress and the President over Foreign Policy-Making* (New York: Harper & Row, 1989), pp. xviii–xix.

21. National Academy of Public Administration, *Beyond Distrust*, pp. 8–9.

22. *National Military Strategy of the United States* (Washington, DC: Government Printing Office, January 1992), pp. 6–8.

23. Gen. Colin Powell, "The Base Force: A Total Force" (Presentation to the House Appropriations Committee, Subcommittee on Defense, September 25, 1991), pp. 1–17.

24. Congressional Budget Office, *The Economic Effects Of Reduced Defense Spending* (Washington, DC: Government Printing Office, February 1992): pp. ix, 22.

25. See William Kaufmann and John Steinbrunner, *Decisions for Defense: Pros-*

pects for a New World Order (Washington, DC: Brookings Institution, 1991), and Representative Les Aspin, "An Approach to Sizing American Conventional Forces for the Post-Soviet Era: Four Illustrative Options" (Washington, DC: House Armed Services Committee, February 25, 1992).

26. Lawrence J. Korb, "The 1991 Defense Budget and the 1991–1995 Defense Program" in Aspen Institute Strategy Group, *Facing the Future*, p. 317.

27. Former U.S. Ambassador to NATO David Abshire, "Testimony before the House Armed Services Committee," Defense Policy Panel, December 11, 1991, mimeo, p. 3.

28. President George Bush, "Aid to the New Independent States: A Peace We Must Not Lose" (excerpts from remarks to the American Society of Newspaper Editors), Department of State *Dispatch*, 3, no. 15, April 13, 1992, p. 1.

29. For more detailed discussion of this challenge, see Steve Fetter, "Ballistic Missiles and Weapons of Mass Destruction: What Is the Threat? What Should Be Done?" *International Security*, 16, no. 1 (Summer 1991), pp. 5–41, and Lewis A. Dunn, "Containing Nuclear Proliferation," *Adelphi Papers* #236. London: International Institute for Strategic Studies, Winter 1991).

30. It is believed that President Harry Truman had picked up on an earlier speech by Ike and paraphrased him in 1955. Truman stated, "A leader is a man who has the ability to get other people to do what they don't want to do and like it." This is from Headquarters, Department of the Army Pamphlet, USMA, *Student and Professional Notebook on Leadership* (Washington, DC: Government Printing Office, November 1986).

7

The Implications of Globalization for U.S. National Security: Defense Industrial Production and the Proliferation of Military Technology

Stephanie G. Neuman

Changes in the economic and political structure of the international system are having dramatic effects on the way states plan for their defense. The purpose here is to analyze the globalization of the defense sector and its implications for U.S. national security.

As defined here, the globalization of the defense sector refers to the growing international character of defense industrial production worldwide and the rapid diffusion of military technology. In the United States, the term generally refers to the import penetration and foreign source dependence in the defense industry, that is, increasing U.S. reliance on foreign military technologies, foreign manufactured products, and items purchased from U.S.-based subsidiaries of foreign corporations.[1] An ancillary trend, one intimately associated with this development, is the proliferation of advanced military items to other countries and regions of the world.

A debate is underway over the implications of globalization for basic U.S. national security interests and over what peacetime policies should be adopted to deal with it.[2] What are U.S. national security objectives in a changing world order? Facing reductions in the size of the U.S. armed forces and the spread of advanced weapons, Presidents Bush and Reagan expressed the view that U.S. national security requires the ability to develop in peacetime advanced weapons and defensive systems, and during crises the ability to obtain sufficient quantities of weapons, ammunition, and other military equipment.[3] To this end, in his 1991 strategy statement, President Bush reasserted the need to maintain "our edge in defense technology" and the capability of "industrial surge."[4] Given these publicly articulated national security objectives, some analysts wonder whether globalization of the defense sector will allow the United States to achieve them.

For deterrence, crisis management and war fighting purposes, technological superiority remains essential to our national security. However, is it realistic to assume
that we can maintain our technological superiority by importing advanced products
and technologies developed overseas?[5]

For other analysts, the effects of unbridled global arms transfers are of
paramount concern.

GLOBALIZATION OF THE WORLD MILITARY SECTOR: DEFENSE INDUSTRIAL PRODUCTION

Consolidation

Shrinking defense budgets and markets are forcing the consolidation and
cooperation of national defense companies worldwide. In an effort to compete
in a contracted world market, these conglomerates are driven to cooperate
in a network of joint ventures.

Industrial cooperation is, of course, not new to the defense sector, but it
now appears to be more concentrated and more international in character.
In the past, cooperation took place on a program-by-program basis. Once
these programs were over, cooperation ended, unless a new program was
agreed to. National industries remained dedicated essentially to fulfilling
the needs of their own military.[6] Although the future is not clear, international industrial cooperation now appears to be more permanent in character—designed to increase military and civilian market share over the longer
term.

Foreign Ownership and Investment

Since the early 1980s, foreign defense companies, especially Western
Europe's, have sought to extend their production lines, create economies
of scale, and generate profits by selling weapons and materiel to the American
military. To do so, a number of countries have bought interests in or ne-
gotiated cooperation agreements with U.S. companies. As one avionics company executive explained, "Even the best European product doesn't stand
much of a chance unless it is bid via an American company, usually with
the pledge of U.S. production."[7]

From 1981 to 1986 (the last year for which there are disaggregated data),
foreign acquisitions of U.S. high-technology firms grew from about 30 to
more than 130 per year.[8] The declining American dollar in recent years has
made investment in the U.S. defense sector a particularly attractive option.

Examples of this development and how it serves to globalize domestic
defense sectors and spin off into the civilian economy abound. The Dowty

(United Kingdom) Group, for example, about ten years ago purchased the small Decoto Company—now Dowty Decoto—of Yakima, Washington. The aim of the purchase was to have a production base for hydraulic actuators close to Boeing so Dowty would not have to rely on a long logistics link to supply Boeing and could thereby reduce its transportation costs. Dowty then enlarged on this concept by purchasing Hydraulic Units, Inc., (HUI) of Duarte, California. As a result, Dowty not only has expanded its sales to the civil market but also has made further gains in U.S. military business.[9]

Another company, Crouzet (France), has teamed with BEI Defense Systems Company of Ft. Worth for manufacturing and marketing helicopter-sighting systems based on Crouzet's Series 100/200 units. From Crouzet's point of view, the linkup with BEI Defense Systems gives the French company an entry into the U.S. market through an American firm that has experience in weapon systems production. Under terms of the agreement, BEI Defense Systems will manufacture and assemble electronic circuitry for the helicopter-sighting systems, while Crouzet will provide sight heads and optical components.[10]

To many this trend raises the specter of foreign ownership of U.S. defense industries. As one military analyst observed: "All small arms being manufactured today for the American forces are manufactured by firms in the U.S. that are owned by European companies."[11] This issue was further dramatized when the French electronics and arms company Thomson-CSF attempted to purchase the missile division of the bankrupt LTV Corporation, marking the first time a major U.S. prime contractor has been up for sale to a foreign corporation. Although the deal was not consummated, French ownership would effectively have guaranteed French acquisition of LTV's classified American defense technology.[12]

Offshore Manufacturing and Procurement

In the United States, declining defense budgets and reduced procurement worldwide are also forcing U.S. defense companies to consolidate, as weaker firms either wither or are absorbed through mergers and acquisitions into stronger ones.[13] For many, economic necessity promotes further globalization. In order to lower labor and transportation costs, widen market share, and enlarge profits, there has been a move toward increased offshore manufacturing. Large transnationals operating in the United States through buy-ins and joint ventures as well as U.S.-owned companies are moving third-tier supply work to countries such as Mexico or Taiwan.

Cost-cutting measures have also prompted the U.S. military to buy components, manufacturing equipment, and certain technologies from these and other foreign corporations.[14] Former Defense Secretary Cheney stated that having the Pentagon buy products exclusively from American manufacturers "would be nice if it were possible to do that." But doing so "raises questions

about my spending money on things I could get cheaper elsewhere, and it
raises the specter of having to rely upon less than first-rate technology in
certain areas."[15]

PROLIFERATION OF ADVANCED MILITARY TECHNOLOGY

The increasing globalization of defense industrial production is closely
associated with the rapid proliferation of advanced technology to other regions of the world. Primary attention has been given to weapons of mass
destruction—nuclear, biological, and chemical. Since the Gulf War, however, concern over the spread of sophisticated conventional weapons has
increased. Although each military service considers different weapon systems
particularly threatening, all are troubled by the rising trade in advanced
military technologies.

Joint Ventures, Collaborative Projects, and Offsets

The drive to enlarge markets and profits has prompted many Western
companies, "usually with the full permission or even at the instigation of
their governments" to enter into collaborative arms projects with Third
World countries. British, French, and Italian companies are cooperating
with the Chinese on various advanced technology projects.[16] American companies, too, "with the blessing of the U.S. government" are collaborating
with China in upgrade programs for the F–8 II and Super–7 combat aircraft
and in a joint U.S.-Chinese main battle tank.[17]

Russia, prompted by economic exigencies, has offered to transfer "advanced defense factories," such as the entire MiG–21 production line, to
India. According to the Russian ambassador, Anatoliy Dryukov, production
of "front-line aircraft" (MIG–29s), tanks (T–72s) and armored personnel car-
riers (APCs) would be available not only for Indian use, but for third party
sales as well.[18]

Third World manufacturers are also part of the process. They too have
established industrial development and arms transfer relationships with
other less industrially capable countries. China, for example, has helped
Algeria and Pakistan build nuclear weapons programs and is now in the
process of helping Iran build a nuclear reactor. It has not only sold ballistic
missiles to several Middle Eastern countries but helped some develop missile
systems of their own. The North Koreans are selling components for the
independent production of Scud-Cs to Iran, and "probably Syria."[19] Brazil,
too, has offered its ballistic missile technology to Iran.[20]

Offsets are another mechanism of proliferation. Buyers are demanding
direct (military-related) offsets, often involving sophisticated equipment, as
the price of doing business. One consequence is that a number of countries

expect to create aerospace industries, although on a global scale there is clearly an overcapacity of such industries. Moreover, when ordering equipment and material for their military, a number of Third World countries expect off-sets in a variety of technological materials. Ten years ago, U.S. companies selling planes in this region bought aircraft seats, tires, or windows from local manufacturers. Now, these states want to supply high-technology night-vision equipment and digital avionics.[21]

"Intellectual" Mercenaries

Aiding and abetting the proliferation of military technology is the rising number of technically capable experts for sale worldwide. Reduced domestic military spending has released onto the global defense market a cadre of "intellectual" mercenaries able and willing to help other countries develop their defense industrial expertise.[22] Largely educated in the West, many of them originating from the Third World, these men and women are returning in the thousands to their own countries or are selling their expertise to the highest bidder in other nations.[23] Their ranks are swelled by former Soviet defense scientists and technicians encouraged to flee their homeland by the economic chaos in the republics, the liberalization of travel restrictions, and continuing cutbacks on the former Soviet military laboratories. Iraq, for example, has recruited more than fifty nuclear scientists from the former Soviet Union. Two of them interviewed by a German paper, *Dresdener Morgenpost*, divulged that they had been given five-year contracts paying $10,000 per month. They had earned the equivalent of $50 a month in the Russian republic.[24]

The Black and Gray Markets

The diminished number of solvent customers and the relatively large number of eager suppliers has created an environment in which the black and gray markets in military equipment are likely to flourish. Equipment sold on the black market is illegal. Gray-market devices are those that elude national and international arms transfer regulations, with or without the collusion of the seller. Often the illegality of the sale is not immediately evident. In general, the black and gray markets are important sources of military technology for politically "incorrect" customers.

Purchasing dual-use technology, that with both military and civilian applications, is an important conduit for the proliferation of military technology. Because it is usually difficult to determine the intended end use of this type of technology, dual-use items imported ostensibly for civilian purposes can easily be diverted to the military sector. For example, civil transports can be used to transport troops, a tractor factor can produce armored vehicles, insecticide plants or chemicals for fertilizer may be used to manufacture chemical weapons.

Although the supplier may be innocent, the diversion of dual-use technology for military purposes often involves the collusion of both buyer and seller. For example, a number of British officials and oil industry experts were willing to attest that the pipes sold to Iraq and seized in Britain in 1990 were for transporting petroleum rather than for a super-gun project. Similarly, a German shipbuilder evaded German prohibitions on defense sales to Taiwan by disguising the sale of four coastal mine hunters as "multipurpose coastal supply ships." The ships were sent to Taiwan without sonar or guns and were later outfitted with defense gear by other suppliers.[25]

This channel of proliferation, too, promises to grow in the future. Until the late 1970s, the military sector led the civilian sector in technological improvements for weapons. Today, because of declining resources and the increasing battlefield role of microelectronics, data processing, and telecommunications, the defense sector is relying more heavily on the civilian sector for many of its high-tech products.[26] Dr. Armindo da Silva of the European Economic Community (EC) noted that 38 percent of systems procured by European defense departments are now classified as dual use.[27] Differentiating between export products with purely military functions and those with civilian functions and controlling their spread is becoming an ever more nettlesome problem.

Whether legal or illegal, third-party transfers are another method of proliferation. In some cases, third-party transfers take place with the agreement of the original supplier. Years may intervene between the original purchase and the transfer, and the supplier may no longer care about earlier restrictions. In other cases, the original supplier may tacitly encourage the retransfer to a politically sensitive friend or ally.

Often, however, third-party transfers involve subterfuge on the part of the seller. Turkey, for example, transferred U.S.-origin spare parts for C–130 and T–37 military aircraft to Pakistan without prior consent from the U.S.[28] More sophisticated equipment was involved in a Japanese third-party transfer. A Japanese electronics manufacturer (Japan Aviation Electronics Industry, controlled by Nippon Electronics Company (NEC) pleaded guilty to having illegally sold navigation equipment for American F–4 fighter jets to Iran through middlemen in Singapore and Hong Kong in 1986. This equipment was made under license from Honeywell, Inc., of the United States.[29]

Measures designed to overtly defraud national and international arms export regulations characterize the black market. Although the line between the gray and black markets is indistinct, black-market transactions involve the conspiracy of buyer and seller. Countless subterfuges have been devised by mercenary, desperate, or unscrupulous actors in the arms trade. Only the most common are described here.

One method is to have a friendly intermediary acquire arms and then clandestinely transfer them to an embargoed country or politically sensitive country. Many states rely on intermediaries without a reportable address, for example, countries that have a strong tradition of banking and company secrecy, such as Switzerland, Belgium, Luxembourg, and Liechtenstein and some Caribbean states.[30] Others use surrogates as intermediaries. China, for example, uses North Korea to sell to politically sensitive states.[31]

Trading intermediaries are also used. Friendly coconspirator countries allow products to be off-loaded at one port and then secretly shipped to another undisclosed port. South Africa used this system through a complex web of trading intermediaries. China, too, has regularly used Hong Kong as a conduit for clandestine imports.

Another device is the use of dummy or front companies to do the purchasing. Iraq, for example, bought foreign companies and used them to purchase technology needed for weapons production. Generally the target company is not the original manufacturer, but a licensee of that company.

Pilfering of arms depots due to limitations of the military accounting and inventory system in many countries is another source of proliferation. U.S. losses are difficult to quantify, but according to one account, during 1970–1975, the U.S. Department of Defense (DOD) reported 11,000 military weapons stolen from military bases. In some years, the recovery rate of these is less than 50 percent. Weapons stolen during this period included Redeye missiles and laser-sighted rifles. In 1985, the U.S. Navy's computer-controlled supply system was tapped into by thieves seeking to divert F–14 parts to Iran.[32]

Other Sources

Surplus weaponry is still another means of technological diffusion. Turkey, for example, will receive 1,057 surplus NATO tanks, which will replace about half of the country's arsenal of 2,795 tanks allowed under Conventional Forces in Europe treaty (CFE). In addition, Turkey will receive 600 armored combat vehicles and 72 artillery pieces by the end of 1993. Greece, Portugal, Spain, Norway, and Denmark are also receiving surplus North Atlantic Treaty Organization (NATO) equipment.[33] The flood of former Warsaw Pact equipment is reported to be so great that former Soviet-manufacture infrared night-vision equipment is "being peddled openly on the streets of Finland."[34]

Weapons captured or acquired in wartime are yet another exchange medium. Although the equipment may not be leading edge, when transferred to a less developed country it often raises the qualitative capability of the recipient's military. Israel, for example, has sold to Latin America captured ex-Soviet equipment, and Iran reportedly has bought Soviet-made Scuds and U.S.-made Stingers from the Afghan mujahadeen.[35] One of the most potent weapons in Iraq's arsenal during the Gulf war was the improved

Hawk anti-aircraft missile Iraq had captured during the invasion of Kuwait in August 1990.[36]

THE NEGATIVE IMPLICATIONS OF GLOBALIZATION FOR U.S. NATIONAL SECURITY INTERESTS

Analysts have focused on many different security interests that are negatively affected by globalization. In this section I have divided their concerns into political, economic, and military, although these categories overlap and are conceptually related to each other.

Political Interests

A major fear of some analysts is that these developments augur less political control over domestic defense industrial policy. They argue that foreign sources of supply and transnational corporations are inherently less reliable than domestic firms because they will act in their own national or corporate interests rather than the national interests of the United States.[37]

There is particular concern that as the foreign component of U.S. defense production rises and the number of producers declines through consolidation, there will be an increasing monopoly of supply. These large transnational or foreign firms, many contend, will have inordinate influence over what and how much is produced for the U.S. military. What will happen, they ask, when U.S. policy and the policy of these corporations diverge? If needed research, development, manufacture, or "surge" production is not profitable, will they be willing to proceed? Similar fears have been expressed in Europe. These analysts point to the recent Gulf conflict "where there were suggestions that the Belgian supplier [of ammunition] was reluctant to fill U.K. orders."[38]

Globalization of the defense sector also is thought to threaten the technological superiority of the United States. In this view, maintaining the technological edge is unlikely without government control over defense companies, which are loath to invest in high-risk projects without substantial incentive.[39] In the past, U.S. military contractors invested their own money heavily in research in hope of winning lucrative production contracts. But with declining procurement dollars and the Pentagon's decision to suspend production of most new weapons after developing test models, it is argued, U.S. companies will be less willing and globalized companies will be unwilling to make the investment in high-end technologies.

Others assert that globalization of defense industries, particularly cooperative ventures and transnational ownership, in turn loosens government control over arms sales by providing companies opportunities to evade domestic arms export regulations. This issue has caused particular concern in the United States. The possibility of a French company trying to buy LTV

Aerospace and Defense Company, for example, raised fears regarding past French export laxity and the emasculation of U.S. arms export controls.[40]

Other analysts stress the importance of arms transfers as a major source of diplomatic leverage.[41] In their view, arms transfers are an effective political tool which the United States needs to persuade other states to follow a certain course of action. If foreign governments have veto power over controversial sales through ownership or monopolistic control over components and subassemblies, how will U.S. foreign policy interests be served? On the other hand, when the United States decides to restrict arms sales to certain countries, will these transnational and foreign companies be willing to cooperate?

For some, domestic political interests are also at stake. How, these analysts ask, will the American electorate respond to the transfer of technology, paid for with U.S. taxpayers' money, to a foreign country or company? In 1992, an election year, this became a major question associated with the LTV sale.[42]

Economic Interests

Economic factors also loom large in the debate. In the sluggish economy of the early 1990s, economic considerations are being used to justify continued domestic production of military equipment. For the same reason, arguments against globalizing U.S. defense industries to keep American jobs safe, stimulate stronger capital investment, encourage technological spin-offs into the civilian sector, and generate export earnings fall upon sympathetic public ears. State governments are particularly loath to give up either the taxes or earnings generated by their local defense industries. Other advocates of autarkic production claim that arms imports pressure the balance of payments and should be avoided at a time of increasing public debt.

The U.S. defense industry is particularly concerned about the loss of civil and military markets to foreign competitors because of increasing globalization. The weak U.S. dollar is prompting more foreign companies to actively bid for the acquisition of U.S. firms. In U.S. industry's dim view, the American operations of a foreign company gives it a direct presence in the U.S. market and positions it to compete for domestic military contracts. Furthermore, industry spokesmen argue, technology transfers through company-to-company deals may be used against U.S. firms in the future in competition for military and civil markets at home and abroad.[43]

These fears have prompted some defense analysts to view globalization with caution—to call for more government regulation of foreign investment and technology transfers and to advocate stronger government support for U.S. military exports.

Military Interests

The capacity to resupply or modify equipment from domestic sources is considered a critical asset during crises.[44] For the reasons stated above, some analysts contend that globalization of defense industrial production through mergers, acquisitions, offsets, and joint ventures threatens U.S. technological superiority in times of crisis.[45] If, as discussed earlier, foreign producers for political or economic reasons decline to increase production or provide needed materiel, the military capability of the United States can be seriously hampered. Domestic production, it is argued, reduces U.S. vulnerability to slowdowns, boycotts, blockades or other forms of foreign punishment and persuasion.

Closely associated with this concern is that expressed over the enhanced firepower the proliferation of advanced military technologies accords other countries. Cited is the increasing number of countries with weapons of mass destruction and advanced conventional weapons in inventory. Much has been written about the former and the problems they present for the United States and the world.[46] I will concentrate here on the diffusion of conventional technologies.

By the late 1980s, nineteen developing countries had acquired large amounts of relatively advanced equipment: sophisticated aircraft, armored vehicles, missiles, submarines, and often ships. The nineteen were: Afghanistan, Angola, Argentina, Brazil, China, Egypt, India, Iran, Iraq, Israel, Libya, North Korea (DPRK), South Korea (ROK), Pakistan, Saudi Arabia, South Africa, Syria, Taiwan, and Thailand.[47]

Submarines. The proliferation of submarines to Third World countries is said to epitomize the threat from the spread of advanced weapons. These vessels, according to Norman Polmar, a naval analyst, can be used to place mines and attack merchant ships and U.S. warships.[48] Over forty countries now have them. In Asia, China, North Korea, South Korea, Pakistan, India, and Taiwan have them and Thailand and Vietnam soon will. In Latin America, Peru, Chile, Venezuela, Cuba, Brazil, and Colombia have acquired submarines. In the Middle East, Libya has submarines and Iran recently acquired three. Turkey and most Mediterranean countries also have them.[49]

Air-launched antiship cruise missiles and photographic satellites. The growing deployment of air-launched antiship cruise missiles and photographic satellites is even more unsettling to naval analysts. India, for example, launched the second of its Intelligence Reconnaissance Satellite (IRS)-photographic satellite in August 1991, and a third followed in 1993. According to Rear Admiral Ted Sheafer, the director of naval intelligence, photographic satellites capable of monitoring large-scale military movements can deny the United States the advantage of surprise. The U.S. flank attack that was secretly prepared during the Gulf War, he contends, would now be more difficult to keep secret.[50]

Space-launch vehicles and services. Other commentators call attention to the proliferation of space-launch vehicles. Because they can provide valuable information for the development of indigenous ballistic missile capabilities, space-launch vehicles are thought to pose an immediate direct military threat. In the hands of U.S. adversaries, they could be used to deliver weapons of mass destruction over long distances. (It is generally accepted that a space-launch vehicle capable of placing 1,000 pounds in low Earth orbit can deliver a 1,000-pound payload in the intercontinental range.)[51] Currently six states in addition to the United States and the former Soviet Union possess indigenous space-launch capabilities: China, France, Japan, India, Israel, and Brazil. Often their programs are interconnected. Brazil's satellite program, for example, is directed by a French ballistic missile expert.[52]

BRIGHT SPOTS IN A GLOOMY PICTURE

This picture of globalization's effect on U.S. security interests is both persuasive and depressing. Yet there are various factors that promise to mitigate the negative impact of these developments on the United States.

U.S. Dominance in a Globalized Defense Sector

Declining competition from other suppliers. If the dollar value of arms sales is an indicator, then competition from other suppliers is declining. Although U.S. arms sales agreements with the Third World fell 26 percent between 1990 and 1991 (from $19 billion to $14 billion), the United States surpassed all other suppliers, accounting for 57 percent of total 1991 world arms agreements with Third World states.[53] (As of this writing, U.S. worldwide arms trade statistics were not yet available for 1990 and 1991.)

The market share of other major suppliers has fallen drastically. Only the United Kingdom registered a small gain in 1991. French arms sales to the Third World fell 87 percent between 1990 and 1991, from $3 billion to $400 million. Chinese sales, too, fell 86 percent, to $300 million from $2.1 billion during the same period.

The greatest drop, however, was experienced by the former Soviet Union. Soviet arms sales to the Third World fell from $11.2 billion to $5 billion between 1990 and 1991 and comprised only 20 percent of total Third World agreements in 1991. U.S. sales to Saudi Arabia alone exceeded the total value of Soviet sales to the Third World.[54] Moscow's attempts to increase hard currency arms sales over the last several years have been, for the most part, unsuccessful. The reduction in grant aid, the poor performance of Soviet equipment in the Gulf War, and the collapse of the former centralized arms sales apparatus have further depressed sales.[55]

Lack of competition from other arms producers. Worldwide military production, too, is expected to drop—some estimate as much as 20 to 30 percent in the 1990s.[56] For arms producers in general, falling defense budgets and contracted demand have had serious negative consequences for their exports and military-industrial infrastructure. In an ever-reiterative downward spiral, the ability of smaller and medium-size states to produce sophisticated weapons is dwindling as their dependence upon the more advanced military production capabilities of others, particularly of the United States, is growing.

In Western Europe, not only is defense production declining for all the reasons stated, but large numbers of domestic as well as collaborative programs are being cancelled, particularly for next-generation platforms, such as tanks and planes.[57] For the smaller producers, the situation is most desperate. The Italian defense industry, for example, is struggling to survive. Because of lower global defense budgets and Italy's relatively high production costs, a number of recent sales have gone to other countries that market more sophisticated equipment at competitive prices.[58] As one analyst observes: "It no longer seems possible to deny that in the short to medium term, aggregate defense production in Europe is declining rapidly and that a major restructuring is underway."[59]

It is not necessary to detail the economic chaos unfolding in the former Soviet Union. Conditions in the military sector have been equally tumultuous in the Soviet Union before its disintegration and in the Russian Republic that inherited over 80 percent of the former Soviet Union's aerospace and defense industries.[60]

Defense spending in the former Soviet Union is estimated to have declined about 6 percent in 1989 and 1990,[61] causing severe production and research cutbacks throughout the industry. Military orders to Soviet defense plants fell by 21 percent in 1991 from the previous year, and in January 1992, the Russian parliament approved a budget that slashed arms purchases to about one-seventh the 1991 level. Research and development funding may fall by as much as 30 percent.[62] Unless the Russian Republic is able to resolve its internal problems and maintain a sophisticated research and development (R & D) and industrial infrastructure over the long term, its role in the world's arms production and transfer system is likely to deteriorate further.

The defense industries in East Europe have been equally hard hit. With the disintegration of the Warsaw Pact, the traditional defense export market for East European military industries, major producers such as Poland and the former Czechoslovakia are struggling. The Polish weapons industry, once a major money-maker, is reportedly near collapse.[63] In Czechoslovakia legal arms exports in 1991 dropped 43 percent below 1990 levels (to $186 million). In 1987, Czechoslovakia delivered arms worth $566 million to Soviet-bloc allies. By 1990 that figure had fallen to $50 million.[64]

A similar state of affairs exists in the Third World. By 1989 imports of weapons had declined 31 percent from 1987 levels and exports had declined 29 percent.[65] For many Third World producers whose defense industries depended upon the Iran-Iraq War for sales, reduced demand has been catastrophic. Brazil is a typical example. Its exports fell by 93 percent between 1987 and 1989.[66] The embargo on Iraq after it invaded Kuwait eliminated Brazil's major market for Astros II rocket launchers and missiles and Urutu armored vehicles. Because exports are vital to the health of Brazil's arms industries—some 90 percent of production is exported[67]—many of these industries were thrown into or near bankruptcy.[68] For the foreseeable future, then, the dearth of customers means that Brazil is unlikely to be a major arms supplier or manufacturer of finished-end items. Even Israel, once considered a major Third World arms exporter, is experiencing difficulty. Israel Military Industries (IMI), the country's second largest defense contractor, announced record losses in 1991.[69]

U.S. economies of scale and large R & D spending. The size of the U.S. military market and the relatively large amount of U.S. research and development spending are major factors promoting U.S. dominance of the world's military market. In Europe, for example, R & D and procurement spending are only 25–40 percent of that of the U.S.[70]

The experience of the American aircraft industry tells the story. Because the United States enjoys the advantage of economies of scale through large production runs for the U.S. military as well as greater R & D spending, U.S. aircraft are the cheapest on the market. The disparity between, for example, the length of U.S. and European production runs creates cost differentials of 20 to 50 percent. Large R & D spending also affords the U.S. about a ten-year lead in aircraft performance. As a result, other Western countries do not compete in the high-end fighter market, nor can the former Soviet Union compete any longer.[71]

Dependence of other states on U.S. military imports. Because of high R & D spending and the manufacture of advanced military products in the United States, most of the world is dependent upon U.S. military technology in some form or other. This is true even for Europe. Although the ratio of European imports to U.S. imports dropped from 8:1 in the late 1970s to 2:1 today, all of Europe, including France and Britain, still relies upon American military imports or the use of U.S. licenses.[72] U.S. military imports, on the other hand, consist largely of components and subassemblies. According to one source, only one "very large" major system, the British Harrier v/STOL fighter, has been imported by the U.S. since World War I.[73] European dependence is likely to continue, as transatlantic trade in subsystems and components is increasing in importance. In other countries with more limited production capabilities, this dependence is even greater.[74]

Dependence of other states on sales to the U.S. military market. As we have seen, because of declining domestic demand and falling orders for military equipment abroad, foreign producers are hoping for sales to the U.S. military, the largest military market in the world. In practice, however, this has not been easy, and the alarm expressed by some regarding U.S. overseas procurement may be exaggerated. Even with an increased emphasis on reciprocal procurement, the United States still awards 94.3 percent of its prime contracts and 92.7 percent of total contracts to domestic sources (dollar value). Out of the total, only 7.3 percent go to non-U.S. companies, most of which are in services, construction, and supplies such as petroleum.[75] U.S. military imports in 1989, for example, amounted to $1.6 billion out of a procurement budget of $79.2 billion, or 2 percent of total U.S. acquisitions.[76]

Foreign investment in U.S. defense industries has also proven difficult, and few have gained significant entrance. To secure part of the market, these companies generally must find an American majority partner to bid on projects.[77] Even then, the likelihood of gaining access to classified or leading-edge U.S. technologies is minimal.[78] The United States does not share its most sophisticated technology, such as Stealth antiradar detection measures or other leading-edge systems, even with its close NATO allies.[79]

Moreover, what is a small sale to the United States is often a major sale for the foreign producer. The sale of even minor weapon systems can have a substantial impact on a defense sector the size of Britain's or France's, for example.[80] The threat of U.S. economic punishment, therefore, is a major deterrent to acts that might deprive the U.S. military of needed equipment during crises. It is also a deterrent to cheating on U.S. arms-sales restrictions and prohibitions.

Dependence of foreign suppliers on the U.S. civilian market. Augmenting the attractiveness of the U.S. military market is the size of the U.S. civilian market.[81] A large number of foreign industries with military contracts have important commercial interests in the U.S. economy as well. These suppliers would be even less likely to imperil those interests by embargoing the United States in time of crisis.

Japan's investments in the United States, for example, were over $70 billion in 1989. Beyond this, Japanese exports to the United States since the 1980s have averaged about $90 billion annually.[82] Other arms producers, such as South Korea, Taiwan, and NATO countries, are almost as involved in the U.S. economy. About 30 percent of South Korea's and Taiwan's exports, for example, go to the United States. In addition, both countries sell components to Japan that are reexported in electronic equipment to the United States.[83] Given the size of their investment in the U.S. economy, these countries are unwilling to place their market and invested assets at risk by withholding critical items from the United States or sabotaging its arms control efforts.

MANAGED ARMS PROLIFERATION

The Invisible Hand of Economics

The proliferation of advanced weapons to Third World states is occurring more slowly than popular accounts would suggest. The weapons available today are undeniably more complex and sophisticated than those in circulation twenty-five years ago, but in the estimation of some analysts the technological gap between the inventories of the industrially advanced and less advanced countries is widening.

The proliferation of diesel submarines, cited by some as a major threat, serves as an example. In fact, the number of submarines in inventory is declining. More submarines are being taken out of service than are entering service around the world because of maintenance problems, obsolescence, and the high cost of new replacements.[84]

Declining defense budgets and the rising cost of advanced technology account for reduced Third World procurement of other high-end major systems, such as aircraft and tanks.

The protective self-interest of the arms producers is a further curb on proliferation. Generally, a manufacturer's disinclination to share its most modern advanced technologies with potential competitors, combined with the military services' fear that their own weapons will be used against them,[85] are powerful incentives for governments to withhold their most sophisticated technologies. Traditionally, the major industrialized suppliers have placed export restrictions on their most advanced weapons:

The USA, for example, may be willing to export its F–15, F–16, or F–18 because, if necessary, it can counter such aircraft with superior aircraft in its inventory; therefore, the USA will not be willing to export its latest Stealth fighters. Most arms exporting nations further secure their technological advantage by either putting their most secret technology in "black boxes" that are not to be opened by the nation to whom that technology has been exported (and which must be repaired only by the nation supplying the technology), or by supplying weapon systems with lesser, "export quality" technology. In these ways various arms exporting nations have attempted to protect their technological lead.[86]

Political Leverage

The economic factors slowing the pace of proliferation are augmented by political factors. Arms marketing patterns are strongly correlated to power status; the dominant position of the United States in the world today suggests it will have a major influence on the character and direction of the arms trade. Its industrial size and technological power relative to those of other countries provide the United States with unique political leverage to slow the proliferation of sophisticated technologies, if it so chooses.

The Gulf War was a watershed that mobilized world public opinion in favor of arms-transfer restraints. Prompted by feelings of moral outrage at the behavior of Saddam Hussein, the war epitomized, particularly to the developed world, the dangers of weapons proliferation to areas of high tension and to aggressive countries such as Iraq. The response of the United States and the coalition forces in expelling Iraq from Kuwait created a climate of opinion concerned about regional stability.

Prospects for the success of arms control are increased by the current configuration of world power. During the period of bipolar competition, arms control was an idealistic hope that could not be realized. Today, the economic and political powers of the United States have reduced the room available for other states to undercut U.S. arms control preferences.

The situation in Eastern Europe and the former Soviet Union illustrates this point. Poland, the former Czechoslovakia, and other East European states have tried to raise cash by selling weapons. They were stopped from doing so by the United States—in the case of Poland, three times.[87] Curbing arms sales from the former Soviet Union is also thought to be possible. Because of the new republics' need for Western aid, U.S. intelligence agencies believe they will be responsive to direct Western pressures to control exports of weapons or military technologies.[88]

The significance of all this for arms control and arms transfers is far-reaching. As international tensions have diminished, tighter arms transfer restrictions have become more attractive to American policymakers. Given U.S. predominance in the system, the preferences of the United States on this issue are likely to receive a favorable response from states now more dependent than ever on U.S. political and economic largess.

CONCLUSIONS

The evidence is overwhelming that current conditions favor U.S. dominance in the world's military sector. This does not suggest, however, that the opportunity to protect U.S. interests cannot and will not be squandered. This chapter merely documents the U.S. comparative advantage and assumes that U.S. policymakers will be able to realistically assess the threat from globalization and choose the necessary policy options to meet it. Next are listed some suggestions as to what might be necessary to do so.

In the 1990s U.S. security and national interests will need good intelligence on the technological inventions of other countries, their arms export and import activities, and their adherence to arms control restrictions and regulations. Reconnaissance, surveillance, signals intelligence, photographic intelligence, and human intelligence resources will be important in tracking these activities.

Diligent counterintelligence will also be necessary to protect government scientific and business secrets from exploitation by foreign governments and businesses attempting to gain technology, economic, and trade information that will aid their own economies or military effort.[89]

U.S. government agencies responsible for the economic well-being, political integrity, and military capabilities of the United States need not only to share information among themselves but to coordinate policies of reward or punishment to implement and support U.S. policies at home and abroad.

Research and development spending, as discussed earlier, is a major requirement for technological superiority. It is also necessary to help protect the United States from its own technological ingenuity. Arms control efforts to slow the proliferation of advanced weapons are likely to be successful in the short term. But technology is fungible and cannot be controlled forever.[90] History proves that military inventions diffuse over time in spite of control attempts, and when they do, the best safeguards are countermeasures against them.

United States policy is already moving in this direction. The Pentagon, concerned that developing countries will be able to greatly enhance the accuracy of older weapons with advanced computer technology, is dealing with the threat by launching a two-pronged research and development effort. It is increasing funding for programs designed to improve U.S. intelligence and Command, Control, and Communications (C3) networks. It is also funding programs intended to destroy an enemy's intelligence and C3 efforts.[91]

Similarly, the proliferation of antiship missiles has prompted the U.S. Navy to focus on missile defenses for non-AEGIS system-equipped ships. This program has become the U.S. Navy's top modernization priority. Mine countermeasures (MCM) is also high on a revised modernization list. The Navy believes all its surface combatants must be able to defend themselves against low-flying and steep-diving, high-speed antiship missiles (ASMs) and aircraft. With the demise of the Soviet submarine threat, antisubmarine warfare (ASW) is no longer considered to be critical. Countermeasures that will allow non-AEGIS vessels to better defend themselves now take precedence.[92]

Ultimately, U.S. technological and military superiority can be maintained only through investment in U.S. technological competitiveness. This will involve long-term planning and cooperation between the American government, domestic industry[93] and foreign suppliers, particularly in areas where a potential monopoly of critical materiel exists. Juggling so many interests will not be easy, and will require direction, determination, and, most important, a strong political will on the part of U.S. policymakers.

Various schemes have been put forth, but most analysts agree that a flexible, diversified industrial policy that devotes significant resources to R & D,[94] maintains alternative sources of supply or finds substitute product,[95] and sustains stockpiles of critical or scarce materiel is a necessary and sufficient antidote to the threat of foreign control over U.S. military industrial and foreign policy.

As Raymond Vernon argues, in the new global economy "no country can hope to maintain an autarkic policy . . . except at significant cost in terms of the efficiency of its military establishment.[96] A 1991 Department of Defense report to Congress expresses optimism that a globalized defense sector can be managed to the advantage of U.S. national security interests. It states that the government has the proper tools to protect U.S. national security from undue foreign control while ensuring domestic defense companies continued access to foreign capital. The Pentagon also states that it can identify and manage the continued supply of critical materiel and is confident of its ability to establish a second, domestic source for critical materials if there is a risk that continued supply from a foreign source may be interrupted.[97] This chapter supports that conclusion. The United States, at this particular juncture of history, is in a unique position to provide leadership in the world's military-industrial sector, the arms trade, and in arms control initiatives. May it use this opportunity wisely.

NOTES

1. Center for Strategic and International Studies (CSIS) Defense Industrial Base Project, *Deterrence in Decay: The Future of the U.S. Industrial Base*, Final Report of the CSIS Defense Industrial Base Project (Washington, DC: Center for Strategic and International Studies, May 1989), p. 2; Defense Science Board, *The Defense Industrial and Technology Base*, Final Report of the Defense Science Board (Washington, DC: Office of the Undersecretary of Defense for Acquisition, October 1988), Vols. 1 and 2.

2. Much of the debate has focused on the U.S. defense-industrial base. See: Undersecretary of Defense (Acquisition) and Assistant Secretary of Defense (Production and Logistics), *Report to Congress on the Defense Industrial Base* (Washington, DC: Office of the Undersecretary of Defense for Acquisition, November 1991); Center for Strategic and International Studies, *Deterrence in Decay*; Undersecretary of State (Acquisition), *Bolstering Defense Industrial Competitiveness* (Washington, DC: Office of the Undersecretary of Defense for Acquisition, July 1988); Final Report of the Defense Science Board 1988 Summer Study on *The Defense Industrial Technology Base*, Vol. 2 (Washington, DC: Office of the Undersecretary of Defense for Acquisition, December 1988); General Accounting Office, *Industrial Base Defense-Critical Industries* (Washington, DC; Government Printing Office, August 1988).

3. The White House, *National Security Strategy of the United States* (Washington, DC: Government Printing Office, January 1987); *National Security Strategy of the United States*, January 1988; *National Security Strategy of the United States*, March 1990; *National Security Strategy of the United States*, August 1991; cited by James Miskel, "Domestic Industry and National Security," *Strategic Review*, 19, no. 4 (Fall 1991), p. 24, notes 2 and 3.

4. *National Security Strategy of the United States*, August 1991, pp. 20 and 30, cited in Miskel, "Domestic Industry," p. 23.

5. Miskel, "Domestic Industry," p. 25.

6. Two or more countries would cofund a particular program, and a number of companies in those countries would develop and produce the system jointly. In Europe this type of cooperation took various forms: binational, transatlantic (NATO programs), intra-European (Independent European Program Group [IEPG]), or a single-country funded program with international participation. (Philippe Cothier, "European Defense Industries: From Traditional Cooperation to a Single European Arms Market," in Wolfgang F. Danspeckgruber, ed., *Emerging Dimensions in European Security Policy*, [Boulder, CO: Westview Press, 1991], pp. 189–231 (quote on p. 189).

7. "European Equipment Industry Changes to Capture International Markets," *Aviation Week and Space Technology*, 129, no. 10 (Sept. 5, 1988), p. 6.

8. Cumulative acquisitions by industry between 1981 and 1986 were: electrical and telecommunications equipment (36 percent); chemicals, pharmaceuticals, and biotechnology (20 percent); computers (16.2 percent); machine tools (13.3 percent); precision instruments (10.9 percent); R & D labs (1.9 percent); and aerospace (1.7 percent) (Defense Science Board, *The Defense Industrial and Technology Base*, vol. 1., fig. 5–1, 5–2, p. 37).

9. "European Equipment Industry Changes," p. 61.

10. Ibid.

11. Cdr. Bernie Grover of the Industrial College of the Armed Forces statement quoted in *Jane's Defence Weekly*, 18, no. 1 (July 4, 1992), p. 43.

12. Thomson, 60 percent of which is owned by the French government, offered $450 million for the purchase, with most of the money being financed by the French government through French banks. About 75 percent of LTV's products are defense related, including such advanced systems as the Multiple Launch Rocket System and the B–2 Stealth Bomber (*Arms Control Monitor*, 15 [May–early June 1992], p. 1).

13. Judith Reppy, "Responses of U.S. Arms Industry," in Michael Brzoska and Peter Lock, eds., *Restructuring of Arms Production in Western Europe* (Oxford: Oxford University Press, 1991), pp. 59–68, p. 66.

14. In 1986 imports of finished systems comprised 14 percent of Department of Defense procurements, and the figure was 19 percent for components and subassemblies (Theodore H. Moran, "The Globalization of America's Defense Industries," *International Security*, 15, no. 1 [Summer 1990], p. 90).

15. John Tirpack, "Cheney Doesn't Expect to Bail Out Industrial Base," *Aerospace Daily*, January 23, 1992, p. 115.

16. See Richard Bitzinger, "China Arms Critics Fail Hypocrisy Test," *Defense News*, 7, no. 2 (January 13, 1992), p. 19.

17. Ibid.

18. Quoted in American League for Exports and Security Assistance Newsletter (hereafter ALESA), June 23, 1992, and July 30, 1992, "Foreign Press Reports," India, June 16, 1992; and *Indian Express*, June 22, 1992.

19. ALESA Newsletter, July 16, 1992, "Foreign Press Reports," Germany (a Hamburg newspaper), July 5, 1992.

20. "Brazil Offers Missile Technology to Iran," *Defense Electronics*, May 1991, p. 12.

21. "Asia Sales Challenge U.S. Firms," *Defense News*, 7, no. 9 (March 2, 1992), p. 1.

22. Tom Clancy and Russell Seitz, "Five Minutes Past Midnight and Welcome to the Age of Proliferation," *The National Interest*, 26 (Winter 1991–92), pp. 3–12.

23. According to Jacques Gaillard, the percentage of the world's scientists and engineers residing in developing countries rose from 7.6 percent to 10.2 percent between 1970 and 1980 and by 1990 exceeded 13 percent (*Scientists in the Third World* [Lexington: University Press of Kentucky, 1991], cited in Clancy and Seitz, p. 4).

24. "Pay Lures 50 Soviet Experts to Aid Iraq's Nuclear Effort," *Washington Times*, March 2, 1992, p. 1.

25. ALESA Newsletter, July 30, 1992, "Foreign Press Reports," Germany DER SPIEGEL, July 20, 1992.

26. Cothier, "European Defense Industries," pp. 189–231.

27. Sharon Hobson, "Picking Your Partner," *Jane's Defense Weekly*, July 4, 1992, p. 44.

28. *Congressional Record*, 102d Congress, Second Session, May 26, 1992, p. H3738.

29. "Japanese Plead Guilty in Iran Arms Sales," *New York Times*, March 12, 1992.

30. In 1989, the Swiss reduced the secrecy of its banks, but other countries such as Sri Lanka, the Cook Islands, and Vanuatu have instituted Swiss-bank-type secrecy.

31. "Controlling the Flow of Sophisticated Arms to the Third World: A Modern Dilemma," *Asian Defence Journal*, June 1992, pp. 28–36.

32. Ibid., p. 32.

33. "NATO Arms Transfer Benefits Turkish Military," *Defense News*, 7, no. 36 (September 6, 1992), p. 7.

34. ALESA Newsletter, June 23, 1992, "Foreign Press Reports," Sweden, June 12, 1992.

35. ALESA Newsletter, June 23, 1992, "Foreign Press Reports," London, June 4, 1992.

36. "Hawk Episode Highlights Risks to U.S. by Captured Weapons," *Defense News*, 7, no. 11 (March 16, 1992).

37. Frank Gaffney, "Bush Must Quash Dangerous LTV Sale," *Defense News*, 7, no. 21 (May 25, 1992).

38. *Jane's Defence Weekly*, 18, no. 1 (July 4, 1992), p. 43.

39. Brzoska and Lock, "Introduction," *Restructuring of Arms Production in Western Europe*, p. 7.

40. Bruce van Voorst, "Giving Away the Weapons Store," *Time*, June 1, 1992, p. 37.

41. Office of Technology Assessment, Congress of the United States, *Global Arms Trade: Commerce in Advanced Military Technology and Weapons* (Washington, DC: Government Printing Office, June 1991), p. 16.

42. "Congress Should Enforce Existing Legislation," *Arms Sales Monitor*, 15 (May–early June 1992).

43. Reppy, "Responses of U.S. Arms Industry," p. 66.

44. Miskel, "Domestic Industry," p. 23.

45. Gaffney, "Bush Must Quash."

46. A flood of publications have appeared on this subject in recent years. Leonard S. Spector and William C. Potter are only two of the many specialists writing on nuclear proliferation. Two of their publications are: Spector, "Threats in the Middle East," and Potter, "The New Suppliers," both in *Orbis*, 16, no. 2 (Spring 1992), pp. 181–210. On chemical and biological weapons, see: "Chemical and Biological Warfare," *The Military Balance, 1988–1989*, pp. 242–249; Edward M. Spiers, *Chemical Weaponry* (New York: Macmillan, 1989); Elisa D. Harris, "Stemming the Spread of Chemical Weapons," *The Brookings Review*, 8, no. 1 (Winter 1989), pp. 39ff.

47. David E. Albright, "Threats to United States Security in a Post-Containment World: Implications for United States Military Strategy and Force Structure," *In Depth*, 2, no. 2 (Spring 1992), p. 71.

48. "Stalking Submarines by Air," *Boston Globe*, April 19, 1992, p. 21.

49. Ibid.

50. "Experts Say Agencies Should Improve Coordination," *Defense News*, 7, no. 8 (February 24, 1992).

51. Technologies for providing reentry vehicles with heat shields need not be sophisticated to assure the survival of a nuclear, chemical, or biological warhead. These technologies are reported to be "readily available" in the Third World. Sufficient accuracy to hit a city—an accuracy measured in miles, not feet, is enough to constitute a major threat ("Space Vehicles Pose Ballistic Threat," *Defense News*, 7, no. 2 [May 18, 1992], p. 31). See also "Letters" and "Satellite Threat," *Defense News*, 7, no. 22 (June 8, 1992), p. 26.

52. "Letters" and "Satellite Threat," *Defense News*, 7, no. 22 (June 8, 1992).

53. Richard F. Grimmett, *Conventional Arms Transfers to the Third World, 1984–1991, CRS Report for Congress* (Washington, DC: Congressional Research Service [CRS] July 20, 1992), p. 49. (Unless otherwise noted, all arms trade statistics are from this source.)

54. Ibid., p. 8.

55. Statement of Kathleen Horste, Special Assistant for Russian/Eurasia-DIA and Joint CIS/DIA Testimony before the Joint Economic Subcommittee on Technology and National Security, in Memo 92–37 distributed by ALESA, June 17, 1992.

56. Keith Krause, "Trends in the Production and Trade of Conventional Weapons" (Paper prepared for the conference "The Supply-Side Control of Weapons Proliferation," Canadian Institute for International Peace and Security, Ottawa, Canada, June 1991), pp. 6–7.

57. "European Plane Hits a Head Wind," *New York Times*, September 7, 1992, p. 37.

58. ALESA Newsletter, July 30, 1992, "Foreign Press Reports," Italy, *-L'Espresso*, July 12, 1992.

59. Edward J. Laurance, "A Model and Some Preliminary Indications" (Paper prepared for the annual meeting of the International Studies Association, Vancouver, March 1991), p. 8.

60. Together, the Russian Republic and the Ukrainian Republic account for 90 percent of the former Soviet Union's military-industrial sector. Nick Cook, "Soviet Aviation Industry Nears Independence," *Jane's Defence Weekly*, 16, no. 21 (November 23, 1991), p. 995; "Drastic Cuts in Weapons Orders Underway," *Aviation Week and Space Technology*, January 27, 1992, p. 34.

61. Interview with Uri Ryzhov, Chairman, Supreme Soviet Science Committee in "One on One," *Defense News*, 6, no. 29 (July 22, 1991), p. 62.

62. "Drastic Cuts in Weapons Orders Underway in Former Soviet Union," *Aviation Week and Space Technology*, January 27, 1992, p. 34; "Wire News Highlights," *Current News*, January 24, 1992, p. 16; "Russia to Cut Arms Orders by 85 Pc This Year," *Daily Telegraph*, January 16, 1992, p. 8.

63. "Polish Arms Industry Collapsing," in "Wire News Highlights," *Current News*, September 24, 1991, p. 16.

64. "Czechoslovaks Find Profit and Pain in Arms Sales," *New York Times*, February 19, 1992, p. A11; and "Focus on the Czechoslovak Defense Industry," *International Defense Review*, 24, no. 8 (August 1991), pp. 862ff.

65. U.S. Arms Control and Disarmament Agency, *World Military Expenditures and Arms Transfers, 1990* (Washington, DC: Superintendent of Documents, November 1991).

66. Ibid. According to the *SIPRI Yearbook, 1991, World Armaments and Disarmaments*, Stockholm International Peace Research Institute (New York: Oxford University Press, 1992), Brazil's exports continued to drop in 1990; it records a 95 percent decline between 1987 and 1990 (p. 198).

67. Ron Matthews, "The Neutrals and Gunrunners," *Orbis*, 35, no. 1 (Winter 1991), p. 41–52 (quote on p. 45).

68. Two of Brazil's three major arms-producing industries faced bankruptcy in 1992 (Testimony of Rear Admiral Sheafer, Director of Naval Intelligence, to the Seapower, Strategic, and Critical Materials Subcommittee of the U.S. House Armed Services Committee, February 5, 1992, excerpted in *Arms Sales Monitor*, 11–12 (January–February 1992, p. 5).

69. "Looking to the State for Salvation," *Jane's Defence Weekly*, 18, no. 15 (October 10, 1992), p. 37.

70. Andy Moravcsik, "1992 and the Future of the European Armaments Industry," in Danspeckgruber, ed., *Emerging Dimensions in European Security Policy*, pp. 199–220 (quote on p. 205).

71. Gansler and Henning (no source cited), references found in Jacques Gansler, *Affording Defense* (Cambridge, MA: MIT Press, 1989), pp. 300–310; Frederick P. Biery and Leonard Sullivan, Jr., *Assessing U.S. Weapons System Modernization Cost and Performance Trends*, Report for the Office of the Secretary of Defense, 1985, (Arlington, VA: TR–3993–3), cited in Moravcsik, "1992 and the Future," p. 204, note 23.

72. These are average figures. Some European countries have larger unfavorable trade balances. Between 1982 and 1986, Switzerland's, for example, was 6.8:1 (David Silverberg, "Domestic Sources Reap Bulk of U.S. Prime Contracts," *Defense News*, 2, no. 40 (October 5, 1987), p. 15). Fifty percent of the missiles procured by European countries are U.S. designs, and between 10 and 30 percent of the Tornado's components (depending on the model) are of U.S. origin. See Moravcsik, "1992 and the Future," p. 210.

73. Moravcsik, "1992 and the Future," p. 209.

74. The five-year (1982–1986) cumulative defense trade balance figures with the U.S. are telling in this regard: Pakistan, 4,147 to 1; Taiwan, 1261 to 1; Egypt, 340 to 1; Greece, 15 to 1; Switzerland, 7 to 1; Australia, 6 to 1; Japan, 4 to 1; Korea, 4 to 1; Israel, 2 to 1 (Silverberg, "Domestic Sources Reap Bulk," p. 15).

75. Ibid.

76. U.S. Arms Control and Disarmament Agency. *World Military Expenditures and Arms Transfers, 1990*; Secretary of Defense Frank C. Carlucci, *Annual Report to Congress: Fiscal Year 1990* (Washington, DC: Superintendent of Documents, 1989).

77. Moravcsik, "1992 and the Future," p. 209.

78. The Department of Defense rules for foreign contractors require either the negotiation of a "special security arrangement" (SSA) or the establishment of a non-voting trust for the foreign parent, with the top management and board of directors of the U.S. subsidiary composed only of U.S. citizens. A new measure to prevent foreigners from "burrowing into" the U.S. defense industrial base is the Exon-Florio amendment. It gives to the President the authority, for national security reasons, to prevent an American company from falling into foreign hands through merger, acquisition, or takeover. Twelve months after the amendment's passage, the government had reviewed more than fifty cases, in contrast to fewer than thirty cases in the twelve preceding years (Theodore H. Moran, "The Globalization of America's Defense Industries," *International Security*, 15, no. 1 [Summer 1990], pp. 94–95).

79. Moravcsik, "1992 and the Future," p. 209. France, for example, tried to arrange a joint venture with Texas Instruments and General Electric to upgrade radars for the French Rafale aircraft. This proposal was apparently turned down by the U.S. government because a sensitive technology, galium arsenide, was involved (*Inside the Pentagon*, October 30, 1987, p. 1).

80. For example, Plessey (U.K.) increased its exports from 10 percent to 50 percent of sales in less than a decade because of U.S. sales. See Moravcsik, "1992 and the Future," p. 210.

81. For further discussion, see S. Neuman, "The Arms Market: Who's On Top?" *Orbis*, 33, no. 4 (Fall 1989), p. 521.

82. Miskel, "Domestic Industry," pp. 30–31.

83. Ibid., p. 31.

84. In Third World and East European countries, submarines in inventory were delivered between 20 and 50 years ago, and new technology has rendered them obsolete. New submarines are too costly for most of these countries (David Silverberg, "Third World Sub Fleets Shrink, Still Pose Small Threat to West," *Defense News*, 7, no. 22 [June 8, 1992], p. 14).

85. Fairly recent experiences include French forces facing their own technology during the Gulf War and U.S. fears about Iraqi missile-delivery capabilities.

86. "Controlling the Flow of Sophisticated Arms to the Third World: A Modern Dilemma," *Asian Defence Journal*, June 1992, pp. 28–36 (quote on p. 2).

87. The agreements were with Iran, Syria, and Myanamar. In addition, Poland honored the sanctions by the U.S.-led United Nations during the Kuwait Gulf War and lost several hundreds of millions of dollars owed it by Iraq (Andrzeh Karakoszka, Comments on "Models for Explaining the Global Spread of Weapons," in *The Global Diffusion of Military Technology*, the proceedings of a workshop held at the University of Wisconsin–Madison, December 6–8, 1991, sponsored by the Center for International Cooperation and Security Studies, p. 14).

88. Statement of Kathleen Horste.

89. See, for example, Jeffrey W. Wright, "Intelligence and Economic Security," *Intelligence and Counterintelligence*, 5, no. 2 (1992), pp. 203–221.

90. "We Have the High-Tech, They Have Not," *The Economist*, September 5, 1992, pp. 12–14.

91. "Third World C3 Potential Concerns Pentagon," *Defense News*, 7, no. 30 (July 27, 1992), p. 8.

92. "ASW Gives Way to Missile Defence as US Priority," *Jane's Defence Weekly*, 7, no. 11 (March 14, 1992), p. 437.

93. Dr. John Starron of the National Defense University observed that because the threat today is unpredictable, the government must "conceive and develop generic capabilities useful in more than one type of response. . . . It is not realistic to distinguish between a US national industrial base and a defence industrial base" (*Jane's Defence Weekly*, 18, no. 1 [July 4, 1992], p. 43).

94. According to the Department of Defense, other budgetary reductions will not greatly affect defense research and development funding, although there will probably be a shift in resources from nuclear forces and weapons to conventional areas. The Bush administration requested $41.4 billion for defense-related R & D in FY 1993, $38.8 billion in Department of Defense and $2.6 billion in the Department of Energy (John D. Moteff, "Defense Research and Development," *CRS Review* (Washington, DC: Congressional Research Service, April–May 1992], p. 24). The Pentagon has stated:

While the Department will produce fewer weapon systems in the future, it must strengthen its research and development efforts. These efforts are essential to: (1) equip the smaller, base force that the U.S. will maintain, (2) preserve the technological capabilities to equip larger forces in a timely fashion in the event that a substantial threat to U.S. interests emerges in the future, and (3) deter potential aggressors (Department of Defense Fact Sheet, "A New Approach to Defense Acquisition," January 1992).

95. Miskel, "Domestic Industry," p. 27.

96. See, for example, Raymond Vernon, "Are Foreign-Owned Subsidiaries Good for the United States?" (Unpublished paper, November 7, 1991), p. 25.

97. Undersecretary of Defense and Assistant Secretary of Defense, *Report to Congress on the Defense Industrial Base*, see particularly pp. 4–7, incl.

8

The Gulf War: Lessons for the Future

Douglas V. Johnson II

The collapse of the bipolar competition of the last forty-five years released long pent-up hostilities, and in place of the anticipated global peace, we now have global war. Despite the sharp reduction in a single-power threat and the obvious consequence of reduced defense requirements, the growth in number of murderous squabbles may require adaptation to pacification or peacekeeping requirements of nearly equal dimensions. To use the Gulf War as a lens through which to view these phenomena, we must first review the war's broadest outlines.

OVERVIEW

On August 2, 1990, after considerable mutual provocation, Iraq's armed forces overran Kuwait in an operation lasting little more than a day. Provocations aside, Iraq's action brought forth immediate international condemnation. While that may have been expected, the collective military response that followed was remarkable. Following a rapid buildup of American military power augmented by international contingents of widely varying combat value, the coalition forces smashed Iraq's armed forces in Kuwait and southern Iraq and dealt devastating blows to Iraq's military infrastructure. The coalition next reestablished legitimate government in Kuwait, tended briefly to refugees in the theater of operations, and then evacuated southern Iraq. What was not done was as remarkable as what was. Iraq was not occupied, nor was its government replaced. Iraqi sovereignty was left essentially intact, although it was found expedient to restrict it above the 36th parallel to provide protection to the Kurds. Although U.S. leadership was crucial in forming and sustaining the coalition, the United States at all times acted under the covering of the United Nations. From a domestic perspective, the military action was supported by a majority of the American people and ultimately by their elected representatives.

As soon as the shooting stopped, the arguments began. Was Operation Desert Storm the first battle of a new era or the last of the old? Most likely, Desert Storm was both the last battle of the past era and the *prototype* battle of the new era. The armies of the Gulf War were those built to prevent the Cold War from becoming hot. They, their command structures, doctrine, logistical support, and alliance linkages developed from a unified focus on a common threat perception. Such a basis for integration, as incomplete as it was, no longer exists with any significant force. Thus, we can draw the conclusion that those armies represent the final scene in the final act of a very long play. On the other hand, the ad hoc nature of the coalition, the sharp technological disparities between participants, friend and foe alike, the covering of the United Nations, and the relative precision and impunity with which American forces operated suggest the emergence of a new style of warfare—perhaps the realization of what has been called the "American Way of War."

THE AMERICAN WAY OF WAR

Professor Russell F. Weigley in 1973 described the American yearning for quick, decisive, low-casualty wars and then detailed all the reasons why this had been unattainable.[1] He concluded the book with this sentence: "Because the record of non-nuclear limited war in obtaining acceptable decisions at tolerable cost is . . . scarcely heartening, the history of useable combat may . . . be reaching its end."[2] What the Gulf War demonstrated was that the potential for "tolerable cost" may now be realizable. This is the physical aspect of the "American Way of War." The issue of obtaining "acceptable decisions" is somewhat more philosophical. If the enemy's will to resist resides in his military instrument, the United States has enough capability to destroy that instrument with relative *impunity* and *precision*. While the political definition of an "acceptable decision" will vary with each situation, the ability of the military instrument to help shape that decision may be improving. At the very least, the American military is now asking the right question: In political terms, what is the world supposed to look like when all the shooting stops? The challenge is to create a coherent vision of the end, something at which we are not particularly good.

Realization of the "American Way of War" may be within reach technologically, but there is much more to it than technology. The observations below suggest that full realization may be somewhat more difficult and distant.

RESPONSES TO AGGRESSION

The Military Instrument

Most peoples of the world acknowledged that aggression of the type Iraq perpetrated against Kuwait is wrong, and wrong enough to lead to the approval of collective military action to reverse it. This view reflects a visceral sensing that must be balanced against the reality that vital national interests were also involved. That there was not unanimous agreement highlights the fact that there are many factors that condition the range of reactions to aggression.

There is little doubt that simple aggression is not enough to motivate the peoples of the world to act together to relieve victims of aggression. The coincidence of vital national interests, media attention, and vigorous leadership were—and are—required.

Simple aggression involves crossing internationally recognized borders, but how many of the world's national borders are subject to dispute in the first place? From an Iraqi perspective, Kuwait has always been an illegitimate artifact of a colonial period. Arguments over the "real" borders are today the most potentially volatile cause of further hostilities with Iraq. Specifically, how can Iraq possibly submit to the division of its sole remaining port, Umm Qasr, as mandated by the U.N. Border Commission?[3]

It is significant that the coalition made no effort to set any goal that placed the Iraqi state at risk as a sovereign nation. In the short run, that decision has been subject to plentiful criticism, but the long run may well prove it to have been an act of wisdom. If nothing else, it suggests that internationally recognized borders will be respected by the United Nations.

What the world faces at the moment, however, is the somewhat more complex problem of peoples deciding to redraw accepted internal borders and, incidentally, deciding who will be allowed to live within them.

Thus, two cases exist: crossing borders and redrawing borders. In the former case, the weight of international law is substantial, though not sufficient to call forth military reaction. In the latter, the actions of the United Nations leave some doubt as to when military intervention may be sanctioned. In the abstract, aggression across a border may be dealt with simply by the destruction of the invading military forces. In the internal process of redefining borders, for all intents and purposes a civil war, humanitarian considerations appear to be driving considerations of military involvement. What is new about all of this is that the television media are now consciously at work to place before the world selected humanitarian situations, seeking to engage as much "expert opinion" and popular emotion as it can gather. Apparently the effect upon governments is somewhat stronger than that of the infamous Yellow Press of the 1890s. If simple humanitarian considerations were decisive, United Nation's forces would be at work in a hundred other places today, most of which are ignored by the media for uncertain reasons.

Why did all the members of the coalition gather as they did to oppose the otherwise naked aggression against Kuwait? The Saudis were clearly frightened, and rightly so. Why did Turkey join in, why Bangladesh, why Egypt, and, most of all, why Syria? Of the lot of them, Syria may have come out the biggest winner. It was immediately given a free hand to dispose of its opposition in Lebanon, it was removed from the list of pariah states supporting terrorism, and its relations with the United States were revitalized with certain economic benefits—on the basis of what? Simple humanitarianism or outrage at violations of international law can both be used as cloaks for other agendas.

The conclusions drawn from all of these developments is not comforting. War remains a political act carried out by the military instrument. The motivation for war in response to naked aggression is not hard to produce, and less so if a threat to a vital national interest can be worked into the fabric of provocation. But because we are moving rapidly into the true information age, there may be other, seemingly humanitarian reasons for initiating military operations. Perhaps, because we are better able to strike with relative precision and impunity, and because there may be more causes where common humanity demands action to halt suffering, the restraints may begin to fall away and risks may not seem to be as great. We may be unconsciously setting the stage for a period of global war, not war against any single power, but wars or operations short of war that leave people dead and wounded all over the globe—in the name of humanity.

If the military instrument has reached a stage of development in which it may be used with greater effect and less indiscriminate damage, it is still looked upon as the instrument of last resort, and the economic instrument has entered stage left.

The Economic Instrument

Economic sanctions are becoming an alternative coercive instrument of choice. The general effectiveness of the embargo against Iraq demonstrated the potential of this weapon. However, there are significant peculiarities to the Iraqi situation. A single-commodity economy is obviously more vulnerable than is a diversified one. But most important of all, it must not be forgotten that the effects of an embargo are dual edged. Had it not been for Saudi and Kuwaiti financial assistance to Iraq's former trading partners, the embargo would have been very leaky. In fact, without Saudi assistance, it is likely that some nations could not have afforded to participate in the embargo; Turkey may have been one of the most important ones. Also, economic sanctions take time, apparently a long time. Political situations do not generally allow too much time to elapse before demands are raised, especially in financial realms, to get back to normal. There is also a problem of focus. Sanctions are supposed to be a relatively humane approach to coercion. While it is not the intent of most sanction programs to attack the general populace, at some point that issue moves out of the hands of the external parties. Saddam Hussein has cynically manipulated the media and the rightly concerned international medical community to portray the ill effects of the U.N. embargo on his people when there is little reason, and almost none related to the embargo, that they should suffer at all.

Is the economic instrument a newly useful tool for future conflict and crisis management? The best that might be said about the use of the economic weapon in an embargo scenario is that we now have a good deal more experience with which to evaluate the instrument. We have yet to demonstrate that we have learned anything, but perhaps the Iraqi and Serbian experiences will add something to our knowledge base.

The Diplomatic and Political Instrument

There is an argument in *Imperial Temptation: The New World Order and America's Purpose*, by Robert W. Tucker and David C. Hendrickson, that there has been a shift in international law that reaffirms the old responsibility of victorious nations to perform certain duties on behalf of the conquered.[4] The argument concludes that occupation and pacification of Iraq would have provided a more stabilizing solution to the region, that the American experience of World War II with Japan and Germany is conclusive evidence of the benefits of such a policy, and that it would have been possible to do the same in Iraq. While one cannot say with certainty that such would have been the case, it is certain that to do so would have been viewed by the American electorate with considerable skepticism, by the Iranians with renewed fury, and by most other Arab nations with deep misgivings. After the fact, it appears that such a course may indeed have been the better route to long-term stability. (It offered, incidentally, the tantalizing prospect of placing the United States in direct control of the world's second largest proven oil reserves.) Would the United States ever again be willing and able to bear the cost of such an undertaking? At the time the answer was clearly, No! In light of the prospects of a need to return to finish the business some time in the indeterminate future, perhaps we were shortsighted once again.

As fascinating as that argument is, there would undoubtedly have been a storm of criticism. Was the United States not doing in reverse what it had just gone to war to correct? Were we not simply restoring a colonial administration to the region as Saddam had said?

If the United States is seriously going to pursue its stated National Security Strategy objectives, then perhaps we should proceed as Tucker and Hendrickson suggest and seek to occupy and pacify all those recalcitrant nations on the globe who otherwise disturb the peace, and make democracies of them all.[5] After all, isn't it conventional wisdom that democracies never go to war against each other? So it takes another forty years to complete the process of democratization—isn't the end result worth it?

THE WEINBERGER DOCTRINE

In 1984, Secretary of Defense Caspar Weinberger delivered a speech setting forth what is now the Weinberger Doctrine.[6] This doctrine suggests the manner in which the United States should approach war and, in so doing, prevent any repetition of the Vietnam debacle. The doctrine is largely inapplicable in practical terms, as Dr. Samuel J. Newland and I argued in *The Recourse to War: An Appraisal of the "Weinberger Doctrine."*[7] Our appraisal notwithstanding, the Gulf War experience and the linkages that have been developed, after the fact, between it and the Weinberger Doctrine suggest that there is likely to be a continued effort to embed the doctrine's six tests into formal decision making. Ironically, the shrinking American defense budget could also tempt us to use Mr. Weinberger's six tests as an excuse for inaction.

The first test is that military forces should not be committed unless the occasion is "deemed vital to our national interest."[8] Ensuring the free flow of low-cost oil from the Persian Gulf was most certainly a major factor in justifying our intervention there and a valid one. This first test goes on to include those interests "of our allies," and the Gulf crisis met that test as well, particularly in regard to Japan's Middle East oil dependency. But there are two problems here that must be seen through the eyes of the American electorate. What are our "vital national interests," and just exactly how many allied interests do we intend to fight for? Unfortunately, the national security strategy of the United States is written in rather broad terms, including statements that we seek "[a] stable and secure world, where political and economic freedom, human rights, and democratic institutions flourish."[9] Was the violation of human rights in Bosnia in 1992 and 1993 sufficiently terrible to cause the United States to deploy forces, as if in defense of a national interest? The Kurdish situation certainly was, and we did, although that case was clearly an extension of our war against Saddam Hussein. Why, one may well ask, have we not, therefore, gone to war in Ethiopia, Sudan, Bulgaria, Azerbaijan, or other places where people are being killed daily in droves? Strictly and cynically speaking, it is because their deaths do not affect our vital national interests. Operation Provide Comfort can easily be seen as a simple extension of our desire to humiliate and destabilize the regime that threatened our oil supplies.

Secretary Weinberger's second test is, "If we decide . . . to put combat troops [in] we should so so wholeheartedly . . . with the clear intention of winning."[10] We got that half right. Desert Storm was a beautiful example of wholeheartedness; only after the shooting stopped did we begin to wonder if we had rightly defined "winning." Tucker and Hendrickson argue that establishing the Middle Eastern Command Headquarters in Baghdad would have been a better solution than simply satisfying the provisions of the United Nations resolution mandating Iraqi withdrawal from Kuwait.[11]

Perhaps we must begin to examine further the business of occupation and pacification. Evidence of the natural progression toward democracy is ambiguous, and the evidence of the Gulf War suggests that without significant outside help, the Iraqis are unlikely to see democracy in the lifetime of this or the next generation. Arguably, the prospects of a Muslim country achieving democracy as we know it are slim. Consequently, what does "winning" mean when dealing with a state like Iraq?

Moving on to Weinberger's third test, we find ourselves constrained to determine beforehand "clearly defined political and military objectives. And we should know precisely how our forces can accomplish those . . . objectives [and] send the forces needed to do just that."[12] Once again we confront the need for a clear definition and description of success. The worst part in this case is the assumed existence of some cosmic calculus that allows us to derive an exact Time-Phased Force Deployment List, the infamous TPFDL, Q.E.D.[13]

Test four is little more than a restatement of the principle of mass with an acknowledgment that the application of that principle entails recognition that the application of force is a dynamic process changing over time. We got that right when the Seventh Corps arrived.

The fifth test, reasonable assurance of the support of the people, is an interesting example of wishful thinking.[14] It is tied directly to the problem that the people may not necessarily see that there is a threat to a vital national interest. As was demonstrated during the prelude to the shooting war, the American people retained a certain skepticism about the vital nature of Gulf oil. Our obvious dependency brought forth a reaction such as, Why don't we do something about the dependency rather than go to war in some godforsaken desert?[15]

The criterion for war that I encountered in central Pennsylvania was, How many people do you expect will be killed? If the figure was about 1,000, war was acceptable; if it rose above 5,000, it was wholly unacceptable despite clear recognition that oil was a vital national interest.[16] This skepticism remained until the reserves were called up and deployed. In retrospect, the congressional debate over the approval of the use of force was one of the most salutatory events of the entire war. It was the democratic process in action in its greatest glory and was one of the few genuinely sincere interchanges to have taken place in the Congress in this decade. Whether Saddam Hussein watched it on CNN along with the rest of the world is unknown. Given his narrow understanding of Americans, its effect, assuming he watched it, was certainly lost to him. In that extended exchange, the Congress satisfied a good part of the last test, for they determined in their minds and by their votes that the use of force was to come about as a last resort.

There is another twist to this proposition. Whereas Presidents Wilson and Roosevelt seemed constrained not to move too far ahead of public opinion as war approached, both eventually began to lead gently until they sensed that the people had begun to decide. Sinking ships served as an excellent catalyst for public opinion in both cases. President Bush, on the other hand, felt the need to seize and shape public opinion directly and fashion it quickly to his stated ends. It may be argued that in moving as rapidly as he did, he defined the issue too narrowly, even though he cannot be faulted for clarity. Arguably, the restoration of Kuwait was insufficient to reestablish peace and stability in the region. But it was certainly consistent with the military principle of war objective, identification of a decisive, attainable goal.

Why this extended review of the Weinberger Doctrine? There is a danger that because this war seemed to satisfy most of its provisions, this doctrine will become established in the minds of policymakers and the people as something more than it is. It may take on legal dimensions not unlike those of the Gettysburg Address, which, some scholars have argued, effectively redefined portions of the Constitution.[17]

Taking the Weinberger Doctrine together with the broad descriptions of our national interests and objectives could lead us into an era where we were obliged to be the global policeman despite the fact that the doctrine was intended specifically to avoid such a role.

JUST WAR

The American in the street does not know much about the concept of just war in particulars, but he readily identifies with the "rightness" of its provisions because they reflect our heritage. In concluding that the Gulf War did meet the requirements of just war, it may be argued that these dictates offer a far more certain and useful guide for action than anything else we currently have available to guide us into and through war or even military operations short of war.

Jus Ad Bellum

The rightness of going to war contains seven provisions, the first of which is a just cause.[18] In a case as overtly contrary to accepted international behavior as was the invasion of Iraq, the principal complaint has been that there may have been an opportunity for sanctions to have worked, but not that there was an absence of just cause. Defensive measures against attack are clearly sanctioned by the just cause provision, and offensive reaction to the loss of territory through attack is likewise accepted.

The fourth provision of *jus ad bellum* is proportionality of ends. This brings us to the heart of the war termination issue so vigorously argued in the media and, frankly, within the U.S. Army. The stated aim of ejecting Iraqi forces from Kuwait was certainly within the limits of a proportional response to aggression. Destruction of the Iraqi military forces in Kuwait and those capable of continuing offensive action from anywhere in Iraq unquestionably fell within the limits. Destruction of Iraqi war-making potential was welcomed by its neighbors, but brought us close to the line.

The criterion of last resort is another problem area. There is always some claim that a few more minutes, hours, or days might have made a difference, but there is no simple equation that will provide that answer. Japan was on its last legs before the atom bombs were dropped. Submarine and mine warfare had reduced import shipping to negligible proportions, but how long it would have taken genocidal starvation to set in and thereby induce surrender was incalculable. In the Gulf War, it should now be perfectly clear that sanctions would have taken years to take effect. How a coalition would have held together that long is an unanswerable question; how long it would have been needed is less uncertain. It is clear that in the Muslim Middle East, obtrusive "infidel" forces can be present for short periods only. Last resort is, therefore, an uncertain equation that must yield to the political and military considerations of the moment. There can be relatively little doubt that nothing short of military action was ever going to cause Saddam Hussein to abandon Kuwait. If that was not clear at the moment, it should be abundantly clear in hindsight, for the Iraqis have renewed their cry for a return of the "19th Province."[19]

Jus ad bellum requires "reasonable hope of success." We see echoes of this in Weinberger's emphasis upon certainty of victory.[20] It is unconscionable for any nation to initiate war without some prospect of successful conclusion. The rapid application of overwhelming combat power is the surest guarantee of quickly stabilizing matters. The greatest captains have generally agreed that the shorter the war, the shorter the campaign, the shorter the battle, the fewer the casualties. In the Gulf, Operation Desert Shield was prolonged for as long as it was for exactly this purpose, to gain a sufficiently large edge in combat power that the fight would be sharp and short. That we were all astounded by the rate of success does not in any way discount the validity of the concept. Should we have gone with less? Why? In order to sustain more casualties, in order to make the fight fair, in order to preserve the enemy's honor? The first of thirteen observations I made after participating in several postwar enterprises is "Never fight fair—combat is for keeps."[21] Everything we do and every effort we can bend to the task must be undertaken to eliminate any chance the enemy might have.[22] The danger that now confronts a high-tech force such as ours is that the three-to-one ratio for success will slip downward to replicate the numerical imbalance of

Desert Storm without consideration of the multitude of other factors that impinge upon the combat power equation, for it is this combat power equation, not simply the numbers, that is the real three-to-one measure.

"Among the ends for which a war is fought should be the establishment of international stability and peace." This is the seventh provision of *jus ad bellum*.[23] Insofar as rhetoric is concerned, the American administration aligned itself perfectly with this provision, stating as its fourth goal, "[p]eace and stability in the region."[24] The implementation of this happy phrase has been somewhat less than satisfying. Peace can be either a simple absence of war or an absence of overt conflict. Stability can mean a return to the status quo, or it can mean a set of conditions that, taken together with an absence of hostilities, produces a situation fundamentally in balance.

Simple maintenance of the status quo may well not lead to any stability at all. This was the case during the Cold War when instability was equated with encroaching communism. Are we prepared to prop up unpopular regimes simply because we cannot be certain of the aims of their successors? When the Communists were seen to be waiting in the wings behind every disturbance, the United States was willing to accept any dictator or tyrant not tarred with the Communist ideology. So long as there is no Communist power waiting to take advantage of any inaction on our part, we ought to consider letting events take their natural course. C. Northcote Parkinson stated a "rule" that it is not in the long-term interests of states to interfere in others' quarrels until one of the parties has established dominance.[25] Premature interference, Parkinson said, artificially froze a situation short of its fundamental resolution, which meant that as soon as the interfering power was removed, the fight would start all over again. "What we really want is a result which eventually produces stability."[26] That recommended course of action—to let the event play itself out to some point of natural stability—is somewhat more difficult in the information age. Since these squabbles tend to spill blood, the television media immediately flock to the scene like so many flies. They capture the conflict in all its dramatic aspects and invariably offer their considerations on the carnage, which are fed into our homes on an hourly basis. Sensitive individuals rightly take up one of the causes and begin to demand action to halt the killing. Fair enough. In fact, when then–Lieutenant General John M. Shalikashvili was sent to Turkey to command Operation Provide Comfort, the order given to him was simply, "Stop the dying."[27] During approximately the same larger time frame, the United States was involved in stopping the dying in Bangladesh, Somalia, Liberia, Kuwait, and along the Iraqi southern border.

Operation Provide Comfort is a good example of just how far one may push the "stability and peace" business. Stability in northern Iraq can be obtained only by killing all the Kurds or by allowing the Iraqis to do so. That is beyond the bounds of what we could morally contemplate, although we have routinely turned blind eyes to similar events in Cambodia and

Ethiopia. How could one obtain peace and stability in a region where the subject peoples were being oppressed, to one degree or another, by each of the four states among which they were scattered—to say nothing of the turmoil caused by their own brutal internecine warfare? Killing them all is certainly the easy way to establish lasting peace and stability in that part of the region. What alternative could be offered that would effect a sufficient change? The United Nations has undertaken a previously unprecedented step in intruding upon a member state's national sovereignty by establishing an autonomous zone. It is not exaggerated to say that Iraq has been, to a limited degree, partitioned. So far, the military guarantee of the security of the Kurds living above the 36th parallel has been sufficient. Iraqi threats have been repulsed by sternly worded warnings to cease and desist from threatening activity, but not without bitter recriminations against the United States and the United Nations for their intrusion upon Iraqi sovereignty. How long will the Iraqi Kurds be safe in their sanctuary? The answer is, as long as the United States has credible forces at hand to deal with any Iraqi mischief. The minute that force is removed, the threats will reappear and will likely result in direct hostile action against the Kurds.

The restoration of the Sabah family rule was not one of the initial objectives of American policy in the Gulf. We demanded the restoration of Kuwaiti sovereignty, but at the outset made little or no particular commitment to restoration of the former government for the very good reason that we were not particularly happy with it. Fledgling representative government had been slapped down by the Sabah family in 1986, and the nation had a "company town" character that is offensive to Americans. The absence of media noise over the lack of progress since the war's end is interesting. Perhaps the magnitude of American investment in restoring the Kuwaiti state has interest groups leaning on either the press or the administration not to upset the very lucrative apple cart. One thing is certain. Peace and stability in Kuwait may arrive, in the long run, under a democratic government, but it is also probable that stability in Kuwait will continue so long as the current government is able to buy off its citizenry with the enormous amount of paternalistic largess it offers as an inducement to keep quiet and continue in the status quo.

Peace and stability, and the entire thorny issue of war termination in this new, multipolar era, demand that thoughtful people in and out of government and the military service begin to consider new approaches. If we do not learn something new, we will continue in the same old circle of retribution, retaliation, and revenge.

CONCLUSIONS

We find ourselves confronted by the interesting phenomenon of potential realization of the "American Way of War" that most find viscerally satisfying and seemingly in harmony with the prerequisites of just war theory. Could this be manipulated to lead us into more rather than fewer wars? It may be possible to wield the military instrument with greater discrimination and selectivity, provided the ends are as thoughtfully considered as the means. However, this increasingly discriminate capability may result in temptations to employ the military instrument more often in support of broader, less cleanly defined national interests.

None of this has a significant impact on U.S. military force posture if the current tenets of readiness, agility, and versatility are maintained. What will be required for the future is greater attention to ends. Of greatest importance is the strategic decision-making process that must produce proper focus and depth of thinking to provide precise direction, right and left limits, and all those other incalculables required for effective prosecution of war that meet just war criteria. We have an increasing capability to conduct war according to just war principles, particularly in terms of proportionality. Structural changes within the services are already underway and will result in more versatile, rapidly deployable forces with ultra-high-tech capabilities. But the most important questions have little to do with technology. Instead we must answer the question: Why apply military power at all? And if it is to be applied, to what long-term end? If we can force ourselves to answer these questions wisely, within the moral limits of just war theory, perhaps we will find ourselves en route to true peace and stability.

NOTES

The views expressed are those of the author and do not necessarily reflect the official policy or position of the Department of the Army, Department of Defense, or the U.S. Government.

1. Russell F. Weigley, *The American Way of War: A History of United States Military Strategy and Policy* (Bloomington: Indiana University Press, 1977). (Originally published as part of The Wars of the United States series [New York: Macmillan, 1973].)

2. Ibid., p. 477.

3. "Iraq," *The Economist Intelligence Unit*, 2 (1992), pp. 12–13.

4. Robert W. Tucker and David C. Hendrickson, *The Imperial Temptation: The New World Order and America's Purpose* (New York: Council on Foreign Relations, 1992). See chap. 12, "The Responsibilities of Victory," pp. 142–151.

5. Ibid., pp. 143 and 145. For a discussion of the prospects of democracy in the region, see Ali Hillal Dessouki, "The Postwar Arab World," *Journal of Democracy* 2, no. 3 (Summer 1991), pp. 63–67.

6. Caspar W. Weinberger, "The Use of Force and the National Will," *Baltimore Sun*, December 3, 1984, p. 11.

7. Samuel J. Newland and Douglas V. Johnson II, "The Military and Operational Significance of the Weinberger Doctrine," in Alan Ned Sabrosky and Robert L. Sloane, eds., *Recourse to War: An Analysis of the "Weinberger Doctrine."* (Carlisle Barracks, PA: Strategic Studies Institute, 1988), pp. 115–142.

8. Ibid., p. 11.

9. *National Military Strategy of the United States* (Washington, DC: Government Printing Office, January 1992), p. 5.

10. David T. Twining, "The Weinberger Doctrine and the Use of Force in the Contemporary Era," in Sabrosky and Sloane, *Recourse to War*, p. 11.

11. Tucker and Hendrickson, *Imperial Temptation*, p. 145.

12. Twining, p. 11.

13. Every cadet at the U.S. Military Academy at West Point concludes his mathematics recitation at the blackboard by underlining the final answer and writing "QED." QED stands for the Latin words *quod erat demonstrandum*, "which was to be demonstrated."

14. Twining, p. 12.

15. The author spoke frequently to civic organizations and college audiences in the months before Operation Desert Storm and came away with these impressions.

16. These figures were a specific focus of discussion with Dickenson College students during a presentation to a newly formed current affairs colloquium.

17. Garry Wills, "The Words that Remade America," *Atlantic Monthly*, June 1992, pp. 57–79.

18. The ordering and general description of these provisions are taken from the chapter written by James Turner Johnson "Just War Thinking and its Contemporary Application: The Moral Significance of the Weinberger Doctrine," in Sabrosky and Sloane, *Recourse to War*.

19. Paul Lewis, "Immovable Object," *New York Times*, July 31, 1992, p. A6, notes that Iraqi television was running a thirty-part series justifying its claim to Kuwait as the 19th province.

20. James Turner Johnson, p. 87.

21. Shortly after the Gulf War, the author felt obliged to gather his thoughts together and provide some colleagues on the U.S. Army War College faculty the benefit of his involvement in the several after-action enterprises in which he had been involved. His thirteen observations are (1) Never fight fair; combat is for keeps; (2) Fight with friends who are filthy rich; (3) Think through to the end before you begin; (4) Keep it simple, seriously, especially in strategy; (5) Liaison leverages through linkages; (6) Nine-tenths of combat is not combat; (7) Space is the high ground; (8) Special operations are special; (9) Call up the reserves, then commit 'em; (10) When you play hardball, use hard balls; (11) Meaningful training makes the most of technology; (12) Combined arms contrive convincing conclusions; (13) "The effectual prayer of a righteous man availeth much."

22. In *Iraqi Power and U.S. Security in the Middle East* (Carlisle Barracks, PA: Strategic Studies Institute, 1990), Dr. Pelletiere and I argue that this is exactly what the Iraqis did to end the Iran-Iraq War, ensure success through overwhelming concentrations of power at the decisive point.

23. James Turner Johnson, p. 87.

24. President George H. W. Bush in a televised public address to the nation. See Arthur H. Blair, *At War in the Gulf: A Chronology* (College Station: Texas A&M University Press, 1992), p. 13. As noted, Col. Blair is indebted to Col. Joseph Englehardt for compiling the initial chronology at the U.S. Army War College (USAWC) in order to keep the faculty and student body informed.

25. Cyril Northcote Parkinson, "The Five Other Rules," *Foreign Policy*, 9 (Winter

1972–73), pp. 115–116. "Avoid any too early interference in an armed conflict which would otherwise lead to a decisive result" (p. 115).

26. Ibid., p. 116.

27. Interview with Lt. Gen. John M. Shalikashvili, October 31, 1991, as part of the Commandant, U.S. Army War College's Senior Leaders Interview Program, whose purpose was to capture the experiences of senior military leaders in the Gulf War for consideration by the USAWC faculty and for the historical record. In August 1993, General Shalikashvili was appointed chairman, Joint Chiefs of Staff, replacing General Colin Powell. Once the project is complete, the interviews will be available to bona fide researcher through the U.S. Military History Institute, Carlisle Barracks, Penn.

Part IV

U.S. National Security: Into the Twenty-First Century

9

Reorganizing America's Security Establishment

Gregory D. Foster

In his immensely insightful book *Images of Organization*, Gareth Morgan characterizes organizations as "psychic prisons" that may trap their members in favored—frequently illusionary—ways of thinking. The metaphor of the psychic prison is rooted in Plato's famous allegory of the cave, where Socrates addresses the relations among appearance, reality, and knowledge. Organizations, suggests Morgan, are psychic phenomena that ultimately are created and sustained by conscious and unconscious processes. People, both those within the organization and those who simply must deal with it, actually can become imprisoned or confined by the images, ideas, thoughts, and actions to which these thought processes give rise.[1]

The United States is trapped in the psychic prison of the Cold War. Change—bewildering in its scope, intensity, and rapidity—is going on all about us. Yet we are stuck in neutral, seemingly mired in a past that is no more, waiting for the invisible hand of evolutionary drift to guide us to some sort of social, political, and economic equilibrium whose contours will be defined *for* us naturally rather than *by* us intentionally. A major culprit for such rearview-mirror thinking is the organizational framework—generally known as the "national security establishment"—set in place in 1947 and maintained essentially unchanged since.

Harvard historian Ernest May has made the telling observation that policymakers often are influenced by erroneous beliefs about what history teaches or portends. The key members of the Truman Administration, who brought us the notion of the Cold War as well as the policies and organizational arrangements that went with it, appear to have thought about the issues before them, suggests May, in a frame of reference made up in large part of narrowly selected and poorly analyzed historical analogies, parallels, and presumed trends.[2]

We can learn two important lessons from our Truman Administration forebears. First, we tend invariably to "face" the future by looking backward. Looking back, of course, is not bad in and of itself; it is a seemingly sound way to impose understanding on the unknown. But it can become a self-deluding crutch to avoid not thinking anew as circumstances change. Thus, a second lesson: thinking and organizing go hand in hand. At some point in time, we organize the way we think; thereafter, however, we tend to think the way we are organized. As inheritors of the Cold War mantle, we are thinking the way we have been conditioned to think by 45-year-old organizational structures. If we want to think differently—and we must if we are to cope with a world that is reconfiguring itself almost daily—then we must organize differently.

STUMBLING INTO THE FUTURE

There are those among us who argue with great certitude that the United States, having emerged victorious from the Cold War, is the world's lone remaining superpower. It seems a fatuous boast, not only because our claim to victory seems to be based primarily on our having outlasted an exhausted foe, but even more so because there is no reason to believe that we can command the automatic deference from the rest of the world that one would expect of a true superpower. If we aspire to superpower status, we must lead. To lead, we must demonstrate vision. In the words of Warren Bennis and Burt Nanus:

The absence or ineffectiveness of leadership implies the absence of vision, a dreamless society, and this will result, at best, in the maintenance of the status quo, or, at worst, in the disintegration of our society because of lack of purpose and cohesion.[3]

Vision requires three things. It requires *foresight*, an ability to look into the future and see possibilities and relationships that others cannot or will not see. It requires *courage*, the strength to stand by that vision in the face of censure and resistance. Above all, it requires *initiative*—even boldness— the willingness to move forward when others shrink from the prospect, to position oneself ahead of events, to create a new reality.

The United States has demonstrated no such traits in the aftermath of the Cold War. We have instead assumed an inertial attitude toward the future that some would characterize as inactivism or reactivism. Inactivists are satisfied with the way things are and the way they are going. They assume a do-nothing posture. Reactivists prefer a previous state to the one they are in. They believe things are going from bad to worse. Hence they not only resist change, they try to unmake previous changes and return to where they once were.[4]

It is interesting to note, for example, that the future of which the Commission on the Year 2000 of the American Academy of Arts and Sciences spoke a quarter of a century ago is now almost upon us. Among the many findings and speculations emanating from that body, one was especially noteworthy: by the year 2000, if not long before, the foreign affairs organization of the federal executive branch would be substantially reconstructed. To date, of course, no such thing has come close to happening.[5]

And in 1975, the Commission on the Organization of the Government for the Conduct of Foreign Policy (the Murphy Commission) submitted its thorough and perceptive final report to the President. The commission's recommendations for reorganization—very few of which ever were implemented—were based on a view of the future that offers a strong taste of déjà vu today:

The most pervasive characteristic of international affairs in the next decades will be the growing interaction and tightening interdependence among the nations of the world. Almost certainly, economic issues will loom larger on the foreign policy agendas of the future. . . . Technological and environmental issues will continue to grow in importance. . . . The frequency and intimacy of contact between societies will also increase. . . . Military power alone cannot provide security. A growing number of conflicts of national interest will take economic form. . . . Important questions will more often be debated or resolved in multilateral as well as bilateral forums. Foreign policy and domestic policy merge. . . . The organization implications of this mingling are numerous and important. They include changes in the number of executive departments involved in foreign policy; the necessity for clearer Presidential oversight and direction; a substantial expansion in the role of Congress in foreign policy; the need for better coordination between the executive and congressional branches; and a new role for public opinion.[6]

One of the things on which leading futurists most agree is that, although almost all human endeavors, institutions, and systems are becoming more complex, current institutional structures, such as government, are not up to the task of managing this complexity. Most such structures are out-of-date, bureaucratic, and sluggish; possess short time frames and attention spans; and lack a coherent worldview.[7]

Sounding this same theme in their popular book *Reinventing Government*, David Osborne and Ted Gaebler contend that traditional bureaucracies increasingly are failing to cope with the dizzying change that surrounds us. Bureaucratic governments focus on supplying services to combat problems rather than anticipating and preventing problems. They develop tunnel vision. They wait until a problem becomes a crisis and then offer new services to those affected. Our fundamental problem today, therefore, is not too much or too little government. It is that we have the wrong kind of government. We need better government—or, more precisely, better governance. We need an American *perestroika*—a restructuring.[8]

BOWING TO THE ORGANIZATIONAL IMPERATIVE

Organization matters because government matters. Government is what enables humans to operate as a group, to make communal decisions. It is, said R. M. MacIver, the administrative organ of the state, the "organization of men under authority."[9]

Government is a collective enterprise that operates through organizations. As some perceptive observers have noted, we live in an organizational society in which organizations are pervasive social and cultural forces that dominate our lives and have critical normative consequences for society.[10]

In the narrowest sense, organization is important for three reasons: it creates capabilities, it vests and weights certain interests and perspectives, and it helps assure the legitimacy of decisions.[11] In a broader sense, though, the way we organize does three other things that are especially important in the context of the national security establishment.

1. Organization influences thought processes by determining who deals how with what issues. Assigning responsibility for a particular issue is a way of prescribing who is and is not permitted even to address it. Further dividing the issue into component parts for managerial purposes is equivalent to defining its nature and specifying how it is expected to be handled.

2. A formal organizational structure institutionalizes and gives permanence to a pattern of relationships and a mix of actors that is intended to be more or less immune to whims of personality or changes in participants.

3. The composition and placement of an organization project an image to outsiders of one's worldview. Organizational schemes, in other words, have symbolic content that, intentionally or not, may influence how others see the organization.

The national security establishment is not simply an organization, although organizational principles clearly apply to its structure and functioning. It is, rather, a *system*, a network of interrelated organizations that presumably share a common purpose. And it is a vital *institution* that both reflects and shapes the dominant values of American society.

The systems perspective is useful in several respects. First, the national security establishment does not exist in isolation. It contains constituent organizations and activities, and is itself part of a hierarchy of higher-order enterprises (see Figure 9.1). As defined here, the *national security establishment* consists of all the organizations of the federal government in both the executive branch and Congress charged with formulating, executing, and overseeing national security policies and programs. The *national security community* includes the national security establishment and those other elements of society (the media, industry, interest groups, think tanks and universities, state governments, and the informed public) that affect, are affected by, and are interested in the establishment's workings. The *inter-*

Figure 9.1
The U.S. National Security Establishment and Its Security Communities

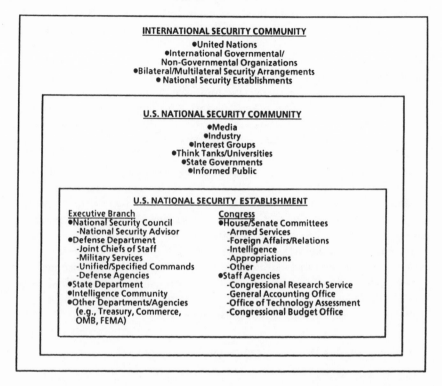

INTERNATIONAL SECURITY COMMUNITY
•United Nations
•International Governmental/
Non-Governmental Organizations
•Bilateral/Multilateral Security Arrangements
• National Security Establishments

U.S. NATIONAL SECURITY COMMUNITY
•Media
•Industry
•Interest Groups
•Think Tanks/Universities
•State Governments
•Informed Public

U.S. NATIONAL SECURITY ESTABLISHMENT

Executive Branch	Congress
•National Security Council	•House/Senate Committees
-National Security Advisor	-Armed Services
•Defense Department	-Foreign Affairs/Relations
-Joint Chiefs of Staff	-Intelligence
-Military Services	-Appropriations
-Unified/Specified Commands	-Other
-Defense Agencies	•Staff Agencies
•State Department	-Congressional Research Service
•Intelligence Community	-General Accounting Office
•Other Departments/Agencies	-Office of Technology Assessment
(e.g., Treasury, Commerce,	-Congressional Budget Office
OMB, FEMA)	

national security community encompasses the world's individual national security communities as well as the entire contingent of supranational or transnational security organizations and activities (including, most notably, the United Nations and its supporting arms).[12]

Second, ideally the cooperative interaction of the national security establishment's constituent elements will have a synergistic effect that exceeds and is qualitatively superior to the mere accumulation of their individual contributions operating in parallel.

Third, the holistic notion that everything is related to everything else provides a robust conceptual underpinning for broadening the notion of national security to encompass a fuller range of concerns than defense, foreign policy, and intelligence—the major organizational elements embodied in the 1947 National Security Act.

Fourth, and perhaps most important, open social systems interact with their governing environments. This suggests that the structure of the national security establishment must be capable of reconfiguring itself, not simply to adapt to its internal and external surroundings but, no less, to influence the direction and shape of those surroundings.

There is a crucial distinction to be made between the rational, means-oriented, efficiency-guided process of the *organization* and the value-laden, adaptive, responsive process of the *institution*. As Robert Bellah and associates have noted, institutions mediate the relations between self and world. Institutions are patterns of normative, or moral, expectations enforced by both positive and negative social sanctions. We create institutions, but they also create us: they educate us and form us, especially through the socially enacted metaphors that provide us our normative interpretations of situations and actions. Institutions today, say Robert N. Bellah and colleagues, have become corrupt because means have been wrongly turned into ends. The institutions set up to fight the Cold War, for example, have partially destroyed the freedom they supposedly were set up to defend. The vast military and intelligence apparatus created to preserve freedom and dignity instead may have smothered the rest of society and sown the seeds of paranoia among its citizens. The connection between government and an enlightened public has been broken, thereby engendering the need to renew a serious public conversation and to strengthen the institutions that nurture and extend it.[13] The national security establishment is the institutional embodiment of the Cold War ethos. If that ethos is to change in an era to which it no longer is relevant, the institution must change.

OLD WAR THINKING—COLD WAR ORGANIZATION

The thinking that spawned America's response to the Cold War and produced the 1947 National Security Act was grounded firmly in World War II, the events that precipitated that experience, and the desire to prevent its recurrence in the form of World War III.

President Truman's advisors, instinctively anti-Communist and anti-Soviet, viewed the Soviet Union as a powerful, ambitious, ruthless, deceitful foe. Relying on the experience of the 1930s' interwar years as their frame of reference, they were convinced that appeasement of totalitarian states during that period had encouraged Axis aggression. They therefore adopted the position that Communist Russia represented an ominous threat that the United States had to resist—by resort to (total) war, if necessary.[14]

French social philosopher Raymond Aron, a devoted Cold Warrior, reflected the tenor of the times in describing the Cold War as a "pretended peace" waged by limited-war means: propaganda, espionage and sabotage, agitation and mass movements, and civil war. An outgrowth of the Soviet design for world conquest, the Cold War represented more a preparation than a substitute for total war—and the threat of total war waged by the West seemed the only convincing way to prevent Communist military expansion.[15]

Such ideas pervaded post–World War II Washington policy circles and magnified the seriousness of the lessons we drew from the war. The 1947 Senate Armed Services Committee report on the proposed National Security Act observed that World War II, however successful in the main, had disclosed a number of fundamental weaknesses in the country's security apparatus that needed to be remedied: a slow and costly mobilization, limited intelligence on the designs and capacities of our enemies, an incomplete integration of political purpose and military objective, and the prodigal use of resources. The counterpart report of the House of Representatives, citing the anticipated totality and rapidity of modern war, called for the creation of a new security structure that would (1) help ensure the coordination of our domestic, foreign, and military policies on an informed basis; (2) facilitate the integration of our military services and their unified strategic direction and command; (3) assist in taking full advantage of our resources of personnel, materials, scientific research, and development; (4) preserve the integrity and more fully exploit the capabilities of all components of ground, sea, and air forces; and (5) provide for continued civilian direction and control.[16]

The resultant National Security Act sought

to provide for the establishment of integrated policies and procedures for the departments, agencies, and functions of the Government relating to the national security; to provide three military departments for the operation and administration of the Army, the Navy (including naval aviation and the United States Marine Corps), and the Air Force, with their assigned combat and service components; to provide for their authoritative coordination and unified direction under civilian control but not to merge them; to provide for the effective strategic direction of the armed forces and for their operation under unified control and for their integration into an efficient team of land, naval, and air forces.[17]

The act established eight organizational entities of enduring importance: the National Security Council (NSC); the Central Intelligence Agency (CIA); the National Security Resources Board (NSRB); the National Military Establishment (Department of Defense), headed by a Secretary of Defense; the Department of the Air Force, headed by a Secretary of the Air Force; the Joint Chiefs of Staff (JCS); the Joint Staff; and the unified (multiservice) and specified (single-service) combatant commands (or at least the authority to create them).

The NSC originally was composed of the President, the Secretary of State, the Secretary of Defense, the secretaries of the three military services, the Chairman of the NSRB, and other specified officers designated by the President with Senate consent. Its function was "to advise the President with respect to the integration of domestic, foreign, and military policies relating to the national security so as to enable the military services and the other departments and agencies of the Government to cooperate more effectively in matters involving the national security."[18]

The CIA was created "for the purpose of coordinating the intelligence activities of the several Government departments and agencies in the interest of national security."[19] Its duties included advising and making recommendations to the NSC on intelligence activities; correlating, evaluating, and disseminating intelligence; and performing "such other functions and duties related to intelligence affecting the national security as the National Security Council may from time to time direct."[20] The act gave special authority for statutory secrecy to the Director of Central Intelligence by making him responsible "for protecting intelligence sources and methods from unauthorized disclosure."[21]

The NSRB was responsible for advising the President "concerning the coordination of military, industrial, and civilian mobilization."[22] This basically meant peacetime planning for wartime production, procurement, distribution, and transportation of all national resources (including stockpiling of strategic and critical materials, economic stabilization, emergency facilities relocation, and the like).

The Secretary of Defense, as the "principal assistant to the President in all matters related to the national security,"[23] was given authority over the military departments, the Joint Chiefs, and all military forces. The JCS, consisting of the Army and Air Force Chiefs of Staff, the Chief of Naval Operations, and "the Chief of Staff to the Commander in Chief, if there be one,"[24] were coequal principal military advisers to the President and the Secretary of Defense. They were charged with, among other things, preparing strategic plans and providing for the strategic direction of the military forces. The Joint Staff, limited in size to one hundred officers (more or less equally apportioned among the three services), supported the corporate JCS.

What the National Security Act produced was an organizational engine to keep the country running in a permanent state of limited mobilization. Several features of this original architecture would have enduring significance. First, in giving new currency to the term "national security," the act thereby implied a more comprehensive orientation—a more internationalist posture, even—toward the outside world than the traditional notion of national defense seemed to suggest. Most policy practitioners of the time, though, crudely conflated the two concepts. The result was a security posture dominated by military concerns and priorities.[25]

Second, the act called for the integration of domestic, foreign, and military policies. The implied emphasis, though, at least with regard to the domestic component of this policy triumvirate, clearly was on ensuring that domestic resources and initiatives were capable of giving way to and supporting emergency military needs. What the relationship was to be between military policy and foreign policy was left unsaid (tacit obeisance, perhaps, to the eternal verities of Clausewitzian thought).

Third, without conscious acknowledgment, the act laid the foundation for (or perhaps merely reaffirmed and codified) what, in the years since, has been our seeming preference for crisis management over crisis prevention. The act assigned responsibility for all strategic planning to the JCS and related the notion of strategic direction purely to military forces.[26]

Fourth, the act institutionalized and legitimized secrecy and covert activities as central features of our national security posture. Among other things, this would have the ultimate effect of fostering a new order of technocratic elitism that removed many facets of our national security posture from the realm of public accountability and discourse.

Fifth, despite numerous positive references to unification and integration, the act actually sought to avoid the oneness most of us would associate with these terms. Instead, drawing a distinction from the more ambiguous concept of "merger," the act legitimized and perpetuated bureaucratic separateness and autonomy, especially of the individual armed services.

Finally, the act was, as much as anything, a paean to the principle of civilian control of the military. By placing civilian authorities in the chain of command, ensuring that the services were independent counterweights to one another, providing originally for no (and later for a weak) military chairman, and limiting the size of the Joint (general) Staff, the authors of the act evinced the obsessive fear of concentrated military power they had inherited from their Constitutional forebears. Unity of action, though ostensibly an important underpinning of the act, really became little more than window dressing.

CHANGED STRATEGIC ENVIRONMENT—UNCHANGED SECURITY STRUCTURE

The world has changed materially since 1947. Most of that change, despite having been underway for many years, has become widely credible (to both ideologues and the general public) only since 1989 and the beginning of the end of the Cold War.[27] James Rosenau has portrayed the turbulent period of profound change we are now in as an era of "postinternational politics"—characterized by sweeping technological breakthroughs, authority crises, consensus breakdowns, revolutionary upheavals, generational conflicts, and other forces that restructure the human landscape in which they erupt.[28]

The obvious changes going on around us require little explication. What was, throughout the Cold War, a seemingly eternal bipolar struggle for survival—U.S.-U.S.S.R., West-East, democracy-totalitarianism, capitalism-communism—has become a multipolar competition involving many actors, employing sundry instruments of power under widely varying conditions, for any of a variety of reasons. Gone are the regularity, simplicity, and discipline of the old order. The discrete, unambiguous, principally military and ideological threats we grew comfortably accustomed to have transmogrified into multiple, ambiguous, largely nonmilitary and nonideological challenges that are difficult to discern and even more difficult to "sell" to the American public.

Notwithstanding the claims concerning America's lone-superpower status and the murkiness of the supporting evidence, it is quite logical to conclude that the United States today is in a state of relative decline—economically, if not in other important respects as well. Military power has shown itself to be increasingly less important—perhaps less useful—as an instrument of statecraft than nonmilitary (especially economic) power. Similarly, unilateralism has shown itself to be increasingly less feasible—perhaps less desirable—than multilateralism. The United Nations has experienced a rebirth of expectations, if not necessarily of confidence and support, from the nations and states of the world long accustomed to answering to (and looking out for) only themselves. Globalization and interdependence in the economic and technological spheres have forged nascent forms of transnational integration that are struggling against contagious disintegrative tendencies to define the new order.[29]

More important perhaps than these obvious changes are the cosmic changes that have taken shape in recent years. The first of these is the progressive fragmentation, or balkanization, of American society and the associated breakdown of the broad-based national consensus that originally galvanized the public in common cause during the first two and a half decades of the Cold War.[30]

A second cosmic change is the seeming obsolescence of major war in the developed world. As John Mueller suggests: "The institution of war has gradually been rejected because of its perceived repulsiveness and futility. In the developed world few, if any, are able to discern either appeal or advantage in war any more; and they have come to value a goal—prosperity—that has long been regarded as incompatible with war."[31] One might even go so far as to suggest that we are witnessing a sort of grand evolution, in which we have passed from an extended historical period of *hot war*, where the actual use of military force was the central element of statecraft, to a highly compressed period of *cold war*, where the threat of force for coercive purposes assumed overriding importance, to the current period of *new war* (or perhaps even *no war*), where nonmilitary instruments of power predominate.

Yet a third cosmic change is the possibility that just as we have seen the end of the Cold War, of containment, and even of Communism as a prospective universal ideology, so too may we have seen the end of realism. What this suggests, among other things, is a complete transformation in the prevailing worldview that has guided our thought and actions for most of the past half century: from the primacy of national interests as a guide to international behavior to the recognition of global (humanitarian, transnational) interests, from military prowess as the primary measure of national power to nonmilitary measures of strength (culture, knowledge, economic well-being), from the irrelevance or inappropriateness of morality as a guide to action to the centrality of moral desiderata, and, most important, from the belief that there is an objective reality (the darkness of human nature, the inevitability of war, the necessity of meeting pervasive evil on its own terms) that exists independent of human perception to the belief that we socially construct the reality we and others see, and that it is within our power as humans to redefine reality.[32]

In contrast to the sweeping changes that have taken place in the governing international environment, the structure of the U.S. national security apparatus has changed relatively little over time. The composition of the NSC—which, for most of the period, has consisted of the President, the Vice President, the Secretary of State, and the Secretary of Defense, with the Director of the CIA and the Chairman of the JCS as statutory advisors—has remained more or less constant. It has been left to presidential prerogative (or whim) to alter that composition and to determine whether and how to use the NSC.[33]

The President's national security advisor, even in cases where individual Presidents have chosen to suppress the profile of the position, has risen to independent prominence and grown in power and stature though this was never actually provided for in law.[34] The Secretary of Defense, by retaining Cabinet status and a seat on the NSC and by acquiring a greatly enlarged staff, has been strengthened (presumably to ensure dominance over both the JCS and the individual armed services). The Chairman of the JCS, established in 1949, long considered technically first among the legally equal joint chiefs and now principal military advisor to the President, the NSC, and the Secretary of Defense as well as sole owner and operator of the Joint Staff, has also acquired added strength. The Joint Staff has increased in size from its original 100 to (officially) 1,627. The unified and specified commanders in chief ostensibly have gained strength at the expense of the services, though in reality the services continue to exert dominant influence, largely through their control of budgets, resources, force planning, and personnel management.[35]

Perhaps the biggest change is the one least acknowledged (or even recognized): the removal of the NSRB (or its successor agencies) from the NSC. The closest approximation of the NSRB today, that is, an activity with a concentrated, centralized focus on national resource management, civil emergency management, and mobilization, is the Federal Emergency Management Agency, a demonstrably minor-league organization that lacks presidential imprimatur, prestige, and command of resources.[36]

A GENERAL FAILURE OF PERFORMANCE

Ideally, the adequacy or appropriateness of organizational structure should be determined by organizational or system performance. Unfortunately, it

is virtually impossible to draw a conclusive link between the effectiveness
of the established national security structure and overall national performance. Was our failure to foresee the breakup of the Soviet Union and the
fall of Communism, for example, due to faulty organizational arrangements?
Conversely, did our Cold War victory have much, if anything, to do with
organization?[37]

To the extent that we can draw a link between organization and performance at the national level, it was the Iran-Contra fiasco that provided
probably the most visible, telling, and disturbing measure of that linkage.
Ironically, the Tower Commission that President Reagan appointed to "in-
vestigate" the affair, though citing "a flawed [decision-making] process,"[38]
exonerated the institution itself—thereby ignoring the insidious effect the
system had had on the thinking and behavior of its operators. A more pointed
assessment came from the joint congressional committee that investigated
Iran-Contra:

> The common ingredients of the Iran and Contra policies were secrecy, deception,
> and disdain for the law. A small group of senior officials believed that they alone
> knew what was right. They viewed knowledge of their actions by others in the
> Government as a threat to their objectives. . . . The Administration's departure from
> democratic processes created the conditions for policy failure, and led to contradic-
> tions which undermined the credibility of the United States.[39]

In the final analysis, process measures provide the best, if not the only,
basis for judging overall system performance. The many process-related
symptoms we see and hear so much about give strong evidence that the
national security system is—and for some time has been—in ill health.[40]

There is, first, the endemic, perpetual conflict between the executive
branch and Congress. In part this reflects the design (some would say the
wisdom) of the Constitutional framers, who sought to enshrine separated or
shared powers and associated checks and balances in our governmental structure, especially in matters of war and peace. In part, though, it also reflects
other factors, not least of which is the growth and diffusion of the imperial
presidency and Congress's related efforts to keep pace, to maintain sufficient
parity to perform its oversight functions.[41]

Then there are the many sources and forms of enduring conflict within
the executive branch itself: between the Departments of State and Defense,
between either or both of them and the President's national security advisor,
between the office of the Secretary of Defense and the JCS, between the
civilian and military staffs in each service, and, of course, between the
military services. Although the framers of the Constitution sought to divide
and balance power between the branches, they also saw the need for a strong
Executive. In Alexander Hamilton's famous words from *Federalist 70*, "Energy in the executive is a leading character in the definition of good gov-

ernment."[42] The first ingredient of such energy, he argued, was *unity*. What we have today, rather than the unity of an energetic executive, is a vast plurality of individuals, organizations, and activities.[43]

Hedrick Smith has perceptively characterized the conduct of U.S. foreign policy (or national security affairs) as "bureaucratic tribal warfare—institutional conflict fired by the pride, interests, loyalties, and jealousies of large bureaucratic clans, protecting their policy turf and using guile as well as argument to prevail in the battle over policy." He describes the recurring clashes that take place between Secretaries of State and Defense as collisions at the tips of bureaucratic icebergs that echo long, bitter feuds within previous administrations and serve as reminders of the institutional competition built into the structure of the Executive Branch.[44]

The fact that open conflict between the President's national security advisor and the Secretaries of State and Defense was generally muted during the Bush and Reagan administrations (albeit for different reasons) did not hide the underlying tension that is embedded in this relationship. Security advisers owe sole allegiance to, meet daily with, occupy the same vantage point as, and speak for the President. Cabinet secretaries are line managers in the chain of command who outrank presidential staff advisers. But they rarely enjoy unlimited access to the President, and they cannot help but represent the frequently self-serving bureaucracies they head. As Zbigniew Brzezinski, President Carter's National Security Advisor, has observed: "Over time the secretary of state or the secretary of defense in every recent administration has become a propagator of his own department's parochial perspective, even to the detriment of the broader presidential vision."[45] The attendant tension that is bound to result when open conflicts break out can be both strategically and politically debilitating.

Perhaps the most commonly recognized and frequently reported source of conflict within the executive branch is the historical rivalry that has always characterized the relationship of the individual armed services to one another. *New York Times* columnist Richard Halloran has noted that the defense establishment, far from being a unified, cohesive institution dedicated to the national security, is a structure in fundamental disarray:

It is a confederation of feudal domains, each struggling to preserve and to enlarge itself. The fiefs within the confederation do not work together for the common good but struggle to advance their own causes. They battle each other over concepts, responsibilities, weaponry, and, most of all, money. Those intense conflicts are not debates over how best to defend the nation but deadly feuds that sap military strength.[46]

No less insidious than the fighting that regularly goes on between the services is their increasing tendency to collude when convenient to protect their collective interests from outside attack. Samuel Huntington has labeled the dual evils of such competition-cum-collusion "servicism," to describe the prevailing condition in which power resides with the services rather than with a stronger military institution. It is servicism, he contends, not the more commonly feared militarism, that today constitutes "the central malady of the American military establishment."[47]

Beyond these deep-seated organizational conflicts, though, there are several other notable features built into the national security structure that are of enduring problematical import. It is a structure that has focused on international affairs to the virtual exclusion of domestic considerations, despite the fact that the NSC, at least, was designed specifically to provide for the integration of domestic, foreign, and military policies. It is a structure dominated by military interests—and, to only a slightly lesser extent, by diplomatic and intelligence interests—while largely ignoring other important dimensions of security, such as economics, the environment, criminal justice, and the like. And it is a structure that has magnified and perpetuated our natural penchant for unfettered unilateral action abroad in lieu of cooperative multilateral enterprises.

Such features, problematical in their own right, nonetheless are merely symptomatic of deeper ills that must be treated if the system is to be brought back to health. In the simplest sense, much of what we see in the functioning of the system is attributable to plain old bureaucratic politics: factionalism and partisanship, parochialism and inertia, self-interested bargaining and compromise, suboptimization and incrementalism. It is no accident that the burgeoning literature on bureaucratic politics is based in large part on observations of the national security establishment.[48]

At a deeper level, the field of national security affairs has long been the arcane preserve of a self-selected, self-protecting group of technocratic elitists who themselves have been the source of many of the system's most fundamental problems. For one thing, they have inbred and produced the sort of lockstep thinking, fear and loathing of outsiders and the Messianic tendencies we now know as "groupthink." For another thing, their elitism has grown out of and further fed a thirst for power, a disdain for the ignorant mass public, and a belief in the efficacy of the "mushroom principle" ("Keep 'em in the dark, and feed 'em manure"—or its scatological equivalent).[49]

Most important, though, this elitist pretense has thrived on and legitimized the secrecy that is the most lasting, visible, and destructive feature of the Cold War ethos. Justified on grounds that (1) national security is more important than the democratic principle of popular consent and (2) our survival could be endangered by exposing privileged information to a public that has neither the need nor the right to know, obsessive secrecy has had the unintended effects of disguising government abuse, obscuring accountability, and engendering public distrust, fear, alienation, and apathy. Garry Wills has characterized the modern presidency as "nyctitropic," a reflection of its tendency to turn toward the darkness, to prefer covert action, to replace accountability with deniability:

In the nyctitropic presidency, secrecy is a source of power as well as its symbol. The wartime justification of secrecy used to run this way: The citizens must be kept in the dark, as a necessary evil, in order to keep the enemy from knowing what one's country is doing and taking action on the basis of that knowledge. The modern presidency takes the old means and makes it the end: The citizens are kept in the dark about what the enemy already knows, lest the citizens take action to stop their own government from doing things they disapprove of.[50]

Ultimately, organizational cultures—the persistent, patterned ways of thinking that distinguish organizations from one another—represent the most fundamental source of problems within the national security establishment. The foreign service has its own distinctive identity, ranging from its elitist tendencies and preference for negotiation and diplomacy to its extreme caution and resistance to change, as do the individual armed services and the member organizations of the intelligence community. Moreover, each culture has its own identifiable subcultures, each subscribing to values and preferences that, while providing the social glue that gives members their sense of solidarity, also can, and usually do, distort their views of reality and impair their ability to accept and work cooperatively with others.[51]

THE IMPERATIVES OF REFORM

Experience has shown that personalities and procedures ultimately determine whether and to what extent formal organizational structures have an enduring relevance or utility.[52] This realization tends, more often than not, to serve as a barrier to fundamental organizational reform (especially where legislation is required). But if we are to effect a fundamental transformation in how we deal with a rapidly changing world, if we are to eliminate the serious organizational shortcomings that have been built into our national security structure, we have little choice but to reorganize. Seven imperatives must guide any such reform effort.

Imperative No. 1: A Reconceptualization of Security

It is inconceivable that we could establish a security apparatus appropriately geared to the modern age unless we first are willing to rethink our entire approach to security. "A word is not a crystal, transparent and unchanged," said Justice Oliver Wendell Holmes. "It is the skin of a living thought and may vary greatly in color and content according to the circum-

stances and the time in which it is used."[53] National security is a regrettably
vague concept that has never been adequately defined nor formally codified
(not even in the National Security Act).[54] We have equated it with defense
and foreign policy and chosen to focus our security concerns almost exclusively on international affairs. Security is not, of course, just defense. Nor
is it the special preserve of international relations. It is, rather, the cardinal
measure of the seamlessness of domestic and foreign affairs. To be hungry
or homeless, to be illiterate or impoverished, to be chronically ill or addicted
to drugs, to be constantly afraid of being robbed or attacked, to be unable
to afford basic medical care, to be exposed to environmental hazards, is to
be no less insecure than to be afraid—however remote the fear—of external
military attack. To counter such conditions, that is, to provide for health
care, welfare, housing, education, or environmental protection, is not to
diminish or endanger security, but to enhance it. To address such needs is
to acknowledge the importance of and to contribute to the national will or
cohesion that is so critical to the effective exercise of power abroad.[55]

Imperative No. 2: Full-Scale Integration

Organizational structure is fundamentally about balancing the competing
aims of dividing the labor or activities of the organization or system (differentiation) and achieving effective coordination of those activities (integration)
in order to achieve unity of effort.[56] Differentiation (specialization) increases
as the organization seeks to cope effectively with the heightened complexity
and demands of the governing environment. The inevitable result—conflict—is what effective integration is designed to resolve. In the case of our
extraordinarily differentiated national security establishment, we must seek
a fuller integration of civil-military, domestic-international, national-supra-
national, government-industry, air-land-sea, and routine-emergency structures and processes than now exists.

Imperative No. 3: Institutionalized Coherence and Consistency

Strategically, it is absolutely essential that the United States speak with
one voice at any given time and that it demonstrate a credible degree of
consistency across changing presidential administrations. What we must
seek, therefore, is a fully institutionalized framework with the following
characteristics: (1) regular, formal consultation between central decision makers and the organizations responsible for conducting or developing policy,
(2) standardized processes for the conduct of such consultations, (3) severely
constrained opportunities for any of the players to set policy in the absence
of regularized consultative procedures (à la Iran-Contra).[57]

Imperative No. 4: Cooperative Checks and Balances

While it is logical to expect that the system of shared powers and checks and balances the Founding Fathers created would produce natural tensions between the branches of government, it does not follow that what they envisioned was a bare-knuckled adversariness that produces only zero-sum stalemate. We might rather think that what they intended was a dialectical process whose outcomes would be higher-order syntheses of opposing points of view. In the words of Justice Robert H. Jackson: "While the Constitution diffuses power the better to secure liberty, it also contemplates that the practice will integrate the dispersed powers into a workable government. It enjoins upon its branches separateness but interdependence, autonomy but reciprocity."[58] If our overall goal is more effective governance, if our more specific goal is enduring security, and if we subscribe to the wisdom of balancing sober deliberation against speed and efficiency—especially in matters of war and peace—then we would do well to seek mechanisms that will facilitate the cooperative pursuit of common interests.

Imperative No. 5: The Reassertion of Civilian Supremacy

Although we have made much of the principle of civilian control in our approach to organizing for national security, there is less there than meets the eye. We maintain a heavy layer of civilian bureaucracy in each of the armed services in the form of the service secretary and his staff, but these politicians are rarely independent authorities, tending all too often to be "captured" by their service.[59] In a similar vein, with minor exceptions (such as our representation in the North Atlantic Treaty Organization), most of our regional "authorities" around the world are the military heads of our combatant commands. Our civilian representatives of the President are predominantly individual country ambassadors with no regional orientation and no authority over U.S. military forces. Such anomalies must be redressed, especially if we are to present a convincing picture of the United States as a peace-loving country that values civilian supremacy.[60]

Imperative No. 6: Informed Public Consensus

Benjamin Barber has distinguished strong, participatory democracy from the thin, representative democracy the United States has. It is such thin democracy—made even thinner by those in power who would deny the public visibility of their actions—that destroys participation and produces the malaise elitists are so fond of decrying.[61] America's true strength rests with the vitality of our political system. What we must have at a minimum, if we are to avoid elite abuse and stupidity, is popular consent for our government's actions, especially in the international sphere. What we must seek at a maximum, if we are to thrive and prosper, is not merely minimalist consent but active consensus: knowledgeable agreement from an involved citizenry exercising public judgment rather than public opinion.[62]

Imperative No. 7: A Post–Cold War Image

As important as anything substantive reorganization might accomplish are the symbolic purposes it must serve. As Kenneth Boulding has observed, the symbolic image of one's own nation is tinged with ideas of security or insecurity depending on one's image of other nations. Country A perceives itself as insecure and hence increases its armaments or maintains an aggressive posture. It thereby seeks to improve its image of its own security; instead, it makes B feel insecure, and so B increases its armaments. This makes A feel more insecure, so A again increases its armaments, thereby further making B feel insecure and increasing its armaments in a never-ending spiral.[63] Throughout the Cold War the United States has preached peace but prepared for war. We have preached multilateralism but practiced unilateralism. We have preached morality but practiced amorality (or even immorality). We have preached openness and democracy but practiced secrecy and authoritarianism. We have preached joint military operations but practiced the evils of servicism. Through organizational reform we can create a new reality about who we are, what we consider important, and how we view the world. We should seek to demonstrate that we truly subscribe to peace and democracy; that our strength and leadership are based on our ability to generate new ideas; that our process for formulating and executing strategy and policy is one of inclusion, cooperation, and comprehensiveness; and that we have moved beyond the Cold War to shape a new world order.

THE ELEMENTS OF A REVAMPED STRUCTURE

The elements of a revamped security structure that supports the foregoing imperatives and provides the foundation for a new American Security Act of 1994 would include the following elements (see Figure 9.2).

U.S. Security Council

This body, replacing the NSC and having a broadened focus, would consist of six members: the President and Vice President; our ambassador to the United Nations, to reflect our heightened commitment to that body; and three new supra-Cabinet officials, all subject to Senate confirmation to demonstrate presidential commitment to bipartisanship and accountability, a Minister of International Affairs, a Minister of Domestic Affairs, and a Minister of National Resources. The Secretaries of State and Defense and a new Director of National Intelligence would report to the Minister of Interna-

Figure 9.2
Proposed National Security Establishment

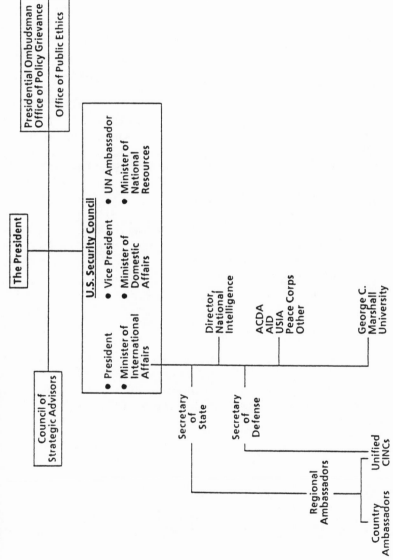

The President

Council of Strategic Advisors

Presidential Ombudsman Office of Policy Grievance

Office of Public Ethics

U.S. Security Council

- President
- Minister of International Affairs
- Vice President
- Minister of Domestic Affairs
- UN Ambassador
- Minister of National Resources

Director, National Intelligence

ACDA
AID
USIA
Peace Corps
Other

George C. Marshall University

Secretary of State

Secretary of Defense

Regional Ambassadors

Country Ambassadors

Unified CINCs

tional Affairs. The Minister of Domestic Affairs would oversee the major domestic departments and agencies—Education, Health and Human Services, Housing and Urban Development, Interior, Justice (including the Federal Bureau of Investigation, the Drug Enforcement Administration, the Immigration and Naturalization Service, and the Coast Guard), and Veterans Affairs—as well as a Director of National Service and a Director of Public Outreach (who would oversee a nationwide network of Citizen Action Councils). The Minister of National Resources would oversee the Departments of Agriculture, Commerce, Labor, Transportation, and Treasury, a newly merged Department of Energy and Environmental Affairs, Federal Emergency Management Agency (FEMA), the Office of Management and Budget, and a new Office of Science, Technology, and Industry (OSTI). OSTI would absorb the current Office of Science and Technology Policy and the (Defense) Advanced Research Projects Agency (ARPA). ARPA would be responsible for guiding national efforts to integrate defense and commercial technologies and for managing a streamlined, consolidated federal laboratory system.[64]

Council of Strategic Advisors

Consisting of ten to twelve distinguished Americans from all walks of life, this permanent body would provide continuing advice and counsel to the President on matters of global strategy. It would absorb the Council of Economic Advisors and the National Economic Council, and it would receive analytical support from the George C. Marshall University.

Presidential Ombudsman

Reporting to the White House Chief of Staff, this senior presidential aide would head a new Office of Policy Grievance, which would provide a formal mechanism outside the normal chain of command for identifying and mediating major policy disputes and bringing alternative policy views to the President's attention.

Office of Public Ethics

An outgrowth and expansion of the current, narrowly focused Office of Government Ethics, this office would be responsible for ensuring consideration of ethical concerns and priorities in major policy issues (both international and domestic) and for governmentwide ethics education.

Elimination of the CIA

This would involve the abolition of the most visible, negative, unaccountable vestige of the Cold War, and the attendant consolidation and streamlining of national intelligence collection and analysis capabilities in the Departments of State and Defense. The Director of National Intelligence would assume authority for determining requirements and priorities and for exercising communitywide product quality control.[65]

Elevation of Second-Tier Agencies

Heretofore second-tier agencies whose functions are likely to assume added importance in the emerging world order—the Arms Control and Disarmament Agency, the Agency for International Development, the U.S. Information Agency, the Peace Corps, and the Overseas Private Investment Corporation—would be accorded greater status and visibility.

Regional Superambassadors

These regionally oriented diplomats would exercise civilian authority over both individual country ambassadors and military commanders in chief in each major region of the world (thereby demonstrating a more expansive regional orientation and asserting true civilian supremacy). Located either in the dominant country of the region or with the regional Commanders in Chief (CINCs) (depending on circumstances), these superambassadors would lead U.S. efforts to establish standing security regimes, arms conferences, and peace conferences in each of the world's regions.[66]

George C. Marshall University

Currently the National Defense University (headed by a three-star military officer who reports to the JCS Chairman), this institution would be headed by a distinguished civilian chancellor who would report to the Minister of International Affairs. It would become the focal point for a dramatically expanded governmentwide education and research program in strategic thinking, executive decision making, and global security affairs. Its research arm would be merged with the defense and foreign affairs arm of the Congressional Research Service to provide common (presumably nonpartisan) analytical support to senior decision makers in both branches of government.[67]

Citizen Action Councils

Headquartered regionally throughout the United States, these permanent bodies would be headed by highly qualified presidential appointees who would report to the White House Director of Public Outreach. The councils would seek to facilitate broad-based strategic consensus through ongoing public education and dialogue on major security issues.

Joint Congressional Committee on Strategic Affairs

To ensure that executive branch integration is matched by commensurate measures in Congress, this committee would be designed to elevate, focus, and streamline congressional oversight and involvement in security affairs.

A Joint Military Establishment

In the interest of breaking the stranglehold of the armed services and achieving true integration of the Defense Department, four measures are in order: (1) completely abolishing the civilian service secretariats, thereby concentrating civilian control in the Secretary of Defense; (2) replacing the JCS with a Council of Military Commanders, headed by a Chief of Military Staff (now the JCS Chairman) and consisting of the commanders in chief of the unified combatant commands; (3) replacing the service chiefs of staff with land, naval, and air deputies to the Chief of Military Staff; and (4) consolidating all common administrative and support functions in joint commands of Defense Department agencies.

AFTERWORD: BOWING TO FUTILITY

In a massive study of institutions in the United States and abroad, two scholars recently observed: "There is widespread agreement that major deficiencies in American governing capacities exist. . . . In particular need of strengthening are the capabilities of the American system to tackle large problems in a coherent and coordinated fashion and to set priorities." They then go on to draw a conclusion, though, that to many of us is all too regrettably obvious: "The prospects for major institutional reforms in the United States are not promising."[68]

Although a reasonably compelling case can be made that the Cold War security structure we have inherited is in need of fundamental overhaul, political feasibility will be the final determinant of whether, how much, and how soon reform takes place. Unfortunately, if we let political feasibility dictate the value of proposed change, then it is senseless even to entertain the proposals I have offered here with any seriousness. Each is sufficiently different from our current way of doing business as to invite only heated debate and intense resistance.

Thus, only strong, assertive presidential leadership, possessed of a coherent strategic vision for the future, can hope to have any chance of overcoming the deep-seated greed, inertia, and parochialism that inevitably will conspire to obstruct sweeping change. But it is only sweeping change that will carry us safely into the next century. Otherwise, the United States could end up being not a superpower, but a superpower emeritus.

NOTES

1. Gareth Morgan, *Images of Organization* (Newbury Park, CA: Sage, 1986), pp. 199–231.

2. Ernest May, *"Lessons" of the Past: The Use and Misuse of History in American Foreign Policy* (New York: Oxford University Press, 1973), p. 51.

3. Warren Bennis and Burt Nanus, *Leaders: The Strategies for Taking Charge* (New York: Harper & Row, 1985), p. 228. Also see Edwin A. Locke et al., *The Essence of Leadership* (New York: Lexington Books, 1991), esp. pp. 49–61; and Burt Nanus, *Visionary Leadership* (San Francisco: Jossey-Bass, 1992).

4. Management theorist Russell L. Ackoff, in his book *Redesigning the Future: A Systems Approach to Societal Problems* (New York: John Wiley, 1974), pp. 22–28, identifies four general attitudes toward planning: inactivism, reactivism (as defined here), preactivism, and interactivism. These latter two orientations would seem most conducive to truly visionary leadership. Preactivists are not willing to settle for things as they are or once were. They believe the future will be better than the present or the past, in direct proportion to how well they predict and prepare for that future. Interactivists similarly are unwilling to settle for the way things were, are, or are going. They try to prevent, not merely prepare for, threats and to create, not merely exploit, opportunities.

5. William M. Capron, "The Executive Branch in the Year 2000," in Harvey S. Perloff, ed., *The Future of the United States Government: Toward the Year 2000* (Englewood Cliffs, NJ: Prentice Hall, 1971), p. 305. The commission, formed in 1965, first published many of its findings in the Summer 1967 issue of the journal *Daedalus.*

6. *Commission on the Organization of the Government for the Conduct of Foreign Policy* (Washington, DC: Government Printing Office, June 1975), p. 2. This commission is also referred to as the Murphy Commission.

7. See Joseph F. Coates and Jennifer Jarratt, *What Futurists Believe* (Bethesda, MD: World Future Society, 1989), esp. pp. 19–20.

8. David Osborne and Ted Gaebler, *Reinventing Government* (Reading, MA: Addison-Wesley, 1992), pp. 23–24.

9. See David Fromkin, *The Question of Government: An Inquiry into the Breakdown of Modern Political Systems* (New York: Scribner's, 1975), p. 91; Osborne and Gaebler, p. xviii; and R. M. MacIver, *The Web of Government* (New York: Free Press, 1965), quotes from pp. 6 and 24. "When we speak of government without a qualifying adjective," says MacIver, "we mean political government, the centralized organization that maintains a system of order over a community large or small" (p. 17).

10. The best-known statement of this theme, of course, is Robert Presthus, *The Organizational Society* (New York: Vintage Books, 1962). Also see William G. Scott and David K. Hart, *Organizational America* (Boston: Houghton Mifflin, 1979).

11. Graham Allison and Peter Szanton, *Remaking Foreign Policy: The Organizational Connection* (New York: Basic Books, 1976), p. 20.

12. The terms "national security establishment" and "national security community" tend to be used interchangeably and imprecisely. When it is singled out, the national security establishment is commonly defined only in terms of the executive branch organs specified in the 1947 National Security Act. For example, see Sam

C. Sarkesian, *U.S. National Security: Policymakers, Processes, and Politics* (Boulder, CO: Lynne Rienner, 1989), esp. pp. 14–19, 61–64, 72–84; and John Allen Williams, "The National Security Establishment: Institutional Framework for Policymaking," in Stephen J. Cimbala, ed., *National Security Strategy: Choices and Limits*, (New York: Praeger, 1984), pp. 323–343. However, because Congress and the President (or, as it has become, the presidency) share virtually all of the Constitutional powers involved in national security affairs, it seems incongruous that both branches would not be considered part of "the establishment." Moreover, the more robustly or comprehensively one defines national security, the more important it becomes to include other executive branch actors (e.g., the Departments of Treasury and Energy, the Federal Emergency Management Agency) in our considerations. The national security community, in turn, must include those numerous other actors outside the federal government that play important roles in the conduct of national security affairs.

13. Robert N. Bellah et al., *The Good Society* (New York: Knopf, 1992), pp. 10–16, 220–229, 287–293. Also see Charles Perrow, *Complex Organizations: A Critical Essay*, 2d ed. (Glenview, IL: Scott, Foresman, 1979), pp. 186–188, for further discussion of the organization-institution distinction.

14. May, *"Lessons" of the Past*, pp. 19–51 (a chapter perceptively entitled "The Cold War: Preventing World War III").

15. Raymond Aron, *The Century of Total War* (Boston: Beacon Press, 1954), pp. 171–173, 226–233.

16. U.S. Congress, Senate, Committee on Armed Services, *National Security Act of 1947*, Report No. 239 to accompany S. 758 (Washington, DC: Government Printing Office, June 5, 1947), p. 2; and U.S. Congress, House of Representatives, Committee on Expenditures in the Executive Departments, *National Security Act of 1947*, Report No. 961, to accompany H. R. 4214 (Washington, DC: Government Printing Office, July 16, 1947), pp. 5–6.

17. Public Law 253, National Security Act of 1947, 61 Stat. 495 (1947).

18. Ibid., p. 496.

19. Ibid., p. 498.

20. Ibid., p. 498.

21. The CIA's so-called fifth function—"to perform such other functions and duties"—has provided authority for the continuing conduct of covert operations ("dirty tricks"). NSC policy paper 10/2 (NSC 10/2), "National Security Council Directive on Office of Special Projects," dated June 18, 1948, assigned the CIA responsibility for covert operations abroad. Portions of NSC 10/2 are contained in Sam C. Sarkesian with Robert A. Vitas, *U.S. National Security Policy and Strategy: Documents and Policy Proposals* (Westport, CT: Greenwood Press, 1988), pp. 32–33. For a fuller discussion of the origins and growth of "the U.S. secrecy system," see Arthur Macy Cox, *The Myths of National Security: The Peril of Secret Government* (Boston: Beacon Press, 1975), esp. pp. 32–60.

22. Public Law 253, p. 499.

23. Ibid., p. 500.

24. Ibid., p. 505.

25. One obvious example of this, of course, was the military-dominated composition of the NSC. Another example was the designation of the Secretary of Defense as the President's principal assistant for national security matters. Yet a third example

was the Senate version of the bill (S.758) leading to the act, which labeled what would become the National Military Establishment the "National Security Organization" and the proposed Secretary of Defense the "Secretary of National Security." As Samuel Huntington points out, for the bulk of U.S. history a sharp distinction was thought to exist between war and peace, and the role of regular military forces in both was limited. After World War II, though, this orientation changed drastically: "National security suddenly became the overriding goal of policy rather than its starting point. Military force came to be viewed as a prime instrument of policy to prevent large-scale war and to deal with small-scale conflicts." See Samuel P. Huntington, "The Soldier and the State in the 1970s," in Andrew J. Goodpaster and Samuel P. Huntington, eds. *Civil-Military Relations* (Washington, DC: American Enterprise Institute, 1977), pp. 5–27 (quote on p. 9).

26. It would not, in fact, be until the passage of the Goldwater-Nichols Department of Defense Reorganization Act of 1986 that there would be a mandated requirement for the President to formulate any sort of strategic guidance at the national level. The resultant annual *National Security Strategy of the United States* has generally not been approached very seriously, however. The latest such report, dated January 1993, is a tribute to superficiality and innocuousness. See The White House, *National Security Strategy of the United States* (Washington, DC: Government Printing Office, January 1993).

27. See William G. Hyland, *The Cold War Is Over* (New York: Random House, 1990).

28. James N. Rosenau, *Turbulence in World Politics: A Theory of Change and Continuity* (Princeton, NJ: Princeton University Press, 1990), pp. 6–8.

29. The most popular, visible, and provocative statement on U.S. decline and the importance of economic power is, of course, Paul Kennedy, *The Rise and Fall of the Great Powers* (New York: Random House, 1987). Perhaps the strongest of the antideclinist rebuttals is Samuel P. Huntington, "The U.S.—Decline or Renewal?" *Foreign Affairs*, 67, No. 4, (Winter 1988–89), pp. 76–96. For a balanced account of America's *relative* economic decline and an important treatment of the growing utility of nonmilitary forms of "soft power," see Joseph S. Nye, Jr., *Bound to Lead: The Changing Nature of American Power* (New York: Basic Books, 1990).

30. On the subject of societal fragmentation, see Kevin P. Phillips, *Post-Conservative America* (New York: Random House, 1982), esp. chap. 6, "The Balkanization of America," pp. 73–87, and, more recently, Arthur M. Schlesinger, Jr., *The Disuniting of America* (New York: Norton, 1992). On the breakdown of the bipartisan consensus spawned by the Vietnam War and other causes, see Richard A. Melanson, *Reconstructing Consensus: American Foreign Policy since the Vietnam War* (New York: St. Martin's Press, 1991), pp. 1–32; and Daniel Yankelovich and Sidney Harman, *Starting with the People* (Boston: Houghton Mifflin, 1988), esp. p. 3. Melanson (p. 2) points to the views of some contemporary and retrospective critics who have argued that Cold War presidents, by baldly and simplistically inflating the communist "threat," manufactured an artificial consensus that stifled domestic dissent, rigidified U.S. foreign policy, and ultimately trapped them in their own rhetoric. Also see Jay Winik, "Restoring Bipartisanship," *Washington Quarterly* 12, no. 1 (Winter 1989), pp. 109–122; and David L. Boren, "Speaking with a Single Voice: Bipartisanship in Foreign Policy," *SAIS Review* 9, no. 1 (Winter-Spring 1989), pp. 51–64.

31. John Mueller, *Retreat from Doomsday: The Obsolescence of Major War* (New

York: Basic Books, 1989), p. 264. Also see Evan Luard, *The Blunted Sword: The Erosion of Military Power in Modern World Politics* (New York: New Amsterdam, 1988). Luard argues (esp. pp. 14–15) that modern conflicts are principally civil wars that take place within Third World states, are determined primarily by political rather than military factors, and generally defy the imposition of superpower will. "Power in modern international relations is no longer primarily a military factor. Increasingly we live in a world of political, not military, conflicts. And it is *political* power—political skills and political influence—not brute military power which is ultimately decisive in these contests" (p. 24).

32. On this last point, see Peter L. Berger and Thomas Luckmann, *The Social Construction of Reality* (Garden City, NY: Anchor Books, 1967), and the discussion of the action frame of reference in David Silverman, *The Theory of Organizations: A Sociological Framework* (New York: Basic Books, 1970), pp. 126–146. For views that run counter to my proposition about the end of realism, see the series of articles by Fareed Zakaria ("Is Realism Finished?" pp. 21–32), Robert W. Tucker ("Realism and the New Consensus," pp. 109–112) in no. 30 (Winter 1992–93 issue) of *The National Interest*.

33. The service secretaries lost their seats on the NSC, as well as their Cabinet status, in the 1949 amendments to the National Security Act.

34. The National Security Act called only for a civilian Executive Secretary to head the NSC staff. Today, the Executive Secretary plays the role of staff administrator or Chief of Staff. For a useful discussion of the different roles—administrator, coordinator, counselor, agent—various National Security Advisors have played, see Cecil V. Crabb, Jr., and Kevin V. Mulcahy, "The National Security Council and the Shaping of U.S. Foreign Policy," *International Journal of Intelligence and Counterintelligence*, 3, no. 2 (1989), pp. 153–168. Also see I. M. Destler, "National Security Advice to U.S. Presidents: Some Lessons from Thirty Years," *World Politics*, 29, no. 2 (January 1977).

35. For contrasting views on the relative strength and influence of the armed services and the commanders in chief, see James A. Blackwell, Jr., and Barry M. Blechman, "The Essence of Reform," in James A. Blackwell and Barry M. Blechman, eds., *Making Defense Reform Work* (Washington, DC: Brassey's, 1990), pp. 1–24, and Admiral Robert P. Hilton, "The Role of Joint Military Institutions in Defense Resource Planning," in the same volume, pp. 151–172. Blackwell and Blechman argue that "the services continue to undercut the real authority of the unified and specified commanders," and "the services continue to exert the predominant influence over military operations" (p. 11). Hilton argues (it appears, on the basis of what was meant to be more than what actually is) that "a major cultural change is under way. The predominance of the services in planning, programming, and budgeting is gradually being modified to give a significant role to the joint military structure, particularly to the chairman, the CINCs and the Joint Staff" (p. 163).

36. The NSRB also became part of the Executive Office of the President in 1949. In 1973, known then as the Office of Emergency Preparedness, it was disestablished, thereby signaling the first time since 1947 that there would be no such representation on the NSC. FEMA was established as a separate agency in 1979. It is headed by an Executive Level II political appointee who does not have a seat on the NSC. For a discussion of the origins and early performance of the NSRB, see Harry B. Yoshpe, *A Case Study in Peacetime Mobilization Planning: The National Security Resources*

Board 1947–1953 (Washington, DC: Executive Office of the President, April 30, 1953).

37. There are those who would argue that our military success in Operation Desert Shield/Desert Storm was due in large measure to the strengthened roles of the JCS Chairman and the CINCs, provided for in the 1986 Defense Reorganization Act. Even if largely true, such appraisals speak only to the military dimension of our response to the situation in the Persian Gulf, not to our overall national (military and nonmilitary) response, nor to the quality of decision making, advice, and counsel that led up to—and may even have encouraged—Iraq's invasion of Kuwait. For a telling portrayal of the flawed thinking that produced Operation Desert Shield/Desert Storm, see Howard Teicher and Gayle Radley Teicher, *Twin Pillars to Desert Storm: America's Flawed Vision in the Middle East from Nixon to Bush* (New York: William Morrow, 1993).

38. The Tower Commission Report, *Report of the President's Special Review Board* (Washington, DC: The White House, February 26, 1987), refers to "a flawed process" (pp. iv–1), but then states (pp. v–5):

The flaws of procedure and failures of responsibility revealed by our study do not suggest any inadequacies in the provisions of the National Security Act of 1947 that deal with the structure and operation of the NSC system. Forty years of experience under the Act demonstrate to the Board that it remains a fundamentally sound framework for national security decision-making. It strikes a balance between formal structure and flexibility adequate to permit each President to tailor the system to fit his needs. . . . We recommend that no substantive change be made in the provisions of the National Security Act dealing with the structure and operation of the NSC system.

It is worth noting that the individuals comprising the Tower Commission—former Senator John Tower, former Senator and Secretary of State Edmund Muskie, and former National Security Advisor General Brent Scowcroft—were traditionalists, nonprovocateurs who were unlikely to challenge the status quo. Their only recourse, if they were to avoid pointing the finger of blame at President Reagan, was to endorse the flawlessness of the system and blame its misuse on the personalities of subalterns.

39. U.S. Congress, *Report of the Congressional Committees Investigating the Iran-Contra Affair*, H. Rept. No. 100–433/S. Rept. No. 100–216 (Washington, DC: Government Printing Office, 1987), p. 11.

40. The general failures that Edgar Schein's "adaptive-coping cycle" (the sequence of organizational activities or processes that begin with some change in the internal or external environment and end with a more adaptive dynamic equilibrium for dealing with the change) is designed to uncover in any system tend to be the specific failures of the current national security establishment: (1) a failure to sense changes in the environment or incorrectly sensing what is happening; (2) a failure to get relevant information to those parts of the system that can act on or use it; (3) a failure to influence the internal system to make necessary changes; (4) a failure to consider the impact of changes on other systems and to achieve stable change; (5) a failure to export the new product, service, or information; (6) a failure to obtain feedback on the success of the change. See Edgar H. Schein, *Organizational Psychology* (Englewood Cliffs, N.J.: Prentice Hall, 1965), pp. 98–103.

41. See Louis Henkin, "Foreign Affairs and the Constitution," *Foreign Affairs* 62, no. 2 (Winter 1987–88), pp. 284–310; Edwin B. Firmage, "To Chain the Dog of

War," *World & I*, August 1987, pp. 561–568; Richard Haass, "Congressional Power: Implications for American Security Policy," in Daniel J. Kaufman, Jeffrey S. Mc-Kitrick, and Thomas J. Leney, eds., *U.S. National Security: A Framework for Analysis* (Lexington, MA: Lexington Books, 1985), pp. 263–306; and the entire collection of papers in Howard E. Shuman and Walter R. Thomas, eds., *The Constitution and National Security* (Washington, DC: National Defense University Press, 1990).

42. Roy P. Fairfield, ed. *The Federalist Papers*, 2nd ed. (Garden City, NY: Anchor Books, 1966), pp. 198 and 199.

43. Bradley H. Patterson, Jr., *The Ring of Power: The White House Staff and Its Expanding Role in Government* (New York: Basic Books, 1988), pp. 16–20. For an excellent discussion of executive energy, see Harvey C. Mansfield, Jr., *Taming the Prince: The Ambivalence of Modern Executive Power* (New York: Free Press, 1989), esp. pp. 266–268.

44. Hedrick Smith, *The Power Game: How Washington Works* (New York: Random House, 1988), esp. chap. 15, "The Foreign Policy Game: Bureaucratic Tribal Warfare," pp. 566–575 (quote on p. 569).

45. Zbigniew Brzezinski, "The NSC's Midlife Crisis," *Foreign Policy*, no. 69 (Winter 1987–88), pp. 80–99. Similarly, Constantine Menges, a former NSC staffer, makes the critical observation that "in foreign policy it is elements within the State Department that most often have decided to ignore, undermine, challenge, and countermand the president" (Constantine C. Menges, *Inside the National Security Council* [New York: Simon & Schuster, 1988], p. 392).

46. Richard Halloran, *To Arm a Nation: Rebuilding America's Endangered Defenses* (New York: Macmillan, 1986), pp. 144–145. Also see Arthur T. Hadley, *The Straw Giant: Triumph and Failure, America's Armed Forces* (New York: Random House, 1986), esp. pp. 23–24, for a detailed discussion of interservice and intraservice rivalry.

47. Samuel P. Huntington, "Defense Organization and Military Strategy," *The Public Interest* 75 (Spring 1984), pp. 20–46. Servicism, says Huntington, is the doctrine or system that exalts the individual military service and accords it primacy in the military establishment. Militarism, on the other hand, is that doctrine or system that, among other things, exalts an institutional structure—the military establishment—and accords primacy in state and society to the armed forces. Of course, if one's concern is civilian control—a concern that recognizably has dominated this country's historical approach to defense organization and civil-military relations—then the fragmentation that accompanies servicism actually could be considered a good thing. Richard K. Betts, for example, in his *Soldiers, Statesman, and Cold War Crises* (New York: Columbia University Press, 1991), takes the position that military disunity actually increases the choices available to decision makers (pp. 115–138):

Although civilian analysts frequently criticize interservice rivalries for the divisiveness, inefficiency, and confusion they cause in defense policy, these disagreements can often help civilians keep the maximum number of choices in their own hands. In the first fifteen years of the cold war, interservice controversy enhanced civilian control by deflecting conflict away from civilian-military lines (p. 116).

48. For a comprehensive recent treatment of the subject, see David C. Kozak and James M. Keagle, eds., *Bureaucratic Politics and National Security: Theory and Practice* (Boulder, CO: Lynne Rienner, 1988).

49. On the subject of groupthink, see, most notably, Irving L. Janus, *Groupthink: Psychological Studies of Policy Decisions and Fiascoes*, 2d ed. (Boston: Houghton Mifflin, 1982). Walter Lippman, from the second decade of this century to the 1950s, gave authoritative voice to much of the elitist and realist thinking that survives today. For an excellent compilation of his writings on elitism, leadership, statesmanship, mass public opinion, and the failings of liberal democracy, see Clinton Rossiter and James Lare, eds., *The Essential Lippmann* (Cambridge, MA: Harvard University Press, 1982). A perceptive contemporary observation is that of Rodney B. McDaniel, former Executive Secretary of the NSC, in Thomas P. Coakley, ed., *C3I: Issues of Command and Control* (Washington, DC: National Defense University Press, 1991), p. 77:

The sociology of the practitioners of foreign policy, and military policy, in my experience, can only be accurately described as elitists who are most comfortable doing business in a back room, talking to nobody, and then after they've done it their notion of the domestic angle is you call in the public affairs guy and flack it up. The notion that you bring a bunch of politicians, Congressmen, and you seriously take what they have to say into account is anathema both to the agency professionals, and the "civilian" policy people—many of whom are cranked out of [Harvard].

50. Garry Wills, "Power Unchecked," *Washington Post Magazine*, June 28, 1987, pp. 31–39. Also see Bill Moyers, *The Secret Government: The Constitution in Crisis* (Cabin John, MD: Seven Locks Press, 1988), pp. 113–115:

It is in secrecy that the bacilli of self-deception thrive unexamined, producing that peculiar Washington disease known as Potomac Fever, which causes one's head to swell and one's mind to shrink. Unless inoculated by facts and informed opinions—rare in the protected coterie of the like-minded—it can rage like an epidemic in the highest realms of government, with devastating costs to the democratic ideal. . . . What is secret is often squalid as well. In the dark, men were able to act contrary to the values they proclaimed in public. Paying lip service to democratic ends, they made league with scoundrels whose interest is anything but the survival of democracy. . . . In secret the road descends from fantasy to fanaticism, from moral relativism to moral hypocrisy. And the United States government becomes the ethical twin of the enemy. *His* rules become the rules of the game.

51. For an excellent discussion of organizational culture, with specific treatment of the State Department, the armed services, and the CIA, see chap. 6, "Culture," in James Q. Wilson, *Bureaucracy: What Government Agencies Do and Why They Do It* (New York: Basic Books, 1989), pp. 90–110. Wilson notes: "A strong sense of mission may blind the organization to changed environmental circumstances so that new opportunities and challenges are met with routinized rather than adaptive behavior. . . . The perceptions supplied by an organizational culture sometimes can lead an official to behave not as the situation requires but as the culture expects" (p. 110). For a thorough treatment of the subcultures of the foreign service, the military, and the intelligence community, see Jerel A. Rosati, *The Politics of United States Foreign Policy* (Fort Worth, TX: Harcourt Brace Jovanovich, 1993), pp. 121–131, 147–169, and 191–223. For one of the best early treatments of the organizational "essences" of these same three groups, see Morton H. Halperin, *Bureaucratic Politics and Foreign Policy* (Washington, DC: Brookings Institution, 1974), pp. 26–62.

52. Probably the most comprehensive treatment of the role of personality in presidential decision making is Alexander L. George, *Presidential Decision Making*

in Foreign Policy: The Effective Use of Information and Advice (Boulder, CO: Westview Press, 1980).

53. *Towne v. Eisner*, 245 U.S. 425 (1918).

54. See Arnold Wolfers, " 'National Security' as an Ambiguous Symbol," *Political Science Quarterly*, 67 (December 1952): 481–502.

55. In an October 1960 interview, shortly before he left office, President Eisenhower observed:

I think you know that I believe we must be strong militarily, but beyond a certain point military strength can become a national weakness. The trouble with collecting military strength beyond our needs is that it tends to become a substitute for all the other things involved in true national security. It fosters the notion that national security is automatically tied to the amount of money spent on arms.

Quoted in Norman Cousins, *The Pathology of Power* (New York: Norton, 1987), p. 80.

56. Henry Mintzberg, *The Structuring of Organizations* (Englewood Cliffs, NJ: Prentice Hall, 1979), p. 2. The classic statement on the nature and importance of differentiation and integration is Paul R. Lawrence and Jay W. Lorsch, *Organization and Environment: Managing Differentiation and Integration* (Homewood, IL: Irwin, 1969), pp. 8–13. The importance of fuller integration to the effective functioning of the national security establishment cannot be overstated. Such integration will require not simply new organizational arrangements, but also other mechanisms for achieving commonality in ways of thinking and doing business (e.g., reeducation, regular and frequent interagency personnel exchanges, and even a coherent grand strategy to guide the nation).

57. These features of effective institutionalization are from Bert A. Rockman, "Institutionalization, Deinstitutionalization, and Leadership," in Shuman and Thomas, eds., *The Constitution and National Security*, pp. 211–230. Terry M. Moe, "The Politics of Structural Choice: Toward a Theory of Public Bureaucracy," in Oliver E. Williamson, ed., *Organization Theory: From Chester Barnard to the Present and Beyond* (New York: Oxford University Press, 1990), pp. 116–153, notes that political opponents want governing structures that work against effective performance. They fear strong, coherent, centralized organization. They like fragmented authority, decentralization, federalism, checks and balances, and other structural means of promoting weakness, confusion, and delay. The task of designing political organization, therefore, is not simply a technical problem of finding an efficient governance structure linking current power holders to their creations. The more fundamental task is to find and institute a governance structure that can protect public organizations from control by opponents.

58. *Youngstown Co. v. Sawyer*, 343 U.S. 579, 635 (1952). Quoted in Louis Fisher, *The Constitution between Friends: Congress, the President, and the Law* (New York: St. Martin's Press, 1978), p. 9.

59. See Arthur T. Hadley's discussion (*The Straw Giant*, p. 126) of what is commonly known as "Operation Pocket": the practice of military professionals trying to put new high-level political appointees at the Pentagon (especially those with little previous military experience) into their pocket.

60. See Kenneth W. Kemp and Charles Hudlin, "Civil Supremacy Over the

Military: Its Nature and Limits," *Armed Forces & Society* 19, no. 1 (Fall 1992), pp. 7–26.

61. Benjamin Barber, *Strong Democracy: Participatory Politics for a New Age* (Berkeley: University of California Press, 1984).

62. See Daniel Yankelovich, *Coming to Public Judgment: Making Democracy Work in a Complex World* (Syracuse, NY: Syracuse University Press, 1991). Public judgment is the state of highly developed public opinion that exists once people have engaged an issue, considered it from all sides, understood the choices it leads to, and accepted the full consequences of the choices they make. This contrasts with "mass opinion," the volatile, confused, ill-formed, emotionally clouded public responses to an issue when underlying value conflicts remain unresolved.

63. Kenneth E. Boulding, *The Image* (Ann Arbor, MI: University of Michigan Press, 1956), pp. 112–113. Murray Edelman, *The Symbolic Uses of Politics* (Urbana: University of Illinois Press, 1985), notes (p. 6): "Every symbol stands for something other than itself, and it also evokes an attitude, or set of impressions, or a pattern of events associated through time, through space, through logic, or through imagination with the symbol." Also see Thomas M. Franck and Edward Weisband, *World Politics: Verbal Strategy among the Superpowers* (New York: Oxford University Press, 1972). The authors argue (p. 118) that verbal weapons are as "real" in their strategic potential as missiles and submarines, and that (p. 128) verbal strategy can be employed to effect fundamental system transformation.

64. Proposals for the creation of supra- or super-Cabinet officials or staffs are anything but new, dating back at least to the 1955 Hoover Commission. The seminal deliberations of the Senate Subcommittee on National Policy and Machinery, more than thirty years ago, assessed Nelson Rockefeller's proposal to create a "First Secretary" of the Government who would be "above the Cabinet" and exercise delegated presidential authority in all areas "of national security and international affairs." Though finding the proposal to have serious shortcomings, the subcommittee made observations that are achingly familiar today:

New dimensions of national security make the proper exercise of the President's responsibility more difficult than ever before in our history. The line between foreign and domestic policy, never clear to begin with, has now almost been erased. Foreign policy and military policy have become more inseparable than ever. The tools of foreign policy have multiplied to include economic aid, information, technical assistance, scientific help, educational and cultural exchange, and foreign military assistance.... Indeed, today, almost every department of our Government, and some 18 independent agencies also, are involved with national security policy. ... The net result is this: The planning and execution of national security policy cuts across the jurisdiction of many departments and agencies. (pp. 15–16)

See U.S. Senate, Subcommittee on National Policy and Machinery, *Organizing for National Security*, vol. 3, *Staff Reports and Recommendations* (Washington, DC: Government Printing Office, 1961), pp. 27–111. For recent supra-Cabinet proposals, see Richard Brown, "Toward Coherence in Foreign Policy: Greater Presidential Control of the Foreign Policymaking Machinery," in R. Gordon Hoxie, ed., *The Presidency and National Security Policy* (New York: Center for the Study of the Presidency, 1984), pp. 324–340, and R. D. McLaurin, "National Security Policy: New Problems and Proposals," pp. 341–354, in the same volume. The question of whether such officials should be subject to Senate confirmation is a contentious one for which there is no simple solution. Brzezinski, "The NSC's Midlife Crisis," has argued that confirmation of the National Security Advisor would make sense only if the President, and perhaps Congress as well, were determined to elevate that person into the key player, designated by law to be the coordinating supervisor of the Departments of State and Defense and the CIA. Clark Clifford, "The Workings of the National Security System: Past, Present, and Future," *SAIS Review* 7, no. 2 (Winter/Spring, 1988), pp. 19–28, contends that Senate confirmation simply wouldn't work: "If these people have to be approved by the Senate then they will just be left out of everything at the White House" (p. 26). Also potentially controversial is the suggestion that these supra-Cabinet officials be called ministers. On the one hand, perhaps there is some lingering philosophical baggage from our colonial heritage that would still make us want to distance ourselves from our European forebears. Lawyers also might make an argument to the effect that it is important not to muddy the semantic waters between executive functions (those requiring judgment and discretion) and ministerial functions (those not allowing discretion). See Fisher, *The Constitution between Friends*, pp. 39–46. On the other hand, to the extent that we see value in more post–Cold War openness, and since "secret" and "secretary" share the same etymological roots, maybe "minister" isn't such a bad label after all.

65. See Marcus Raskin, "Let's Terminate the C.I.A.," *The Nation*, June 8, 1992, pp. 776–784. For just one of what undoubtedly is an infinitude of contrasting views on the subject, see Loch K. Johnson, *America's Secret Power: The CIA in a Democratic Society* (New York: Oxford University Press, 1989), pp. 10–11: "To abolish or emasculate the CIA would be an act of folly, for while the Agency can pose a threat to democracy from within [a not-insignificant concession], it provides a vital protection for democracy against serious threats from abroad."

66. There does not appear to be any provision in the 1961 Vienna Convention on Diplomatic Relations that would preclude the establishment of regional superambassadors. (1961 Vienna Convention on Diplomatic Relations, Padua, CEDAM, 1961). In fact, Article 5 of that protocol states: "The sending State may, after it has given due notification to the receiving States concerned, accredit a head of mission or assign any member of the diplomatic staff, as the case may be, to more than one State, unless there is express objection by any of the receiving States."

67. Although the Constitution prohibits individuals from holding office in both the executive branch and Congress at the same time, there is no obvious reason why both branches of the government could not—or should not—be served by the same analytical arm. The intent of such a proposal is to strive for objective analysis over advocacy research, and thereby to expose obvious partisanship.

68. R. Kent Weaver and Bert A. Rockman, "Institutional Reform and Constitutional Design," in R. Kent Weaver and Bert A. Rockman, eds., *Do Institutions Matter? Government Capabilities in the United States and Abroad* (Washington, DC: Brookings Institution, 1993), pp. 462–481 (quotes, pp. 467 and 472).

10

Total Force Policy

Charles E. Heller

As the nation and the U.S. Army approach the twenty-first century, opportunities exist to build an unprecedented effective peacetime force. Such a prospect might realize the dreams of Army reformers in the ranks and in Congress whose intellectual roots stretch back to the beginning of the century. The key to the future rests in how the Total Force Policy is implemented over the decade of the 1990s. How the U.S. Army will proceed in refining this policy is stated in its Fiscal Year 1993 posture statement. In this document, Chief of Staff General Gordon R. Sullivan refers to "enabling Strategies to meet the challenge of the future." And he states that the Army's policy will be

to **Strengthen the Total Force** by fully integrating our active and reserve components, keeping early-deploying units fully "mission ready," establishing strong training relationships and by fully integrating Total Army readiness standards and operating systems.[1]

This enabling strategy may be best defined by the U.S. Army's Reserve Forces Policy Board. According to the board, Total Force

means the integration of planning, programming and budgeting for the manning, equipping, maintaining and training of a mix of active and reserve forces essential for meeting initial contingency demands for forces. The Total Force Policy implies an increased interdependence of active and reserve forces. It absolutely requires that the availability and readiness of reserve forces must be as certain as the availability of active forces.[2]

The roots of the policy stretch to an earlier period of Army reform focusing on creating a modern American Army. These roots began to grow after the Civil War, when Emory Upton reported to General of the Army William

T. Sherman that the Europeans, specifically the Germans, found an answer to reducing the increasing costs of modern war. Their solution, he observed, was the creation of an integrated army of both regulars and reservists. In 1903 Secretary of War Elihu Root, who read and admired Upton's work, in conjunction with Congress, began a series of reform measures that have continued to today. The most significant of the early reforms dealt with reserve issues, the 1903 Dick Act, the 1908 creation of a federal medical reserve, and the 1916 National Defense Act. It is the 1916 act that gave birth to what we now call the Total Force. Specifically, the act defined the organization of the Army as follows:

The organized peace establishment, including the Regular Army, the National Guard and the Organized Reserves, shall include all of those divisions and other military organizations necessary to form the basis for a complete and immediate mobilization for the national defense in the event of a national emergency declared by Congress.[3]

However, over the following decades, the intent of the early reformers was never completely fulfilled. In looking at the mobilizations that followed, the experience was mixed. It is obvious that mobilization readiness improved with each conflict, yet the key ingredient, completely integrating the three components into one Total Force, continued to elude the Army. Numerous pieces of legislation have helped the regular Army make inroads on improving its peacetime combat readiness and the posture of the two reserve components, the state Army National Guard (ARNG), formed under the militia clause of the Constitution, and the United States Army Reserve (USAR), established in 1908 under the Constitution's Army clause.

There have been setbacks, some significant, as during the Vietnam War. For the first time in the twentieth century, the reserves did not mobilize early for a major war. When a reserve call-up was announced after the 1968 Tet offensive, it was too little and too late. This hesitant and halfhearted mobilization gave rise to a common belief, both inside and out of the military establishment, that the reserve components would never be used in anything short of a global war. Critics of the reserves declared Vietnam proved that a Chief Executive would lack the political will to order these military assets mobilized. Therefore, money expended on their readiness was wasted. Amidst this controversy, the Army demobilized while refocusing on the Soviet threat.

ENTER THE TOTAL FORCE POLICY

In 1970, Secretary of Defense Melvin Laird, concerned about the impact of the coming Vietnam War demobilization, gave new life to the Army's early twentieth-century reform by introducing what he called a Total Force concept. However, it took the final withdrawal of American forces in 1972 and President Richard M. Nixon's promise to replace Selective Service with an all-volunteer force for the concept to become official policy for the U.S. Army.

Beginning in May 1973, the new Secretary of Defense, James R. Schlesinger, supported Chief of Staff General Creighton Abrams in his efforts to reshape the Army. A young officer in World War II, Abrams's perspective on demobilization and postwar downsizing following World War II and Korea probably had a significant impact on his planning for the Army's future. It was not just the Army's unpreparedness following Vietnam that drove Abrams to embrace the Total Force Policy. It was also living through the experience of President Lyndon Johnson's policy decision not to call up the reserves and the escalating lack of public support for the war that shaped Abrams's thinking.

General Abrams identified three significant problems that required resolution in order to create an Army that would break the paradigms of the past and be ready to fight its next first battle without the usual cost in young American lives. The first was the inevitability that the regular Army's combat power would be reduced because there was a lack of a perceived immediate threat. Second, the cost of an all-volunteer force and new weapons systems was taking a greater percentage of the Army's appropriations and would by necessity be paid for by reducing end strength. Lastly, the anguish of Vietnam weighed heavily on his mind. The American public had turned on its Army as a visible target for its frustration over the lengthy war. To Abrams's way of thinking, the Total Force Policy was the vehicle that would solve these three problems. After taking his own counsel, it was the Chief of Staff, according to Lieutenant General ("Hook") Almquist, then Assistant Chief of Staff for Force Development, "who planned the Army structure."[4]

At the commencement of Abrams's tenure, the Army's post-Vietnam planning called for thirteen divisions. Abrams announced, to the surprise of his staff, that the ultimate goal was to field sixteen divisions. Secretary Schlesinger knew in advance of Abrams's plans to reach that objective, and supported him. The reason he did so is that the Chief proposed to use reserve component units as an inexpensive way to maintain what he believed was the correct number of combat divisions in a Cold War environment. Abrams's second objective of finding additional appropriations for rearmament was reached by including the reserves in a Total Force, shifting not only combat (Infantry and Armor) missions, but also Combat Support, or CS (Military Police, Signal, Combat Engineers, Chemical, and Artillery), and Combat Service Support, or CSS (Civil Affairs, Ordnance, Transportation, and Medical), missions to the less expensive reserves. The last objective was achieved by solving the other two problems, thus ensuring that, as Abrams explained to General Walter Kerwin, "If we're ever going to war again, we're going to take the reserves with us." He wanted to make certain that any administration had to be confident enough in its political objectives to call on the citizen-soldier to serve.[5]

Abrams set about structuring the Total Army as "an interrelated structure that could not be committed to sustained combat without mobilizing the reserves."[6] His legacy clearly exists in the Army's dependency on the reserves in a number of areas. For example, the reserve component portion of the force structure in combat divisions is 44 percent; in nondivisional combat units, 72 percent; in its Tactical Support Increment, 73 percent; in Special Theater Forces, 38 percent; and in General Support, 38 percent.[7] Within these categories, some specific types of units are 100 percent reserve, for example, Chemical Brigades, Water Supply Battalions, Enemy Prisoner of War Brigades, and Training Divisions. Today's Total Army cannot go to war for any length of time, including a contingency, without units of the USAR or the ARNG.

To accomplish the transition to a Total Force, the Army under Abrams's guidance developed a number of supporting programs and concepts. The most familiar is the Affiliation Program. In 1973 it "was conceived to improve the mobilization and deployment readiness of selected RC (reserve components) units and provide added combat power earlier in the execution of contingency plans."[8] Reserve combat units were the initial target of this program and were to "round out" active component divisions as part of Abrams's initial concept of creating the prerequisite number of units. Under roundout (the Army combines the words) these reserve combat units would have the same priority of funding as the parent unit. Later, other reserve units in CS and CSS areas were added to the program. It is an indisputable fact that in the early years of the Total Force Policy, there was general agreement that roundout units "were scheduled to deploy with the parent unit, or soon as possible thereafter" to meet "initial contingency demands for forces."[9] This concept was made policy and appears in Army Regulation 11–30, *The CAPSTONE Program*, which further defines Affiliation and other programs.

The other programs appeared soon after Affiliation. The AC/RC (active component/reserve component) Partnership Program aligned certain large combat formations with Special Forces units. Then there was the Counterpart Program, initially geared to bring together reserve and active component attack helicopter units and later expanded for other types of units. CORTRAIN (Corps and Division Training Coordination Program) allowed active and reserve combat units to participate in command post exercises with a corps in the continental United States (CONUS). Another program, initiated in 1979, was CAPSTONE. This established a wartime organizational structure for active and reserve component units designed to deploy in a contingency operation to Europe, Southwest Asia, or the Pacific. Later, Latin America was included as well as the CONUS-sustaining base forces. The CAPSTONE program allowed the components to conduct planning and training together for their wartime missions. There were other initiatives as well. Never in peacetime had the Army focused so much of its resources on its reserve components.[10]

As a consequence, the Total Force Policy increased the mobilization readiness of reservists to an unprecedented degree. Dedicated appropriations flowed into the reserves, although, as in the active force, the beneficiaries were more likely to be the Combat Arms branches rather than the less glamorous CS and CSS areas. In the massive defense buildup begun in 1979 by President Jimmy Carter in response to the Soviet invasion of Afghanistan, there were dollars enough for all. This wealth also bought surface harmony between the three components. Below the surface, however, the problem of integrating what amounted to three separate armies remained.

Thus, the Total Force Policy failed to accomplish the integration of the Army's three components. While there was much talk about "One Army," the basic attitudes and structural divisions between active and reserve personnel still existed. In the former, it has remained difficult for some regulars, who devote a full career to the military, to accept the fact that a part-time "weekend warrior" could be his or her equal on the battlefield after mobilization. Yet there are reservists using the same skills in their civilian occupations as in their CS or CSS military specialties who are as proficient as their active counterparts. On the other side, the reservist's distrust and resentment of the regular for real and imagined slights must not be overlooked as a factor creating divisiveness.

Then, too, few systems of any type interface between the two components. Each has its own personnel management systems, which are further fragmented in the reserve components, especially the ARNG. There continues to be a running debate over training standards, with an acceptance of the fact that the Total Army has two standards, one for the active forces and one for the reserves. It may be that the Army leadership has failed to instill in the ranks a one-Army mind-set. The failure to develop a Total Army attitude and to provide all types of interface systems was readily apparent during two significant global events, the end of the Cold War and the Gulf War.

THE GULF WAR

The end of the Cold War and the simultaneous outbreak of the Gulf War provide a significant backdrop for an analysis of the Total Force Policy and its future. It was the Gulf War that finally destroyed the lingering doubt that an administration would possess the political will to mobilize the reserve components for anything less than a global war threatening the survival of the United States. Saddam Hussein's brutal invasion of Kuwait tested the will of the United States and the Total Force Policy in every way. In doing so it made clear the strengths and weaknesses of a policy in existence for almost twenty years.

On August 2, 1990, President George Bush ordered the deployment of active component units to Saudi Arabia. The defense establishment then recommended a reserve call-up. On August 23, 1990, the President, invoking his authority under Title 10, U.S. Code 673b, which allows for the mobilization of selected reservists (those who have made a commitment to serve voluntarily) for 90 days with a 90-day extension option, ordered to active duty no more than 25,000 Army reservists in CS and CSS units. It should be noted that as result of Secretary of Defense Robert McNamara's Army reorganization in the early 1960s, most of the USAR is in these two categories, while the bulk of the reserve combat power resides in the ARNG.

From the end of August on, there was a creeping mobilization of both ARNG and USAR CS and CSS units, with a November authorization that raised the Army ceiling to 80,000. Congress became increasingly concerned by the Army's failure to mobilize the ARNG roundout combat brigades, which had absorbed a large percentage of the reserve appropriations during the Total Force buildup in the 1970s and 1980s. As a consequence, it passed the Department of Defense FY1991 Authorization Act with a section allowing combat units to be activated for an initial 180 days and an additional 180-day extension if required. In late November and early December, the three ARNG roundout brigades were activated, with the ceiling on the Selected Reserve call-up raised to 115,000. Finally, in January, with indications that Kuwait would have to be liberated by force, the President used the authority under Section 673 to raise the Army ceiling to 220,000. With a national emergency already declared in August to freeze Iraqi assets in the United States, the Army, with Presidential approval, ordered to active duty the USAR's Individual Ready Reserve (IRR), an inactive, pretrained individual manpower pool of prior service members.

Ultimately, the USAR deployed to the Gulf 94 percent of all the Civil Affairs units, 89 percent of the prisoner-of-war military police elements, 69 percent of the postal units, 65 percent of the petroleum assets, 63 percent of the psychological-operations elements, and 59 percent of the water-handling units. Other significant support area elements deployed to the Gulf included chemical decontamination, transportation, maintenance, and engineer assets. Noticeably absent from the Gulf or late on the scene, however, were several major reserve headquarters, such as the 377th Theater Army Area Command, which had a CENTCOM (Central Command) wartime mission and was never called, and other forces that were mobilized belatedly, such as the 335th Signal Command and the 416th Engineer Command. Over 25 percent of the vast USAR medical assets were mobilized for duty in the Gulf and in the United States. Some fifty USAR unique units, such as replacement battalions, garrison commands, training groups, schools, and reception stations were deployed in the United States. Additionally, the IRR provided 130 percent of the filler and estimated casualty replacements. The USAR's Individual Mobilization Augmentee and Retiree Recall programs also made available several thousand individuals in the theater of operations and elsewhere.[11]

The ARNG contributed to the flow of CS and CSS individuals and units to the Gulf. Among those units were six artillery battalions, two field artillery brigades, twelve hospitals, four medical battalions, and three medical groups. Additionally, there were three engineer groups, one group each of Air Traffic Control, Theater Area Support, and Corps Support. Four Maintenance, three Transportation, two Supply and Service, two Ammunition, one each Petroleum and Quartermaster, and five Military Police battalions also deployed to the Gulf. As with the USAR, other ARNG CS and CSS units deployed in the United States and Europe.[12]

The ARNG combat maneuver elements did not deploy to the Gulf. Unlike the CS and CSS units of the ARNG, the combat units required significant postmobilization training. Only one, the 48th Brigade, Georgia National Guard, roundout to the deployed 24th Infantry Division, was certified as deployable, but at the end of hostilities. Army Inspector General and General Accounting Office (GAO) reports were critical of the brigade's postmobilization readiness. In its February 1991 report the GAO mentioned faults noted in three previous studies that had yet to be corrected. Its criticism echoed active-component complaints that the 48th Brigade "suffered from deficient leadership and training, poorly maintained equipment and key personnel sidelined with medical conditions."[13] The author of this chapter personally visited the National Training Center and conducted interviews with several observers/controllers. All were unanimous in their praise of the enlisted soldier's enthusiasm and willingness to learn. However, significant criticism was leveled at the ARNG officers and senior noncommissioned officers.[14]

The National Guard responded to the criticism in their own after-action report: "There is a perception on the part of many in the Defense community and within the media that three Roundout Brigades were incapable of deploying. The facts are that they met the Army's deployability criteria but were never given the mission to deploy." The report claimed a double standard existed: "A significant number of active units did not meet AMOPS [Army Mobilization and Operations Planning System] criteria before they deployed but their readiness ratings were subjectively upgraded to meet deployment requirements."[15] However, the issue is cloudy. A Congressional Research Report, *The Army's Roundout Concept after the Persian Gulf War*, says, "The problem of readiness evaluation and reporting actually appears to be much more complicated than charges of 'double standards' may indicate."[16] The Reserve Forces Policy Board, whose members represent both the ARNG and the USAR, are the source of this assessment. The board's FY1990 report states: "Intangible factors, such as leadership, morale, cohesiveness, skill retention as well as physical fitness, strength, and stamina of the individual members also affect combat readiness of a unit. . . . Measuring the readiness of a reserve component unit or an active component unit remains a complex issue."[17]

Aftermath of the Gulf War

This first measure of the Total Force Policy was a qualified success. Creighton Abrams would have been pleased in a number of areas. His vow never again to go to war without mobilizing America's citizen-soldier was fulfilled when the President authorized activation of the reserves within several weeks of the deployment of active component units to Saudi Arabia. When the creeping mobilization began to impact on communities around the United States, support for the war mushroomed. General Crosbie E. Saint, Commander in Chief, U.S. Army Europe, shared his "Thoughts on the Victory in Desert Storm":

The early victory to call up the reserves, while probably motivated by necessity, turned out to be a major catalyst in consolidating American public opinion firmly behind our strategy in the Gulf. The size of the call-up meant that everyone had players from their state. The moral ascendancy that US troops had when they knew their country was behind them cannot be discounted.[18]

The reserve call-up ensured that the United States was united and committed.

From most accounts, the reserve CS and CSS units were successful in completing their missions. Yet the creeping mobilization hindered their full potential in several areas. First, in order to stay within the manpower ceilings established, a significant number of units were gutted to form basic essential cells. Derivative UICs (unit identification codes) were established while the parent units remained on later deployment lists. The problem was that there was no way of determining what equipment or manpower remained in the parent unit when it was activated later. Also, many headquarters and their staffs were not mobilized with their field units. Larger organizations were created in the theater of operations and commanded by active component officers. As indicated previously, the 377th Theater Army Area Command with its CENTCOM wartime mission did not deploy. Only specific individual reservists of its staff were mobilized, and they became part of a patchwork logistics command in the Gulf.[19]

The reserves in the CS and CSS areas, when mobilized, performed as well or better than their active component counterparts. Then–Secretary of Defense Dick Cheney remarked of the reservists in these areas, "[W]e could not have done the operation" without them.[20] Indeed, the Secretary's comments were echoed within and outside of the defense community. It was clear that in these areas, according to a defense analysis, "The reserves responded, by and large in an exceptional way. . . . For combat support and combat service support forces, their performance, when activated, was often indistinguishable from that of the active forces, in part a reflection of the frequent congruences between what they did in civilian life and their military duties."[21] This experience, then, should have been influential in determining a Base Force for the future, yet it appears to have had little impact on the Army as it began Cold War demobilization.

COLD WAR DEMOBILIZATION—THE BASE FORCE

After the startling changes heralding the end of the Cold War began to occur in 1989, President Bush delivered a major policy statement. On August 2, 1990, the day Kuwait was invaded, he announced a new military strategy for the postwar era. There would be reductions to a level "no more than the forces we need to guard our enduring interests." He warned against a "scaled back or shrunken-down version" of Cold War military forces. Instead, "What we need," the President declared, "are not merely reduction—but restructuring."[22]

The Army began building a Force-Generation Model for the future. As planning evolved through Total Army Analysis (a multiphased force-structuring process that includes force guidance, qualitative and quantitative analysis, and senior leadership review), the resulting early-deploying contingency forces were close to entirely active component, and the reserve components were placed further back in the deployment schedule. When it became apparent that the Army's portion of the defense budget in the out years would not support such a large number of active personnel in the contingency force, reserve CS and CSS were substituted to 5 percent in the forward-deployed forces and 60 percent in the rapidly deployable categories. What has resulted in the FY1993 Army posture statement is a twenty-division Base Force: ten active, two active with reserve roundout brigades, six reserve, and two reserve cadre divisions planned for FY1995. The Army's Base Force is approximately 535,000 active and 567,000 reserve soldiers and maintains the same ratio between the components as during the latter part of the Cold War.[23]

Previously, the Department of Defense planned in its FY1992 military authorization request to reduce all three components' end strength to meet the new global order. The approach taken was to share the burden equally, that is, to maintain the Cold War ratio. The cuts to the USAR and the ARNG were, for the most part, restored by Congress. Yet, in the FY1993 request, the Army ignored history and congressional guidance concerning end strength and pursued significant reserve reductions.[24] What irked Congress, in addition to political pressure from reservists, was that the Base Force appeared as a downsized Cold War Army and not a restructured force.

SEARCHING FOR THE TOTAL FORCE POLICY IN THE NEW WORLD ORDER

At the conclusion of the Gulf War, there was a flurry of articles and statements concerning the demise of the Total Force Policy.[25] However, then–Secretary of Defense Dick Cheney and General Colin Powell, Chairman of the Joint Chiefs of Staff, made it clear that the policy that helped to win the 100-hour war in the Gulf is here for the foreseeable future.[26] Nevertheless, if one examines the Army's Base Force structure closely, it becomes readily apparent that it is a smaller Cold War version of itself. But the issue is not merely end strength; it is also a matter of providing national security and at the same time keeping the Army relevant as well as preventing an unacceptable financial burden for the American public. All of these things can be accomplished, but only if the Total Force Policy fully integrates the Army's three components by restructuring to capitalize on the demonstrated strengths of each.

The Gulf War provided a reasonable test of the Total Force Policy. While the war itself should not be construed as the model for future conflicts, the way the policy impacted on the use of the Army is significant. What is at issue is deciding what worked and what did not, what can be fixed or improved, and what should be discarded in restructuring a new Total Army. The current global situation, the state of the U.S. economy, and the traditional American approach to defense in a peacetime environment combine to make a national security planner's nightmare. The best means to avoid the mistakes of the past, when the active component was drawn down to a state of impotence and the reserves were ignored until they become useless on mobilization, is to restructure an integrated Total Force to meet future defense and societal needs.

In the future, without an immediate threat to its national security, the American public will not support large defense budgets regardless of which political party is in the White House or controls Congress. Defense appropriations in future years will continue to decline, as they have in all peacetime environments. Historically, Americans have ignored the regular establishment, preferring to keep it small yet always expecting it to be ready to build a citizen army and lead that army to victory. Even in wartime, the regulars' role is downplayed and citizen-soldiers become the real victors. One must remember also that in 1945 the United States Army, including the Air Force, was 8 million strong, yet only 16,000 officers and enlisted personnel were regulars.[27]

The American public has never been willing to pay for a large standing army in peacetime. Therefore, a less expensive and more acceptable alternative is necessary. There is a need for the Total Army to evolve, assigning greater roles and missions to the reserve components.

The insistence on maintaining the same ratio between active and reserve forces not only is doomed to meet continual congressional resistance, but will ultimately weaken the readiness posture of all three components. The Army appears to be applying bandages to the Total Force Policy when what is needed is major surgery. Take, for example, a U.S. Forces Command training initiative called Bold Shift. Active-component criticism has focused on the reserve component's senior leadership, especially in the three round-out brigades, specifically, on the inability of senior ARNG combat officers to conduct combined-arms-maneuver warfare. There was also a lack of confidence in reserve senior leaders not only in combat units, but also in logistic functions, as evidenced by the refusal to activate the 377th Theater Army Area Command. Yet Bold Shift is focused on the smallest units and the most junior officers in the reserve and in areas that do not have a high skill-decay rate. By all accounts, reserve enlisted soldiers and small units required little postmobilization training, especially in the CS and CSS arenas, during Operations Desert Shield and Desert Storm. However, the effort should be focused on effective restructuring and integration, rather than on mobilization issues.[28]

Even congressional reformers have failed to grasp the essence of the problem and have introduced legislation that only makes worse the separation and divisiveness working against a Total Force. Then–Chairman of the House Armed Services Committee Les Aspin declared that "Operation Desert Storm showed us that the reserve components can work. It also showed some individual things were broken." Yet Aspin completely ignored what worked and focused on what did not work, the ARNG roundout brigades. He followed up his statements with legislation aimed at reforming the ARNG at the expense of the USAR. Aspin appeared to have an incomplete understanding of past attempts to gain more federal control over the ARNG and of the fact that modern combat maneuver warfare practiced at brigade and division level may well be beyond reserve training time constraints. By apparently ignoring his own advice, Aspin bucked not only the tide of past experience but of the increasing complexities of warfare in the future. It may not be possible to have reserve combat brigades and divisions in a contingency force with little or no postmobilization training. What the well-intentioned former Congressman did was pit the USAR against the ARNG, which probably will further retard revitalization of the Total Force Policy. How Aspin could have ignored the Gulf War success of the USAR's CS and CSS units is difficult to comprehend. The National Guard Bureau and the National Guard Association have made it clear that they oppose a number of the reform measures in the package. Previous attempts to reform the ARNG have failed. It is unlikely that Aspin's current effort will fare any better.[29]

In the Senate there appears to be a more balanced approach to the future of the Total Force Policy. Senator Sam Nunn, Chairman of the Senate Armed Services Committee, took a "top to bottom look at military 'roles and missions,' " including "the domestic and national security missions of the reserve forces."[30] In other words, he is pushing for significant restructuring.[31] Senator Strom Thurman, a member of the Armed Services Committee, sent a letter to his colleagues explaining that "the House Defense Authorization Bill virtually ignored the contributions of the Army Reserves in the Total Force" and enclosed not only a "report" citing the reserves' role in the Gulf War, but also a proposal "for a restructured Total Army acceptable to the American public" that "capitalizes on the strengths and minimizes the weaknesses of each of the Total Army components by using the Gulf War experience."[32]

AN UNCERTAIN FUTURE

What the Total Army will look like in the future has yet to be decided. Uncertainty hangs in the air to such a degree that readiness of all three components may eventually be affected, as it has been following all demobilizations. Former Secretary Cheney appeared to be firmly committed to the Base Force and maintaining a "share the burden," downsizing without restructuring. His stand was remarkably similar to that of former Secretary of War Newton Baker who, in 1919, with his Chief of Staff, insisted that the nation must have for the new world order, a regular army of 500,000 with virtually no role for the reserves in national defense. Congresses and administrations that followed had differing ideas. By 1927 the regular Army was at 133,949 and only reached an end strength of 188,565 in 1939, the year prior to U.S. mobilization for World War II. In 1993, the Army was struggling to develop an effective Total Force policy. This was complicated by Congress, which had decided not to reduce Reserve Component end strength recommended by the Department of Defense. Moreover, considerable debate and disagreement continued over the Base Force concept and the nature of future contingencies.[33] Secretary of Defense Les Aspin and his bottom-up approach to force composition and reduction appeared to continue the Base Force concept proposed in the Bush Administration. Yet the Clinton Administration may reduce forces even further than envisioned in the 1994 Defense Budget.[34] In any case, restructuring and integrating the Reserve Components with the Active Force remain outstanding issues.

As noted previously, there seems to be a consensus in both houses of Congress that something needs to be done to restructure all of the armed forces not only to meet the new world order but to come to grips with growing domestic problems with less dollars. However, there is no consensus in Congress as to exactly how all of this is to be accomplished. The problem is made worse because staffers cannot obtain any new ideas from the Army staff. However, Congress is aware of the cost savings to be accrued by greater reliance on the reserves and will continue to press for greater strength reductions in the active component and additional roles and missions for all the components. Because of the situation, the future of the Total Force

Policy appears bleak. If history repeats itself, Army readiness, recruiting, and retention may suffer because of the uncertainty about the future.[35]

REVITALIZATION OF THE TOTAL FORCE POLICY

Restructuring must take place, not the current reshaping to create a smaller Cold War Army. The Army Base Force is difficult to support, given an absence of a direct and immediate threat to national security and highly visible domestic problems. For those reasons it appears unacceptable to Congress; in essence, it is too expensive. Congress will not agree to maintaining the same percentages between active-component and reserve-component end strength. Members of Congress and the American public believe that an increased reliance on reserve forces is sufficient, given the state of the new global order. The Army, for its part, has initially resisted suggestions that it make itself relevant to the nation in areas other than war fighting.

To decide on the direction the Total Force Policy should take, a more objective analysis needs to be made of Operations Desert Shield and Desert Storm. Active-component combat maneuver elements worked well, as did the reserve forces CS and CSS. The roundout concept at combat brigade level failed the test.

A restructured Army must play on the strengths and minimize the weaknesses of the current Total Force. Therefore, what is needed is restructuring in a number of areas. First, the CONUS-based contingency force should be composed of entirely active-component combat maneuver units unless the ARNG is willing to roundout these units at company and battalion level. The CS and CSS for the contingency force, echelons above division and corps, must come from the reserves, more specifically the federal USAR. ARNG combat maneuver brigades and divisions now mirror the active-component force structure, and they should continue to do so. In addition to engaging in state missions, they should be ready for the wartime missions of reinforcement and reconstitution. Their real contribution is deterrent strength. By fulfilling this role, they will have the postmobilization time General Sullivan believes is needed. The support base in the United States must also be integrated, and the reserve components must assume greater mission responsibility in such areas as training and logistics.

Senator Nunn has also hit on an area that must be part of a twenty-first-century Total Force, that is, the area of domestic missions. It is no secret that the armed forces, especially the Army, were reluctantly dragged into the war on drugs. Historically, however, the Army has spent more of its time conducting peacetime missions than fighting wars. Soldiers have built roads and railroads, explored and mapped vast areas of the globe, delivered the mail including the first airmail, conducted medical research, established national parks, fought forest fires, engaged in major engineering projects, delivered humanitarian aid for natural and man-made disasters, and run youth and work programs. In brief, the Army has done all that was expected of it by the American public. Yet these peacetime missions do degrade readiness, and General Powell was correct in one sense when he said, "[W]e exist to fight. . . . We exist to go kick someone's butt if necessary." On the other hand, he was wrong when he said, "We are not a social agency."[36] As the armed forces of a democracy, by their very nature the forces are social agencies, and they should be proud of their contributions to the society they represent. Because of their community base, peacetime missions logically belong to the reserve components. In 1934 it was natural for the Army to turn over to the Organized Reserve Corps (today's USAR) the New Deal Civilian Conservation Corps mission. The acceptance of peacetime missions by the Total Army should have no great impact on contingency force readiness, since such missions are well suited to the CS and CSS units of the reserves.

An analysis of past demobilizations and the periods of peace that follow indicate that the Army today must use the Total Force Policy to break old paradigms. Restructuring and the acceptance of peacetime missions within the framework of the policy may ensure that future generations of young Americans will not have to pay in blood for what this nation has traditionally failed to accomplish in peace, that is, maintaining a cost-effective, highly efficient Total Army.

NOTES

1. U.S. Department of the Army, Michael P. Stone, and General Gordon R. Sullivan, *Strategic Force Strategic Vision for the 1990s and Beyond: A Statement on the Posture of the United States Army, Fiscal Year 1993* (Washington, DC: Government Printing Office, 1993), p. 9.

2. U.S. Department of Defense, Reserve Forces Policy Board, *Annual Report of the Reserve Forces Policy Board, FY 1975* (Washington, DC: Government Printing Office, 1965), p. 2.

3. U.S. Congress, *The National Defense Act, Approved June 1916 as Amended* (Washington, DC: Government Printing Office, July 1924), p. 1.

4. Quoted in Lewis Sorley, "Creighton Abrams and Active-Reserve Integration in Wartime," *Parameters*, 21 (Summer 1991), p. 44.

5. Quoted in ibid., p. 46.

6. Harry G. Summers, Jr., "The Army after Vietnam," in Kenneth J. Hagan and William R. Roberts, eds., *Against All Enemies* (Westport, CT: Greenwood Press, 1986), p. 363.

7. Department of Defense, "Reserve Component Programs, Fiscal Year 1991," in *Report of the Reserve Forces Policy Board* (Washington, DC: Government Printing Office, February 1992), p. 11.

8. Robert B. Tinsman, ed., *Army Command and Management: Theory and Practice* (Carlisle Barracks, PA: U.S. Army War College, 1991), p. 13.

9. U.S. Department of Defense, Reserve Forces Policy Board, *Annual Report, FY 1975*, p. 2.

10. U.S. Department of the Army, *The CAPSTONE Program* (Washington, DC: Government Printing Office, September 1, 1985).

11. Department of the Army, Office, Chief Army Reserve, *U.S. Army Reserve Report '91* (Washington, DC: Office, Chief of Army Reserve [OCAR], 1991), pp. 1–2.

12. National Guard Bureau, *Army National Guard After-Action Report, Operation Desert Shield/Desert Storm, Executive Summary* (Washington, DC: National Guard Bureau, n.d.), p. 3.

13. Alex Prud'homme, "Lessons of Desert Storm: Phantom Army," *Time*, June 10, 1991, pp. 19–20.

14. Bernard E. Trainor, "Guard vs. Army: Bad blood is boiling," *Atlanta Journal & Constitution*, May 7, 1991, p. C1; Charles E. Heller interviews conducted with Observer/Controllers of the Cobra Team, National Training Center, Mojave Desert, CA, March 10–11, 1992.

15. National Guard Bureau, *After-Action Report*, p. 7.

16. Robert L. Goldich, *CRS Report for Congress: The Army's Roundout Concept after the Persian Gulf War* (Washington, DC: Congressional Research Service, October 22, 1991), p. 37.

17. U.S. Department of Defense, *Annual Report of the Reserve Forces Policy Board, Reserve Component Program, Fiscal Year 1990*, (Washington, DC: Government Printing Office, 1991), p. 135.

18. U.S. Army, Message from CINCUSAREUR to CINCEUR and CSA, Subject: Thoughts on the Victory in Desert Storm, March 26, 1991.

19. Office, Chief Army Reserve, *Army Reserve Special Report: A Statement by Major General William F. Ward before the Committees and Subcommittees of the United States Senate and the House of Representatives, First Session, 102nd Congress* (Washington, DC: (Office, Chief of Army Reserve) [OCAR], 1991), p. 5; Henry Mohr, "Cannibalizing the Reserves?" *Washington Times*, January 7, 1991, p. D4.

20. Barton Gellman, "Cheney Says Guard Units May Need Reorganizing," *Washington Post*, March 15, 1991, p. 34.

21. Lewis Sorley, "National Guard and Reserve Forces," in Joseph Kruzel, ed., *American Defense Annual, 1991–1992* (Lexington, MA: Lexington Books, 1992), p. 201.

22. U.S. Executive Branch, "Reshaping Our Forces," (speech delivered at the Aspen Institute Symposium," Aspen, CO, August 2, 1990), *Vital Speeches of the Day*, 1990, p. 677.

23. Department of the Army, Office Deputy Chief of Staff, Operations and Plans, Discussion Paper, Subject: The Nation's Strategic Land Force, DAMO-SSW, August 28, 1990; Department of the Army, *Posture Statement FY 93*, p. 20; Department of the Army, Office Deputy Chief of Staff, Operations and Plans, Information Paper, Subject: Endstrength, DAMO-SSW, June 2, 1992.

24. Eric Schmitt, "A New Battle Is Ahead for Powell: The Budget," *New York Times*, January 17, 1992, p. 16.

25. Caleb Baker and Philip Finnegan, "U.S. Questions War Role of Reserve Combat Units, *Defense News*, April 15, 1991, p. 34; Andy Pasztor, "Pentagon Drafting Plans to Restrict Army Reserve Use," *Wall Street Journal*, January 7, 1991, p. 4; J. Paul Scicchitano, "Total Force Policy Takes a Beating," *Army Times*, February 25, 1991, p. 12.

26. Dick Cheney and Colin Powell, "Reducing and Reshaping the Reserves Makes Sense, Sound Policy"' (based on a news briefing at the Pentagon, March 26, 1992), in *Defense '92* (Washington, DC: Department of Defense, May–June 1992), pp. 2–3.

27. John C. Sparrow, *History of Personnel Demobilization in the United States Army* (Washington, DC: Government Printing Office, 1952), p. 139.

28. Commander, Forces Command to Chief of Staff, Message, Subject: Reserve Component Enhancement Action Plan, "Bold Shift," September 17, 1991.

29. Les Aspin, "A Total Force for America," *National Guard Magazine*, July 1992, pp. 27–28.

30. John Boatman, "Nunn Urges Major US Role Review," *Jane's Defence Weekly*, 18, no. 3 (July 18, 1992), p. 7.

31. John Lancaster, "Hill Takes Aim on Duplication in Military Services," *Washington Post*, August 8, 1992, p. A1.

32. Letter, Strom Thurman to Trent Lott, July 14, 1992; a copy of the letter is in possession of the author.

33. See for example, James C. Hyde, "Uncertainty Clouds Future for USAF and Army Reserve," *Armed Forces Journal International*, 130, no. 6 (January 1993), p. 29; Steven L. Canby, "Preserving Forward Presence by Radically Rebasing the Force: The European Case," and Mark J. Eitelberg, "Military Manpower and the Future Force," in Joseph Kruzel, ed., *American Defense Annual 1993*, 8th ed. (New York: Lexington Books, 1993), pp. 77–102 and 135–154, respectively. See also Charles E. Heller, *Twenty-First Century Force: A Federal Army and a Militia* (Carlisle Barracks, PA: Strategic Studies Institute, U.S. Army War College, June 14, 1993).

34. See for example, William Matthews, "Aspin Seeks More Cuts, and Ways to Avoid Them," *Army Times*, June 21, 1993, p. 3. See also Rick Maze, "Dellums Calls for Deeper Defense Cuts," *Army Times*, August 9, 1993, p. 23.

35. The author has had a number of conversations with staff members of both the Senate and the House Armed Services Committees and a number of Congressional Fellows during fiscal year 1993. All confirm this impression of the Army staff.

36. Colin L. Powell, "Let's Not Break the Force, in *Defense '92*, (Washington, DC: Department of Defense, March–April 1992), p. 20.

11

Civil-Military Relations in the New Era

Sam C. Sarkesian and John Allen Williams

As the United States enters a new security era, it is faced with restructuring the military and positioning most of the U.S. Army in the continental United States. As a consequence, the U.S. military must rethink its strategic orientation and its force structure. In turn, there will be important consequences for civil-military relations. The purpose of this chapter is to examine the new security landscape, study the changes imposed on military professionalism, and analyze the impact on civil-military relations in the United States in the context of historical patterns.

It is important to recognize that military professionalism and civil-military relations are inextricable. Civil-military relations concerns the civil control of the military, which is affected by the military's view of society and the political system, the military professional ethos, and the legitimate role of civilian leaders in the control and supervision of the military.[1] A study of civilian control of the military cannot be solely from a civilian perspective.

HISTORICAL OVERVIEW

The fundamental principles governing the relationship between the military and American society were established during the American Revolution and the framing of the U.S. Constitution. The debate over standing armies centered on two alternatives: the complete abolition of standing armies or the combination of a small standing Army and the state militia. The founding fathers were eventually convicted that a small standing army was a necessary evil, and a small standing army augmented by a force of citizen-soldiers remained the general organization of the military system until the end of the Vietnam War, with periodic surges in the size of the military during wartime. Regardless of the ebbs and flows of civil-military relations in American history, the basic principles evolving from the Constitutional Convention govern the role of the American military in society and its relationship to the political system and the general populace.

America had a difficult experience with standing armies during British rule, and this influenced civil-military relations from the postrevolutionary period until the Civil War. The British military was a highly visible sign of British rule and a constant reminder to the colonists of their subordinate position. The fear of standing armies was reinforced by an incident at Newburgh, New York, in which Washington's Army was on the verge of mutiny. This incident frightened members of Congress and reinforced the view that an important measure of control for a standing Army was to keep it small and ensure that the state militias remained a basic part of the military establishment. The fear was summed up by Samuel Adams:

> It is a very improbable supposition, that any people can long remain free, with a strong military power in the very heart of their country: Unless that military power is under the direction of the people, and even then it is dangerous. . . . Even when there is a necessity of the military power, within the land, which by the way but rarely happens, a wise and prudent people will always have a watchful and jealous eye over it; for the maxim and rules of the army, are essentially different from the genius of a free people, and the laws of a free government.[2]

Over sixty years later, Alexis de Tocqueville wrote, "After all, whatever one does, a large army in a democracy will always be a serious danger, and the best way to lessen this danger will be to reduce the army. But that is not a remedy which every nation can apply."[3] In 1821, Congress passed legislation reducing the Regular Army to 6,000 enlisted men. The memories of the War of 1812 and wartime nationalism had faded, and the Congress and the American people were concerned more with business and commercial interests and the extension of the nation westward. But even though the new Regular Army was reduced in strength, the groundwork was established for a concept that emerged in the nineteenth century, championed by Brevet Major General Emory Upton: an expandable Regular Army in time of war and the main reliance on a regular military establishment.[4] The concept of militiamen called to service for short periods of time became a basic element of the nation's military posture as the fear of large armies continued to be part of the American psyche.

Sparked by a depression in 1819 and fostered by a populist surge in the 1820s, the egalitarian criticism of the military took on a new life. While the fear of standing armies was part of the revolutionary period, the later criticism, at least by some, broadened to include a fear that the military would oppose democracy and become a threat to freedom. Regardless of the presumed organizational and training advances made later in the regular military establishment, however, criticism of the military continued into the immediate pre–Civil War period.

One element of this criticism was based on the view that the citizen-soldier was motivated and skilled enough in warfare to defend the United States, and therefore a large cadre of military professionals was not required. As C. Robert Kemble points out,

Fundamental to this attitude was America's growing faith in the common man. War, the democrats reasoned, was an occasional and short-lived emergency that could be met by nonprofessionals. Any good white Anglo-Saxon male could, on short notice, be a successful general—or, for that matter, president of the United States.[5]

During the Jacksonian era, the military, and West Point in particular, was attacked as incompatible with republican institutions. The U.S. Military Academy became the focal point for critics of the Army. A standing Army smacked too much of the Old World social order and an Old World aristocracy bent on subduing democracy. West Point was seen as an aristocratic social hierarchy fostering an authoritarian notion of government reflective of the Old World military.

One of the facets of Jacksonian democracy was deep mistrust of professional soldiers and a consequent desire to get rid of the Academy, where, Jacksonians were sure, an aristocratic tradition was being bred. Foes contended that Academy-trained regulars were incompetent as Indian fighters, and that their monopoly cost lives in fights with the red men.[6]

Until the Civil War, professional Army officers were separated from society not only by education and training but by economic status. The professional values evolving from such a separate and closed military system placed little trust in citizen-soldiers or in the efficiency and effectiveness of "democratically" composed armies. Separation between enlisted men and officers compounded the separation from society and the perpetuation of a distinct professional value system.

This separation was particularly sharp during the period between the War of 1812 and the Civil War. As John K. Mahon concludes,

[I]n their own realm the officers were kings. They considered themselves to be, and were, a class apart from the enlisted soldiers. They were carefully educated and drawn from well-placed families, whereas the enlisted men were usually ignorant, dredged up from the outcast elements of society. Most of them, indeed, were foreigners who enlisted because the transition from the culture of the Old World to the New was too hard.[7]

On the eve of the Civil War, American military posture and the military's relationship to society had changed little from the 1820s and 1830s. What had changed was the composition of the officers corps. As the Civil War was to prove, the outcomes of battles and the general conduct of the war were determined primarily by graduates of the U.S. Military Academy. This experience developed a professional dimension within the officers corps that would carry into the next century.

The Civil War was the dividing line between postrevolutionary and industrial America. In the postwar period, American society underwent great changes, as did the American military system. While the country moved into a period of industrial and urban growth and westward migration, the military, although considerably reduced in strength, was faced with missions ranging from Reconstruction in the South to conducting Indian wars on the frontier.

Following the Civil War, an advanced military school system was created to train officers in military skills. By the beginning of the twentieth century, these schools, field experience, and the emergence of the United States as a world power combined to focus the attention of the profession on the external world. By the turn of the century, the United States had gained possessions in the Philippines and in the Caribbean. The broadened responsibilities and worldview that had developed in the officers corps made it essential that military officers focus attention on the military implications of the new national posture. Professionalism now demanded concentration on military skills and battlefield competence at a higher and broader level than in the past. At the same time, a professional military ethos emerged that viewed political involvement as more than a distraction from military professionalism, rather, as a denigration of it. This perspective reinforced the prevailing view in the officers corps that politics should be disdained and the military should keep its distance from domestic politics and the political process. Civil-military relations as established by the framers of the Constitution remained virtually unchanged well into the twentieth century.

With the major exception of the Civil War, the American system of civilian control did not appreciably change or face any critical challenges during the "era of free security" (1815–1914). The institutional relationships established by the constitution, abetted by the patronage system and the minuscule size of the regular Army and Navy, ensured civilian control.[8]

Following World War I, the Army was again reduced in strength as America withdrew into isolationism. Yet the Army officers corps, and military professionals in general, managed to develop the skills and intellectual competence to design far-reaching doctrine that served the nation well in World War II. In addition, the military education of officers provided a cadre of combat leaders for World War II. As a young Army officer of our own era noted, "Clearly, it was the education and expertise of the officers corps that ensured Army readiness to transition from insular isolation to global responsibility and conflict."[9]

Regardless of the efforts in the 1920s and 1930s to create the basis for a new modern Army, America reverted to its historical posture. Following victory in World War I and a return to domestic issues, trade, and commerce, the military was allowed to languish.

So unpopular did military strength and training become that government action on defense was pushed from the back porch into the dog house. Many persons and organizations, who after the World War had savagely demanded a protection for our country, grew absorbed in other pursuits and were lulled by general prosperity. Indeed we resembled our decadence between the Revolution and 1812, with, of course, advanced intelligence.[10]

The depression in the 1930s and the rise of militarism in Germany, Italy, and Japan combined to focus some attention on international security issues. One result was that in 1935, the military received relatively large appropriations from Congress, which sparked an upgrading in combat effectiveness. This helped the Army emerge from its dark ages and try to rebuild. But the fact remained that throughout the 1920s and 1930s the main task of the Army was survival under the pressure of economics and antimilitary attitudes of society. The Navy fared better, primarily because it was relatively isolated from public view and it was supported by business interests concerned with trade and commerce. There was also a prevailing notion that the Navy constituted the first line of defense, a tradition that Navy and Marine Corps leaders would like to reinforce in the present era.

Needless to say, the major change in civil-military relations occurred with the U.S. entry into World War II. Much has been written about American political-military dynamics and the military role in the war, and little review is necessary. But it is important to point out the impact of the war on civil-military relations. This is well summarized by Allan Millett:

World War II marked a watershed in the history of American civil-military relations, but it was no less marked by ambiguities than were earlier periods. . . . While the JCS had reached a role in diplomatic-strategic policy-making that their predecessors would have found amazing, the military had played only a supporting role in deciding how the nation's resources would be applied to the war effort. Even under the extraordinary stresses of global war, the American system of civil control had not been appreciably altered.[11]

At the same time, citizen-soldiers and the populace did not change their views of the military as a national institution: the citizen-soldier, after all, was the primary manpower in the war.

The Postwar Years

From the beginning of the Cold War to Vietnam, civil-military relations were characterized by an increasing interpenetration between civilians and the military. The global strategic interests of the United States demanded a more coherent and integrated political-military effort, which was partially met by the creation of the civilian-run Department of Defense. Moreover, a number of nongovernment organizations emerged with major interests in national security matters to offer advice, act as consultants, and offer services as experts on military matters. This same phenomenon took place in academia. In sum, civil-military relations expanded considerably beyond the military's relationship with government institutions. These relationships not only permeated various sectors of society, but began to take on a political coloration as Congress extended its outreach into military matters ranging from research and procurement to military operations.

Congressional involvement in the military establishment and its concern with the political implications of using the military instrument reached a peak during the Vietnam War. What began as a commitment to save democracy with the full support of the American people turned into a political-military disaster. The American people, led by a number of elected officials and influential persons in society, savaged the Johnson Administration for its conduct of the war and turned their wrath on the military itself as a visible symbol of the "wrong war." Many military professionals became convinced of political and societal malfeasance—sending the military into Vietnam and, when things got tough, withdrawing support, leaving the military "holding the bag."

In the post-Vietnam period, civil-military relations hit a low point. The American military withdrew from Vietnam completely by 1973, leaving it to be defeated in 1975. But as Millett concludes,

From the historical perspective, what is most significant about the post-Vietnam period is not the "new" disillusionment with government *per se* or erosion of respect for the military, but the reassertion of traditional American attitudes about the military and the revitalization of a complex, pluralistic system of civil-military relations.[12]

THE PROFESSION AND THE POLITICAL SYSTEM

Military professionals historically have been suspicious of politicians and contemptuous of political activity. Bargaining, negotiations, compromises, and consensus building have been seen as self-serving and contrary to professional principles. Order, stability, and predictability have been seen by military professionals as the characteristics of effective political systems. Accordingly, discipline, skill, loyalty, and obedience are the preferred basis for responding to challenges and for solving problems.[13] These professional characteristics were summed up by C. Wright Mills, who wrote, "Inside their often trim bureaucracy, where everything seems under neat control, army officers have felt that 'politics' is a dirty, uncertain, and ungentlemanly kind of game; and in terms of their status code, they have often felt that politicians were unqualified creatures inhabiting an uncertain world."[14]

One result of this political perspective is that the military world attempted to keep its distance from the civilian world and from politics in general. This is not to say that military professionals isolated themselves completely from the civilian political realm. Early in U.S. history, military officers not only engaged in internal politics but also did not hesitate to attack elected officials. In the first half of the nineteenth century, Army officers periodically attacked fellow officers or disparaged politicians whom they felt knew little of the military. "While military men might disagree on politics, almost all took a dim view of politicians, who appeared ever ready to interfere in Army matters beyond their ken. The attitude persisted despite most officers' belief that they themselves had every right to participate vigorously in the political process."[15] There were times when some professional officers entered the political arena themselves, most notably Ulysses S. Grant and Dwight D. Eisenhower.[16] But in general, the military has carefully avoided involvement in electoral politics.

In any case, the relationship between politicians, the political system, and Army professionals has been (and is) an uncomfortable one. In the contemporary period, the traditional military distaste for politics and dislike of most politicians continues. There are exceptions, depending on the nature of the times and whether or not a politician has served in the military. But the ingrained antimilitary tradition in America as a liberal society is not lost on most Army professionals. This remains true even when public opinion polls are favorable to the U.S. military. Whatever the opinion polls, antimilitary sentiments seem to be persistent themes in academia and in some political quarters.

Earlier Years

The view of many military professionals rested on the belief that there is an inherent antimilitary theme in American politics and attitudes.

American attitudes toward the military services and the role played by the military in the social and political systems of the United States have deep roots in the American heritage. . . . From England the colonists inherited a distaste for a professional military and a distrust of a standing army. These attitudes have permeated American civil-military relations ever since.[17]

During the same period, the operational doctrine and force organization evolved following the European model. As Russell Weigley notes,

The United States Regular Army was patterned sufficiently on British and European models, in fact, that in 1835 it was not much better prepared for guerrilla warfare against the Seminoles in Florida than Napoleon's soldiers had been for guerrillas in Spain. This was true despite experience in fighting forest Indians and the irregular campaigns that Americans themselves had sometimes waged during the Revolution.[18]

Nevertheless, the military emerged from World War II with the highest accolades from the American people. The fact that this was a war requiring national mobilization against an enemy perceived to be a threat to all that was good made the military effort a common one for the American people. Indeed, most look back at World War II as a moral crusade. Even populist author Studs Terkel calls it the "Good War."[19] Almost immediately following World War II, the U.S. military was virtually dismembered. Selective service ceased, albeit for only a short time, and the massive forces organized for the war were demobilized, following the historical pattern of attempts to return after war to the "normalcy" preceding it. The military was virtually forgotten, and Army professionals seemed to return to the prewar years. All of this lasted but a short period of time, ending with the onset of the Cold War.

The Postwar Years

The Cold War increased the demands of national security and foreign policy on a global scale, eroding the gap between the military and politics and reshaping the notion of military professionalism. No longer could military leaders concentrate solely on military matters. Political factors became closely linked with military considerations. Military professionals could no longer carry out missions or prepare for various contingencies without considering the political and social dimensions of foreign involvement. Participation in the North Atlantic Treaty Organization (NATO) and the need to consider European views and develop interrelationships within a circle of allies were the most visible manifestations of the emerging new professionalism.

In the aftermath of World War II, a new national security establishment was created. Part of this new establishment, the Department of Defense, attempted to meld civilian and military expertise into a working system. At the same time, Congress became a more important player in the national security policy process. The highest levels of military leadership were pushed into a partnership with civilian experts and elected officials.

The new civil-military environment encompassed the nuclear era and the beginning of the technological age. This became part of the strategy and force structure components of the military institution. At the same time, equipment, training, and operations became more expensive. Not only were more demands placed on the military profession but, increasingly, professionals recognized that resources allocated by elected officials were a critical element in the military's ability to perform its missions and prepare for a variety of contingencies.

The U.S. military became a political as well as military institution, in the sense that congressional committees and committee chairmen dealing with the armed forces became critical players in the overall political-military equation. The military profession could not ignore this development if it intended to maintain competence and readiness in responding to global challenges. National security emerged as a term that became an important part of the military professional's lexicon.

Defense policies, needless to say, involve considerations that go beyond explicitly military concerns, but for too long a sophisticated discussion of military affairs has been stifled by the application of politically motivated restraints upon such exposure of views, restraints imposed both from outside and inside the Department of Defense.[20]

For most of the 1950s, the military received virtually all it asked for in resources from Congress, although Army and Navy officers chafed at the Air Force emphasis of President Eisenhower's "New Look." Draftees and volunteers provided enough recruits to allow the military to maintain distance from domestic issues. During this period of time the military was implementing the 1948 desegregation order of President Truman. During the Korean War civilian control of the military was reinforced by President Truman's removal of General Douglas MacArthur as Commander of U.S. Forces in Korea. But the energy and perspectives of military professionals remained focused on external matters, with the primary concern Soviet military power projection. The policy of containment had its national security dimensions, which shaped much of the thinking of the professional military. The Army, in turn, developed doctrine and experimented with organizational structures based on nuclear weaponry and major war in Europe aimed primarily at the only serious enemy, the Soviet Union.

At the same time, subtle changes were taking place in the relationships between military professionals and civilians involved in the political process. The result was a close linkage of the military with politicians and the national security policy process. This became apparent during the Vietnam War.

In the period after the Korean War, the works of Samuel P. Huntington and Morris Janowitz brought scholarly attention to the study of civil-military relations and the military profession.[21] Huntington's study pointed to a gap between a liberal society and the disciplined and authoritative military system. He wrote, "The tension between the demands of military security and the values of American liberalism can, in the long run, be relieved only by the weakening of the security threat or the weakening of liberalism."[22] He pointed to the need for a political separation between the military and society in order to maintain proper civil-military relations in a liberal system. Huntington's study of civil-military relations remains essential reading for those studying the subject.

Janowitz studied the differences between what he termed "absolutists" and "pragmatists" in the military profession as well as the need for a constabulary force.

The constabulary force is designed to be compatible with the traditional goals of democratic political control. The constabulary officer performs his duties, which include fighting, because he is a professional with a sense of self-esteem and moral worth. . . . He is amenable to civilian political control because he recognizes that civilians appreciate and understand the tasks and responsibilities of the constabulary force. He is integrated into civilian society because he shares its common values.[23]

Political knowledge and limited political involvement are important elements in Janowitz's constabulary force. As in the case of Huntington's writings, Janowitz's work is critical in the study of military professionalism.

Later, Sam C. Sarkesian argued that the military is indeed a political instrument as well as a military one and that military professionals need to study, understand, and become involved in the political system.[24] This involvement, however, is not based on partisan politics but on education and enlightened advocacy. According to Sarkesian, the military professional is in the best position to advocate a military perspective in political circles. Such a nonpartisan posture is critical in the proper functioning of the military in a democratic society.

[T]o appreciate the need for such a professional perspective will require professional military men who are enlightened and educated. . . . [T]o presume somehow that the military perspective should not include the bringing to bear of a military intellectual focus that appreciates and understands the consequences of military decisions upon the political and social life of the system is to deny the very criteria of a "profession."[25]

All of these views are a far cry from the Uptonian model that held a prominent place in U.S. military circles in the early twentieth century.[26] With battle experience in the American Civil War, Emory Upton advocated a military system based on the German model. He urged the establishment of a general staff and stressed that military institutions and the military profession stood above and separate from the political system. Later, as America's system proved effective in World War I, the Uptonian model lost its credibility. Nonetheless, traces of this model remain, echoing to some extent in the work of Samuel P. Huntington.

Historically, military professionals have been involved from time to time in the political realm, not generally to seek partisan political goals but to protect their careers and the position of the military. How these political efforts were undertaken and for what purposes are critical to the study of military professionalism and the concept of self-image and perceptions of the outer world. It was in the Vietnam period that these elements went through serious changes, making a major impact on how professionals viewed politics, politicians, and political-military policy.

The Vietnam Era

The Vietnam War marks a watershed in the shaping of civil-military relations. After 1965, the war triggered a variety of protests and political opposition in the United States. This domestic turmoil crystallized into attacks on President Lyndon Johnson and his leadership in what many came to believe was a wrong war. Domestic politics not only affected military operations in Vietnam but had an impact on military professionals and their sense of mission. Many of them felt that they were committed to the war with the initial support of the American people and its elected officials only to find themselves isolated later as Americans withdrew their support.[27]

After the Tet Offensive in 1968, American strategy in Vietnam shifted to Vietnamization. U.S. ground forces withdrew from an active combat role, turning this function over to the South Vietnamese Army. This development ultimately led to withdrawal of American forces in 1973 and the collapse of South Vietnam in 1975. The act of Congress that cut off all aid and assistance to South Vietnam in 1973 was the final bitter pill that Army professionals swallowed regarding their role in the Vietnam War.[28]

AMERICAN POLITICS AND THE MILITARY: A VIETNAM LEGACY?

American attitudes and levels of support for U.S. involvement in the Vietnam War have been tracked by a number of opinion polls and examined by various studies.[29] A serious study of these materials is important for developing an understanding of the changes in American domestic politics and their impact on the conduct of the Vietnam War. In brief, during the initial years of U.S. involvement, there was widespread support for engaging in the war. But in the aftermath of the Tet Offensive in 1968, most Americans felt that U.S. policy and strategy were on the wrong track and the war was too costly.[30] These changing views eventually led to the American withdrawal from Vietnam. From 1968 to 1973, the U.S. political-military policy focused on Vietnamization and disengagement. American national will, political resolve, and staying power eroded precipitously following the Tet Offensive, followed by signs of Army disintegration and ineffectiveness.

The changing opinions of the American public regarding the conduct of the war and U.S. purpose in Vietnam correlated with increasing frustrations in the military regarding the effectiveness of American political leadership. These developments seem to correlate with the anger expressed regarding the behavior of senior Army officers. One must be careful in drawing firm conclusions from such observations, but it seems reasonable to assume that the perceptions of Army professionals regarding American domestic politics and the policy process were negatively affected by the rising tide of antiwar sentiment and the opinions of the American public, which widened increasing dissatisfaction with U.S. military measures and the conduct of the war.

The Post-Vietnam Period

Shortly after Ronald Reagan was elected President in 1980, a reconciliation began to bring together the American people and its military over the Vietnam War. President Reagan's view that the U.S. effort in Vietnam was a "noble cause," the Vietnam Memorial in Washington, the efforts of veterans groups to recast the image of the military and the cause of Vietnam, and a victory parade in Washington began to shape more positive images of those who fought in the war, despite continuing reservations about the war itself. This reconciliation reached its high point with the U.S. success in the Gulf War in 1991.

Following the withdrawal from Vietnam, the U.S. military turned its attention to military doctrine and training, focusing on the air-land battle doctrine and a European battle scenario. This refocusing on the Soviet threat marked a return to a posture that was understood and appreciated by most Americans. The European orientation continued even though a number of lesser military operations were conducted (most notably Grenada and Panama). Throughout this period, the U.S. military enjoyed a comfortable and favorable relationship with society. The reliance solely on volunteers to fill the ranks in all of the services reinforced this relationship.

There were clear signs before the Gulf War that the end of the Cold War had opened a new era.[31] And as Gary Guertner points out, congressional power in control of the armed forces is vast, and there is public support for a peace dividend. These views were apparent before the Gulf War.

Growing public support for retrenchment from global commitments as a superpower is reinforced by a long, continuing cycle of congressional dominance of the policy-making process.... Strategic victory in the cold war has not resulted in any perceivable diminution in congressional power. Institutionally, Congress holds the key to the future of our military forces.[32]

THE NEW ERA

The Gulf War marked the beginning of a new era for the U.S. military. For many, it not only relegated Vietnam into the dustbin of history but highlighted the renewed effectiveness of the U.S. military. This new era is an important reference point in coming to grips with civil-military relations and Army professionalism in the remainder of this decade and into the next. It is at this point in time that a new research project to assess Army professionalism was coming to fruition. While this research focused on full-time civilian graduate education for Army officers, it revealed attitudes and opinions on a variety of political and social subjects.[33]

This research revealed that even with changes in world perspectives and more sensitivity to domestic political issues, most Army professionals perceive the world through orthodox lenses and from traditional value systems. As such, politics is seen as one separate arena and the military as another. However, some reports indicate that this separation does not prevail at the highest ranks, particularly among these serving inside the Washington beltway.[34] Nonetheless, even with the changes in the security landscape that occurred in 1989 through the first months of 1991, Army professionals saw little change in their own professional status, while continuing to view domestic politics and the policy process according to long-established professional frameworks. This is true even though a body of professional views surfaced which was more concerned about the nature of the political system and the policy process than were mainstream professional views. Such concern was expressed primarily by Army professionals who had recently completed full-time civilian graduate education or who were in such a program.

Yet the plans for reducing the military and repositioning most of the U.S. Army in the United States are sure to have an impact on civil-military relations. The new military posture entails not only longer tours of duty at one location, but more stringent enlistment criteria. Combined with serious debate about the role of women in combat and the role of homosexuals, these changes are also sure to affect the military professional ethos.

Military professionalism remains fixed in the notion of "duty, honor, country." While there remains a conservative bent in the concept of military professionalism, it is not rigid and does not preclude a diversity of ideas, particularly among those officers who have completed full-time civilian graduate education. Also, military professionalism and civil-military relations may be evolving toward a qualitatively different interpretation of "duty, honor, country" from that presumed to exist a generation ago. While in part this is due to the changing nature of modern war, it is also due to the intellectual stimulus injected into the military institution by the input of a select number of officers completing full-time graduate education.

Where the new security landscape and the changing military force structure will lead in terms of military professionalism and civil-military relations is not clear. This uncertainty is complicated by the drawdown and downsizing of the U.S. military, which is having a particularly great impact on the Army. The training and education of military professionals must go beyond battlefield competence in the traditional sense. The "fog of peace" has brought with it innumerable benefits, but also a number of confusing and ill-defined threats and challenges to U.S. security. To be well-prepared for both international and domestic demands, the U.S. military must expand its professional horizons and its intellectual competence. As a recent study has shown, civilian graduate education provides the necessary dimension for military professionalism to place it in the best position to respond to the new strategic landscape and the American domestic milieu. At the same time civilian leaders, academicians, media "experts," and citizens in general must expand their own horizons and understanding of the military. Without this mutual effort, civil-military relations could well lead to a military isolated from society and remote from the realities of the international security landscape.

In the final analysis, civil-military relations in a democracy necessitates a close linkage between the people and the military. This also means that military contingencies and the use of military force must be closely linked to the American people. This is not a new phenomenon. Indeed, an Army officer reflecting about the Russo-Japanese War of 1904–1905 wrote the following in 1928:

[This] war shows that wars may be won or lost in the home country as well as on the battlefield and that no government can go to war with hope of success unless it is assured that the people as a whole know what the war is about, that they believe in this cause, are enthusiastic for it, and possess a determination to win. If conditions are not present the government should take steps to create them or keep the peace.[35]

The Vietnam War proved this point only too well. The U.S. military must not forget this inextricable linkage with the American people. Given the uncertainties of the new security landscape, this linkage has become the most critical in committing U.S. military forces to any conflict. The American people must also be aware that the world remains a dangerous place. Economic strength and skilled diplomacy are not always enough to ensure success of American national interests. Whether Americans like it or not, military force may be the only recourse in some instances. This is reason enough for the American people and their elected officials to develop a broader and more sensitive understanding of the realities of military professionalism and what this means in a democratic society.

NOTES

1. Sam C. Sarkesian, "Military Professionalism and Civil-Military Relations in the West," *International Political Science Review*, 2, no. 3 (1981), p. 285.

2. As quoted in Clinton Rossiter, *The Political Thought of the American Revolution* (New York: Harcourt, Brace and World, 1963), p. 126.

3. Quoted in J. P. Mayer, ed. *Alexis de Tocqueville, Democracy in America* (Garden City, NY: Doubleday Anchor Books, 1969), p. 651.

4. Emory Upton, *The Military Policy of the United States from 1775* (Washington, DC: Government Printing Office, 1904).

5. C. Robert Kemble, *The Image of the Army Officer in America* (Westport, CT: Greenwood Press, 1973), p. 36.

6. John K. Mahon, *History of the Second Seminole War, 1835–1842* (Gainesville: University of Florida Press, 1967), p. 118.

7. Ibid., p. 117.

8. Allan R. Millett, "The American Political System and Civil Control of the Military: A Historical Perspective," (Mershon Center Position Papers in the Policy Sciences, Ohio State University, No. 4, April 1979), p. 11.

9. Captain Mark D. Redina, "An Officer Corps for the 1990s," *Military Review*, 70, no. 10 (October 1990), p. 65.

10. William Addelman Ganoe, *The History of the United States Army* (New York: Appleton-Century, 1942), p. 482.

11. Millett, "The American Political System," p. 34.

12. Ibid., pp. 59–60.

13. The ideas in this paragraph are those of Robert A. Vitas, one of the consultants for this research.

14. C. Wright Mills, *The Power Elite* (New York: Oxford University Press, 1980), p. 174.

15. Col. Stanley L. Falk, USA (Ret.), "Feudin' and Fussin' In the Old Army," *Army*, vol. 34, no. 11 (November 1984), p. 58.

16. See also A. J. Bacevich, *Diplomat in Khaki: Major General Frank Ross McCoy and American Foreign Policy, 1898–1949* (Lawrence: University of Kansas Press, 1989).

17. James Alden Barber, Jr., "The Military Services and American Society: Relationships and Attitudes," in Stephen E. Ambrose and James A. Barber, Jr., eds., *The Military and American Society: Essays and Readings* (New York: Free Press, 1972), p. 290.

18. Russell Weigley, *History of the United States Army* (New York: Macmillan, 1967), p. 160.

19. Studs Terkel, *The Good War: An Oral History of World War Two* (New York: Pantheon Books, 1984).

20. Donald Atwell Zoll, "The Moral Dimension of War and the Military Ethic," in Lloyd J. Matthews and Dale E. Brown, eds., *The Parameters of Military Ethics* (Washington, DC: Pergamon-Brassey, 1989), p. 122.

21. Samuel P. Huntington, *The Soldier and the State: The Theory and Practice of Civil-Military Relations* (New York: Vintage Books, 1964), and Morris Janowitz, *The Professional Soldier: A Social and Political Portrait* (New York: Free Press, 1971).

22. Huntington, *The Soldier and the State*, p. 456.

23. Janowitz, *The Professional Soldier*, p. 440.

24. Sam C. Sarkesian, *Beyond the Battlefield: The New Military Professionalism* (New York: Pergamon Press, 1981).

25. Sarkesian, *Beyond the Battlefield*, p. 188.

26. Upton, *The Military Policy*.

27. A survey of over 900 student officers and faculty at the U.S. Army Command and General Staff College, Fort Leavenworth, Kansas, in 1972 showed, among other things, that many felt that antiwar and antimilitary sentiments affected the Army's

effectiveness in Vietnam. Also see Lieut. Col. John H. Moellering, "Future Civil-Military Relations," *Military Review*, 53, no. 7 (July 1973), pp. 68–83.

28. Nguyen Cao Ky, *How We Lost the Vietnam War* (New York: Stein and Day, 1984), pp. 7 and 9. See also General Cao Van Vien, *The Final Collapse* (Washington, DC: Government Printing Office, 1983).

29. See, for example, Albert H. Cantril, "The American People, Viet-Nam and the Presidency" (Paper prepared for presentation at the Sixty-sixth Annual Meeting of the American Political Science Association, Los Angeles, California, September 8–12, 1970).

30. Cantril, "The American People," pp. 3–5. Ironically, Tet marked a significant military defeat for Viet Cong forces, which were decimated once they exposed themselves. It was, nevertheless, a significant political victory for them and the North Vietnamese due to its effect on the American people. The misleading media reports from South Vietnam about the effectiveness of the Viet Cong and North Vietnamese forces was a major factor in reinforcing the negative American political views regarding the conduct of the war. See Peter Braestrup, *Big Story: How the American Press and Television Reported and Interpreted the Crisis of Tet 1968 in Vietnam and Washington* (Boulder, CO: Westview Press, 1977).

31. John J. Mearsheimer, "Why We Will Soon Miss the Cold War," *Atlantic Monthly*, August 1990, pp. 35–50.

32. Gary L. Guertner, *The Armed Forces in a New Political Environment*, Monograph of the Strategic Studies Institute, U.S. Army War College (Carlisle Barracks, PA: Strategic Studies Institute, March 2, 1992), p. 4.

33. Sam C. Sarkesian, John Allen Williams, and Fred B. Bryant, "Civilian Graduate Education and the U.S. Military Profession" (Paper prepared for presentation at the American Political Science Association Convention, Chicago, Illinois, September 3–6, 1992).

34. See, for example, Bob Woodward, *The Commanders* (New York: Simon & Schuster, 1991), and the politics of the Gulf War as reported in "The Generals' War," *Army Times*, March 2, 1992.

35. From Major G. P. Baldwin, U.S. Army, writing as a student at the War College in 1928, as quoted in David Richard Palmer, *Summons of the Trumpet: A History of the Vietnam War from a Military Man's Viewpoint* (New York: Ballantine Books, 1984), pp. 341–342.

Part V

Conclusions

12

Into the Twenty-First Century

John Mead Flanagin

In recent years there have been frequent calls in the international relations literature for a new strategic doctrine to replace containment.[1] Many in the community of policymakers and policy analysts who shape national strategy are looking for a comprehensive assessment—both interpretive and prescriptive—that will guide the United States through the post–Cold War era. One sees repeated references to George Kennan and Paul Nitze, who articulated the strategy of containment so forcefully during the initial stages of the Cold War. Their arguments had a catalytic power that fused together domestic and international politics in the minds of opinion leaders, who then set about building a public consensus in support of an internationalist, anti-Communist national strategy.

Consensus will be more difficult to achieve in the post–Cold War era, and for that we can be thankful. In the absence of an immediate and massive threat to U.S. national security, there is an opportunity to reexamine assumptions about the sources of national strength and the responsibilities of international leadership. The process of reconciling our domestic needs with international objectives has proven to be a lengthy one, and there is still a great deal of uncertainty.

The debate over how domestic and international priorities should be reordered, to which this volume contributes, began without an accepted premise about how states will interact in the future. Yet, in a multipolar world, U.S. national strategy does not necessarily need to follow a global logic (except, perhaps, on the question of environmental degradation). Regional politics have come to the fore in U.S. national strategy, and the distinction between internal and external factors has diminishing importance. Changes in the U.S. labor force cannot be understood without reference to Asia's manufacturing boom. Domestic drug abuse cannot be understood without reference to the Latin American economy. Domestic energy costs cannot be understood without reference to Middle Eastern politics. There are numerous cross-cutting strategic issues that cannot be adequately explained in global terms.

At the regional level, political, military, and economic trends are more distinct. However, midrange strategic planning for major regional conflicts calls for a high degree of abstraction. The force planning models devised by Les Aspin while he was Chairman of the House Armed Services Committee were based on generic threats and contingency equivalents to Operations Desert Storm, Just Cause, and Provide Comfort. By contrast, the Joint Chiefs of Staff postulated a set of specific conflict scenarios as a basis for force planning and found that Congress and the national security policy community were skeptical about this approach. William Taylor and Don Snider observe that the U.S. will need to balance cooperative and competitive strategies in regional contexts where our security interests diverge from our economic interests, as in Asia and Europe.

At present, the emphasis is on strategic flexibility. However, as variables multiply, the prospects for a stable domestic political consensus on foreign and defense policies decrease. With all this complexity and ambiguity, the United States may have to forge ahead into the twenty-first century without the benefit of a well-defined strategic doctrine.

SOURCES OF CONFLICT

Having noted some of the changes that have taken place since the end of the Cold War, it is also helpful to identify some lines of continuity. The same question that was frequently asked at the beginning of the twentieth century could be asked now, at the end of the century: How will nations liberate themselves from the age of imperialism? Today, the question has direct bearing on the futures of Central Asia, Kashmir, and Hong Kong. World War I was ignited by friction between imperial powers. Recall that President Wilson refused to intervene on behalf of the Allies until a democratic government—the ill-fated Kerensky government—took control in Russia in 1917. World War II resulted from imperialist designs, even as monarchy and formal colonialism were on the way out. Fascism was, among other things, a brutal form of economic imperialism, as was the Greater East-Asia Co-Prosperity Sphere. The Cold War was fought over this question, without resolving it. The Persian Gulf War, which has been described as the first post–Cold War conflict, can also be viewed as the consequence of imperialism. To some, Iraq is a descendant of the Ottoman Empire, jealous of its more prosperous cousins. Others see vestiges of Soviet imperialism in Iraq's rise to power.

During the Gulf War, President Bush echoed Wilson's emphatic belief that an international coalition can defeat aggression and enforce international law. Many interpreted this as the renaissance of liberal internationalism.

Others criticized Bush for cynically disregarding the undemo,ratic character of Kuwait's political culture. However, if the Wilsonian brand of liberal internationalism is examined more carefully, there is no real inconsistency. Wilson did not declare that America would make the world democratic, but only that America would make the world safe for democratic states. Upholding international law, disarming a cruel and reckless dictator, and securing the oil supply upon which the Western industrial democracies depend are objectives that would have made as much sense in 1917 as they did in 1990.

Put another way, the United States has sought to make the world *safe for diversity*. The United States intervened in World War I, World War II, Korea, Vietnam, and the Persian Gulf in the belief that it was defending the principle of self-determination. In the tense, Cold War atmosphere of nuclear rivalry, this principle was sometimes wrought into tragic contortions, especially when the United States intervened in civil wars in Asia and Latin America. But in each case U.S. strategy was designed to halt the advance of an expansionistic regime or ideology, be it imperialist, fascist, or Marxist. From an American perspective, geopolitical balance, reflected in diversity, is safer.

However, it may not be safer for the people who live along the fault lines of the nation-state system. Around the world nationalist movements seek to carve a political culture of their own out of larger political entities. Here, again, is the legacy of imperialism. Americans have been encouraged to see totalitarian regimes brought down by popular political movements, but some hard truths have emerged from these upheavals. The quest for national liberation subsumes a drive for ethnic or religious homogeneity among some peoples, and civil conflict is just as bloody as conflict between states.

As Douglas Johnson observes, we have moved from a period of superpower confrontation to a period of systemic conflict. The Cold War discipline of bipolarity is gone, and without the threat of escalatory spirals, deterrence is relatively weak. U.S. national strategy cannot possibly anticipate the particular causes of many conflicts. However, John Lewis Gaddis has offered a theoretical perspective on post–Cold War conflict that may help us adjust our expectations to the new security environment.[2] Gaddis believes that the burden of statesmanship is to strive for an equilibrium between two concurrent processes: fragmentation and integration. These phenomena are value-neutral. Fragmentation can lead to greater freedom, as in the former Soviet Union, or bloodshed, as in former Yugoslavia. Integration can liberalize the political economy of a supranational entity, as in the European Community, but can also convey a sense of exclusion to outsiders, as it has to the countries on the periphery of the European Community. This apparent paradox—that self-determination leads to fragmentation while trade liberalization leads to integration—is a characteristic of liberalism that has not been fully understood until recently. Nineteenth-century liberals believed that a community of self-determined nation states trading freely with each other under the rule of international law could eventually eliminate war. On the contrary, argues Gaddis, Iraq was fully integrated into the international economy and was a signatory to the Nuclear Non-Proliferation Treaty. Yet neither Iraq's trading partners nor the International Atomic Energy Agency could restrain Saddam Hussein and his regime. Likewise, the principle of self-determination has been wielded to tragic effect in the Balkans and the Horn of Africa, and intervention by the United Nations, the North Atlantic Treaty Organization (NATO), the European Community, and other multinational organizations representing integrated power is required to restore order in both of those regions.

So, a national strategy designed to preserve stable geopolitical diversity will need to embrace both self-determination and supranational integration. Such a strategy will also need to be able to differentiate between friends and foes. As Adda Bozeman points out, a realistic appreciation for cultural barriers and cultural antagonisms leads one to conclude that the United States and its Western allies will continue to be the objects of aggression. In assessing this threat, she recommends that Western nations think of cultural (or ideological) conflict in gradients, rather than in the traditional binary sense of war and peace. Bozeman also urges that Americans keep firmly in check the impulse to mount democratic crusades. Since geopolitical conformity is not a realistic strategic objective for a post-imperial age, the United States must make judgments about the reliability and cooperativeness of foreign governments that reflect different political cultures. Neither Saudi Arabia nor Iraq are liberal democracies, yet the United States allied with one to fight against the other. Both Singapore and North Korea have single-party rule, but the United States Navy visits one and conducts patrols against the other. The concept of "legitimacy" is one way to categorize foreign regimes. Where there is a high degree of repression, there is a low degree of legitimacy, and illegitimate regimes are dangerous neighbors. A government that does not respect limits at home is not likely to respect limits abroad.

PERCEPTIONS OF CONFLICT

Can the United States make firm alliances with nondemocratic regimes in the post–Cold War era? Should the United States defend nondemocratic regimes against aggression? The United States allied itself with a number of dictatorships during the Cold War, but those alliances were justified, at the time, by the threat of international Communism. Can the U.S. government mobilize public opinion for a politico-military strategy not based on ideological affinity?

These questions are a function of how conflicts are defined rather than how conflicts are caused. The editors of *The Economist* remind us that there are two different types of conflict: "wars of interest" and "wars of conscience."[3] While these are not discrete categories, the distinction will be important in the realm of American public opinion. As it moved to intervene in the Persian Gulf War, the Bush Administration faltered in its attempt to frame its purposes. The American people heard mixed messages that emphasized, variously, oil, jobs, nuclear weapons proliferation, international law, and atrocities against innocents. Eventually, the Bush Administration came to rely heavily on emotive arguments to build public support for the intervention, but it is questionable whether such a foundation would have held in the event that the war could not be won quickly and decisively.

During the Cold War, the distinction between interest and conscience was frequently blurred, much to the frustration of the political realists. Arguably, that distinction is more important now than ever. When the United States pursued an isolationist (or unilateralist) foreign policy in the eighteenth, nineteenth, and early twentieth centuries, it did not have the power to intervene decisively in wars of conscience. During the latter half of the twentieth century—when the United States achieved hegemonic power—interest and conscience were rhetorically interchangeable. Now that power disparities have narrowed and ideological conflict has abated, the U.S. electorate will need a more explicit justification for intervention. Is it a result primarily of national interest or of conscience? There will be elements of both in most cases, but delineating between them will be important if the government wants to preserve its credibility with the public.

To what extent do these categories—interest and conscience—overlap? The plight of the Kurds is instructive. The Kurdish independence movement in Iraq sought, with some outside encouragement, to exploit the outcome of the war of interest between Iraq and the U.N. coalition. Hussein's counterattack on the Kurds prompted U.N. intervention in their defense—as a matter of conscience. However, the United States and its Western allies do not favor the creation of an independent Kurdish state, for reasons of national interest.

Thus, wars of interest and wars of conscience are connected in ways that should be clear to the American public. When peaceable nations choose appeasement rather than intervention against an aggressor in a war of conscience, there is a demonstration effect that other potential aggressors notice. As he formulated his plans for total war in central and eastern Europe, Hitler is reported to have remarked, "Who remembers the Armenians?"[4]—a reference to the near extermination of the Armenians by the Turks a generation before. While planning his conquest of Kuwait, Saddam Hussein may have asked himself, "Who remembers the Kurds?" Certainly the United States and its allies will have to be selective about intervention where there is no vital national interest threatened. Pacification is a hazardous undertaking. More American military personnel were killed in 1984 during the Beirut peacekeeping operation than were killed in combat with Iraq.

As Harvey Sapolsky and Douglas Johnson point out, U.S. strategy in the Persian Gulf reflected an understanding that the American public demands a quick and decisive victory with low levels of casualties. The U.S. military achieved the capability to fight and win a major regional conflict on these terms by preparing for superpower conflict on a global scale.[5] When the next major regional conflict breaks out, the United States will have a somewhat reduced capability. Will there be a gap between public expectations, based on the performance of the U.S. military during the Gulf War, and actual power projection capability? The United States will likely retain clear technological superiority, according to Stephanie Neuman. However, if technological superiority is necessary, it is not sufficient. Other, more mundane factors, such as training and transportation, were critical to victory in the Gulf and will be critical in future conflicts. Unfortunately, operations and maintenance accounts are likely to be cut drastically in order to meet budget reduction targets. These cuts can be made without the political struggle that attends base closings or the cancellation of weapons programs. It remains to be seen if the security commitments made by the U.S. government and made credible by the U.S. military are consistent with the diminishing level of defense spending.

In this time of severe budgetary constraints, described by Stephen Daggett as "redistributive politics," spending programs for national security are in direct competition with spending programs for other social needs. Under these circumstances, policymakers can take one of two courses. They can understate the implications of defense cuts, in which case the United States will not have the resources to fulfill its stated strategic goals. Or, they can subject defense spending plans, and the politico-military judgments that inform those plans, to rigorous scrutiny in order to ensure that the United States is not strategically overextended. If history is a guide, there will be a reckoning. It should take place before American forces are sent into battle.

NOTES

1. Articles addressing this topic include, Edward N. Luttwak, "Do We Need a New Grand Strategy?" *The National Interest*, 15 (Spring 1989), pp. 3–14; Burton Yale Pines, "Searching for Mr. X," *Policy Review*, 49 (Summer 1989), pp. 2–6; Zbigniew Brzezinski, "Selective Global Commitment," *Foreign Affairs*, 70, no. 4 (Fall 1991), pp. 1–20; James Schlesinger, "Quest for a Post–Cold War Foreign Policy," *Foreign Affairs: America and The World 1992/93*, 72, no. 1 (1993), pp. 17–28; Malcolm Wallop, "Needed: A Post-Containment Doctrine," *Orbis*, 37, no. 2 (Spring 1993), pp. 187–204.

2. For a brief version of his analysis, see John Lewis Gaddis, "Toward the Post–Cold War World," *Foreign Affairs*, 70, no. 2 (Spring 1991), pp. 102–122.

3. "A Survey of Defense in the 21st Century," *The Economist*, 324, no. 7775 (September 5, 1992), pp. 4–5.

4. Kevork Dardakjian, *Hitler and the Armenian Genocide* (Cambridge, MA: Zoryan Institute, 1985), p. 81.

5. Patrick Glynn, "The Storm after the Storm," *The American Enterprise*, 3, no. 5 (September/October 1992), pp. 34–43.

Select Bibliography

BOOKS

Ackoff, Russell L. *Redesigning the Future: A Systems Approach to Societal Problems.* New York: John Wiley, 1974.

Allison, Graham, and Peter Szanton. *Remaking Foreign Policy: The Organizational Connection.* New York: Basic Books, 1976.

Allison, Graham, and Gregory Treverton, eds. *Rethinking America's Security: Beyond the Cold War to New World Order.* New York: Norton, 1992.

Aron, Raymond. *The Century of Total War.* Boston: Beacon Press, 1954.

Bacevich, A. J. *Diplomat in Khaki: Major General Frank Ross McCoy and American Foreign Policy, 1898–1949.* Lawrence: University of Kansas Press, 1989.

Baker, Susan P., Brian O'Neill, Marvin J. Ginsberg, and Quohua Li. *The Injury Fact Book.* New York: Oxford University Press, 1992.

Barber, Benjamin. *Strong Democracy: Participatory Politics for a New Age.* Berkeley: University of California Press, 1984.

Barber, James A., Jr., ed. *The Military and American Society: Essays and Readings.* New York: Free Press, 1972.

Bennis, Warren, and Burt Nanus. *Leaders: The Strategies for Taking Charge.* New York: Harper & Row, 1985.

Berger, Peter L., and Thomas Luckmann. *The Social Reconstruction of Reality.* Garden City, NY: Anchor Books, 1967.

Betts, Richard K. *Soldiers, Statesmen, and Cold War Crises.* New York: Columbia University Press, 1991.

Binkin, Martin. *Military Technology and Defense Manpower.* Washington, DC: Brookings Institution, 1986.

Blackwell, James A., Jr., and Barry M. Blechman, eds. *Making Defense Reform Work.* Washington, DC: Brassey's, 1990.

Blair, Arthur H. *At War in the Gulf: A Chronology.* College Station: Texas A&M University Press, 1992.

Blechman, Barry M. *The Politics of National Security: Congress and U.S. Defense Policy.* New York: Oxford University Press, 1990.

Bowman, William, Roger Little, and G. Thomas Sicilia, eds. *The All-Volunteer Force after a Decade.* Elmsford, NY: Pergamon-Brassey's, 1986.

Bozeman, Adda B. *Conflict in Africa: Concepts and Realities*. Princeton, NJ: Princeton University Press, 1976.

——. *The Future of Law in a Multicultural World*. Princeton, NJ: Princeton University Press, 1971.

——. *Strategic Intelligence and Statecraft*. Washington, DC: Brassey's (U.S.), 1992.

Braestrup, Peter. *Big Story: How the American Press and Television Reported and Interpreted the Crisis of Tet 1968 in Vietnam and Washington*. Boulder, CO: Westview Press, 1977.

Brzoska, Michael, and Peter Lock, eds. *Restructuring of Arms Production in Western Europe*. Oxford: Oxford University Press, 1991.

Calleo, David O. *Beyond American Hegemony: The Future of the Western Alliance*. New York: Basic Books, 1990.

Cimbala, Stephen, J., ed. *National Security Strategy: Choices and Limits*. New York: Praeger, 1984.

Coakley, Thomas P., ed. *C3I: Issues of Command and Control*. Washington, DC: National Defense University Press, 1991.

Coates, Joseph F., and Jennifer Jarratt. *What Futurists Believe*. Bethesda, MD: World Future Society, 1989.

Cox, Arthur Macy. *The Myths of National Security: The Peril of Secret Government*. Boston: Beacon Press, 1975.

Crabb, Cecil V., and Pat M. Holt. *Invitation to Struggle: Congress, the President, and Foreign Policy*. Washington, DC: CQ Press, 1989.

Danspeckgruber, Wolfgang F., ed. *Emerging Dimensions in European Security Policy*. Boulder, CO: Westview Press, 1991.

Deitchman, S. J. *Beyond the Thaw: A New National Strategy*. Boulder, CO: Westview Press, 1991.

Edelman, Murray. *The Symbolic Uses of Politics*. Urbana: University of Illinois Press, 1985.

Fisher, Louis. *The Constitution between Friends: Congress, the President, and the Law*. New York: St. Martin's Press, 1978.

Franck, Thomas M., and Edward Weisband. *World Politics: Verbal Strategy among the Superpowers*. New York: Oxford University Press, 1972.

Fries, James F. and Lawrence M. Crapo. *Vitality and Aging*. San Francisco: Freeman, 1981.

Fromkin, David. *The Question of Government: An Inquiry into the Breakdown of Modern Political Systems*. New York: Scribner's, 1975.

Gaddis, John Lewis. *Strategies of Containment: A Critical Appraisal of Postwar American National Security Policy*. New York: Oxford University Press, 1982.

Ganoe, William Addelman. *The History of the United States Army*. New York: Appleton-Century, 1942.

Gansler, Jacques. *Affording Defense*. Cambridge, MA: MIT Press, 1989.

George, Alexander L. *Presidential Decision Making in Foreign Policy: The Effective Use of Information and Advice*. Boulder, CO: Westview Press, 1980.

Gilpin, Robert. *The Political Economy of International Relations*. Princeton, NJ: Princeton University Press, 1990.

Gold, David, and Gordon Adams. *Defense Spending and the Economy: Does the Defense Dollar Make a Difference?* Washington, DC: Defense Budget Project, 1987.

Goodpaster, Andrew J., and Samuel P. Huntington, eds., *Civil-Military Relations.* Washington, DC: American Enterprise Institute, 1977.

Grant, Lindsey, ed. *Elephants in the Volkswagen.* New York: Freeman, 1992.

Hadley, Arthur T. *The Straw Giant: Triumph and Failure, America's Armed Forces.* New York: Random House, 1986.

Hagan, Kenneth J., and William R. Roberts, eds. *Against All Enemies.* Westport, CT: Greenwood Press, 1986.

Halloran, Richard. *To Arm a Nation: Rebuilding America's Endangered Defenses.* New York: Macmillan, 1986.

Halperin, Morton H. *Bureaucratic Politics and Foreign Policy.* Washington, DC: Brookings Institution, 1974.

Heller, Charles E. *Twenty-First Century Force: A Federal Army and a Militia.* Carlisle Barracks, PA: Strategic Studies Institute, U.S. Army War College, June 14, 1993.

Heller, Walter W. *New Dimensions of Political Economy.* Cambridge, MA: Harvard University Press, 1966.

Hoxie, R. Gordon, ed. *The Presidency and National Security Policy.* New York: Center for the Study of the Presidency, 1984.

Huntington, Samuel P. *The Soldier and the State: The Theory and Practice of Civil-Military Relations.* New York: Vintage Books, 1964.

Hyland, William G. *The Cold War Is Over.* New York: Random House, 1990.

Janowitz, Morris. *The Professional Soldier: A Social and Political Portrait.* New York: Free Press, 1971.

Janus, Irving L. *Groupthink: Psychological Studies of Policy Decisions and Fiascoes.* 2d ed. Boston: Houghton Mifflin, 1982.

Johnson, Loch K. *America's Secret Power: The CIA in a Democratic Society.* New York: Oxford University Press, 1989.

Kaufman, Daniel J., Jeffrey S. McKitrick, and Thomas J. Leney, eds. *U.S. National Security: A Framework for Analysis.* Lexington, MA: Lexington Books, 1985.

Kaufmann, William, and John Steinbrunner. *Decisions for Defense: Prospects for a New World Order.* Washington, DC: Brookings Institution, 1991.

Kemble, C. Robert. *The Image of the Army Officer in America.* Westport, CT: Greenwood Press, 1973.

Kennedy, Paul. *The Rise and Fall of the Great Powers: Economic Change and Military Conflict from 1500 to 2000.* New York: Random House, 1987.

Kozak, David C., and James M. Keagle, eds. *Bureaucratic Politics and National Security: Theory and Practice.* Boulder, CO: Lynne Rienner, 1988.

Kruzel, Joseph, ed. *American Defense Annual, 1993,* 8th ed. Lexington, MA: Lexington Books, 1993.

Ky, Nguyen Cao. *How We Lost the Vietnam War.* New York: Stein and Day, 1984.

Link, Eugene Perry. *Democratic-Republican Societies 1790–1800.* New York: Octagon Books, 1965.

Lippmann, Walter. *U.S. Foreign Policy: Shield of the Republic.* Boston: Little, Brown, 1943.

Lowi, Theodore J. *The End of Liberalism,* 1st ed. New York: Norton, 1969.

Luard, Evan. *The Blunted Sword: The Erosion of Military Power in Modern World Politics*. New York: New Amsterdam, 1988.

MacIver, R. M. *The Web of Government*. New York: Free Press, 1965.

Mahon, John K. *History of the Second Seminole War, 1835–1842*. Gainesville: University of Florida Press, 1967.

Mansfield, Harvey C., Jr. *Taming the Prince: The Ambivalence of Modern Executive Power*. New York: Free Press, 1989.

Matthews, Lloyd J., and Dale E. Brown, eds. *The Parameters of Military Ethics*. Washington, DC: Pergamon-Brassey, 1989.

May, Ernest. *"Lessons" of the Past: The Use and Misuse of History in American Foreign Policy*. New York: Oxford University Press, 1973.

Mayer, J. P., ed. *Alexis de Tocqueville, Democracy in America*. Garden City, NY: Doubleday Anchor Books, 1969.

Melanson, Richard A. *Reconstructing Consensus: American Foreign Policy since the Vietnam War*. New York: St. Martin's Press, 1991.

Menges, Constantine C. *Inside the National Security Council*. New York: Simon & Schuster, 1988.

Mills, C. Wright. *The Power Elite*. New York: Oxford University Press, 1980.

Mintzberg, Henry. *The Structuring of Organizations*. Englewood Cliffs, NJ: Prentice Hall, 1979.

Morgan, Gareth. *Images of Organization*. Newbury Park, CA: Sage, 1986.

Moyers, Bill. *The Secret Government: The Constitution in Crisis*. Cabin John, MD: Seven Locks Press, 1988.

Mueller, John. *Retreat from Doomsday: The Obsolescence of Major War*. New York: Basic Books, 1989.

Nanus, Burt. *Visionary Leadership*. San Francisco, CA: Jossey-Bass, 1992.

Nye, Joseph S., Jr. *Bound to Lead: The Changing Nature of American Power*. New York: Basic Books, 1990.

Oksenberg, Michael, and Robert B. Oxman, eds. *Dragon and Eagle: United States–China Relations: Past and Future*. New York: Basic Books, 1978.

Olson, D., and M. Hanson. *2001: Preparing Families for the Future*. Washington, DC: National Council on Family Relations, 1990.

Osborne, David, and Ted Gaebler. *Reinventing Government*. Reading, MA: Addison-Wesley, 1992.

Palmer, David Richard. *Summons of the Trumpet: A History of the Vietnam War from a Military Man's Viewpoint*. New York: Ballantine Books, 1984.

Patterson, Bradley H., Jr. *The Ring of Power: The White House Staff and Its Expanding Role in Government*. New York: Basic Books, 1988.

Perloff, Harvey S., ed. *The Future of the United States Government: Toward the Year 2000*. Englewood Cliffs, NJ: Prentice Hall, 1971.

Perrow, Charles. *Complex Organizations: A Critical Essay*. 2d ed. Glenview, IL: Scott, Foresman, 1979.

Phillips, Kevin P. *Post-Conservative America*. New York: Random House, 1982.

Presthus, Robert. *The Organizational Society*. New York: Vintage Books, 1962.

Roherty, James M. *State Security in South Africa: Civil-Military Relations under P. W. Botha*. Armonk, NY: M. E. Sharpe, 1992.

Rosati, Jerel A. *The Politics of United States Foreign Policy*. Fort Worth, TX: Harcourt Brace Jovanovich, 1993.

Rosenau, James N. *Turbulence in World Politics: A Theory of Change and Continuity.* Princeton, NJ: Princeton University Press, 1990.

Rossiter, Clinton. *The Political Thought of the American Revolution.* New York: Harcourt, Brace and World, 1963.

Sabrosky, Alan Ned, and Robert L. Sloane, eds. *The Recourse to War: An Analysis of the "Weinberger Doctrine."* Carlisle Barracks, PA: Strategic Studies Institute, 1988.

Sarkesian, Sam C. *Beyond the Battlefield: The New Military Professionalism.* New York: Pergamon Press, 1981.

———. *U.S. National Security: Policymakers, Processes, and Politics.* Boulder, CO: Lynne Rienner, 1989.

Sarkesian, Sam C., with Robert A. Vitas. *U.S. National Security Policy and Strategy: Documents and Policy Proposals.* Westport, CT: Greenwood Press, 1988.

Sarkesian, Sam C., and John Allen Williams, eds. *The U.S. Army in a New Security Era.* Boulder, CO: Lynne Rienner, 1990.

Schaffer, Ronald. *Wings of Judgment: American Bombing in World War II.* New York: Oxford University Press, 1985.

Schlesinger, Arthur M., Jr. *The Disuniting of America.* New York: Norton, 1992.

Scott, William G., and David K. Hart. *Organizational America.* Boston: Houghton Mifflin, 1979.

Shuman, Howard E., and Walter R. Thomas, eds. *The Constitution and National Security.* Washington, DC: National Defense University Press, 1990.

Smith, Hedrick. *The Power Game: How Washington Works.* New York: Random House, 1988.

Snow, Donald M. *National Security: Enduring Problems in a Changing Defense Environment.* 2d ed. New York: St. Martin's Press, 1991.

Spiers, Edward M. *Chemical Weaponry.* New York: Macmillan, 1989.

Teicher, Howard, and Gayle Radley Teicher. *Twin Pillars to Desert Storm: America's Flawed Vision in the Middle East from Nixon to Bush.* New York: William Morrow, 1993.

Terkel, Studs. *The Good War: An Oral History of World War Two.* New York: Pantheon Books, 1984.

Tucker, Robert W., and David C. Hendrickson. *The Imperial Temptation: The New World Order and America's Purpose.* New York: Council on Foreign Relations, 1992.

Upton, Emory. *The Military Policy of the United States from 1775.* Washington, DC: Government Printing Office, 1904.

Vien, General Cao Van. *The Final Collapse.* Washington, DC: Government Printing Office, 1983.

Warburg, Gerald. *Conflict and Consensus: The Struggle between Congress and the President over Foreign Policy-Making.* New York: Harper & Row, 1989.

Weaver, R. Kent, and Bert A. Rockman, eds. *Do Institutions Matter? Government Capabilities in the United States and Abroad.* Washington, DC: Brookings Institution, 1993.

Weigley, Russell F. *The American Way of War: A History of United States Military Strategy and Policy.* Bloomington: Indiana University Press, 1977.

Williamson, Oliver E., ed. *Organization Theory: From Chester Barnard to the Present and Beyond.* New York: Oxford University Press, 1990.

Wilson, James Q. *Bureaucracy: What Government Agencies Do and Why They Do It*. New York: Basic Books, 1989.

———. *On Character*. Washington, DC: American Enterprise Institute, 1992.

Yankelovich, Daniel. *Coming to Public Judgment: Making Democracy Work in a Complex World*. Syracuse, NY: Syracuse University Press, 1991.

Yankelovich, Daniel, and Sidney Harman. *Starting with the People*. Boston: Houghton Mifflin, 1988.

GOVERNMENT DOCUMENTS

Collins, John M. *Special Operations Forces; An Assessment, 1986–1993: CRS Report for Congress*. Washington, DC: Congressional Research Service, July 30, 1993.

Goldich, Robert L. *The Army's Roundout Concept after the Persian Gulf War: CRS Report for Congress*. Washington, DC: Congressional Research Service, October 22, 1991.

Grimmett, Richard F. *Conventional Arms Transfers to the Third World, 1984–1991: CRS Report for Congress*. Washington, DC: Congressional Research Service, July 20, 1992.

National Guard Bureau. *Army National Guard After-Action Report, Operation Desert Shield/Desert Storm, Executive Summary*. Washington, DC: National Guard Bureau, n.d.

National Science Board. *Science and Engineering Indicators, 1991*. Washington, DC: Government Printing Office, 1991.

Office of Technology Assessment, Congress of the United States. *Global Arms Trade: Commerce in Advanced Military Technology and Weapons*. Washington, DC: Government Printing Office, June 1991.

Secretary of Defense. *Annual Report to Congress: Fiscal Year 1990*. Washington, DC: Government Printing Office, annual publication.

U.S. Arms Control and Disarmament Agency. *World Military Expenditures and Arms Transfers, 1990*. Washington, DC: Government Printing Office, November 1991.

U.S. Bureau of Census. *Household and Family Characteristics 1990 and 1989*. Washington, DC: Government Printing Office, 1990.

U.S. Department of Commerce. *Statistical Abstract of the United States, 1991*. Washington, DC: Government Printing Office, 1991.

U.S. Department of Defense. *Defense 92; Almanac*. Washington, DC: U.S. Government Printing Office, September/October 1992.

———. *Population Representation in the Military Services, FY 1990*. Washington, DC: Government Printing Office, July 1991.

———. *Report of the Reserve Forces Policy Board*. Washington, DC: Government Printing Office, February 1991.

U.S. Department of the Army. *The CAPSTONE Program*. Washington, DC: Government Printing Office, September 1, 1985.

U.S. Department of the Army, Michael P. Stone, and General Gordon R. Sullivan. *Strategic Force Strategic Vision for the 1990s and Beyond: A Statement on the Posture of the United States Army, Fiscal Year 1993*. Washington, DC: Government Printing Office, 1993.

U.S. Departments of Labor, Education, and Commerce. *Building a Quality Work-force*. Washington, DC: Government Printing Office, July 1988.

U.S. Senate, Subcommittee on National Policy and Machinery. *Organizing for National Security*. Vol. 3: *Staff Reports and Recommendations*. Washington, DC: Government Printing Office, 1961.

The White House. *National Security Strategy of the United States*. Washington, DC: Government Printing Office, annual series from 1987.

Index

About the Editors and Contributors

ADDA B. BOZEMAN is Professor Emeritus at Sarah Lawrence College. She has published numerous articles and books on international history, foreign policy, and intercultural relations, including her most recent book, *Strategic Intelligence and Statecraft*. Ms. Bozeman is a member of the board of founding directors of the Consortium for the Study of Intelligence and was a barrister at the Middle Temple Inn of Court, London.

STEPHEN DAGGETT is a specialist in National Defense in the Foreign Affairs and National Defense Division of the Congressional Research Service at the Library of Congress. He was previously affiliated with the Center for Defense Information, where he served as a budget analyst, and he has written extensively on defense budget issues.

MARK J. EITELBERG a nationally recognized authority on military manpower policy, is currently Associate Professor of Public Administration in the Department of Administrative Sciences, U.S. Naval Postgraduate School, Monterey, California. Dr. Eitelberg is author or coauthor of more than fifty publications and several books on military manpower topics. He is coauthor of *Marching Toward the 21st Century* (Greenwood, 1994).

JOHN MEAD FLANAGIN is Research Director at the National Strategy Forum in Chicago. Trained in U.S. Diplomatic History at the American University and the University of Chicago, he writes frequently on foreign affairs and the policy-making process.

GREGORY D. FOSTER is J. Carlton Ward Distinguished Professor and Director of Research at the Industrial College of the Armed Forces, National Defense University. He is also an adjunct faculty member at Johns Hopkins University. His numerous publications include *The Strategic Dimension of*

Military Power and *Paradoxes of Power: The Military Establishment in the Eighties*.

RICHARD E. FRIEDMAN is President and Chair of the National Strategy Forum and Of Counsel to Rosenthal & Schanfield in Chicago. He is a member of the American Bar Association Standing Committee on Law and National Security.

CHARLES E. HELLER, Colonel, U.S. Army Reserve, is currently the U.S. Army Reserve Advisor to the Strategic Studies Institute, U.S. Army War College. He is a graduate of the institution and holds a Ph.D. in U.S. History from the University of Massachusetts—Amherst. He has authored numerous publications on national security issues and military history.

DOUGLAS V. JOHNSON II is currently an Associate Professor of National Security Affairs at the Strategic Studies Institute, U.S. Army War College. He served thirty years in the U.S. Army, retiring in September 1992.

STEPHEN L. MEHAY is Professor of Labor Economics in the Department of Administrative Sciences, U.S. Naval Postgraduate School, Monterey, California. He is widely regarded for his research and writing in the fields of military manpower and public choice. The author or coauthor of over twenty articles in professional journals and two books, Dr. Mehay is coauthor of *Marching Toward the 21st Century* (Greenwood, 1994).

STEPHANIE G. NEUMAN is Senior Research Scholar and Director of the Comparative Defense Studies Program at Columbia University. She also teaches courses on Third World security issues at Columbia as Adjunct Professor. Professor Neuman writes widely in the field of international security, particularly on international arms trade, defense industries, and Third World security issues.

HARVEY M. SAPOLSKY is Professor of Public Policy and Organization at Massachusetts Institute of Technology (MIT) and Director of the MIT Defense and Arms Control Studies Program. A specialist in the interaction of government and technology in various areas of public policy including defense, health, and science, Professor Sapolsky has served as a consultant to various agencies and commissions. He is author of *The Polaris System Development: Bureaucratic and Programmatic Success in Government* and numerous other works.

SAM C. SARKESIAN, Professor of Political Science, Loyola University of Chicago, chairs the Academic Advisory Council of the National Strategy Forum and the Research Committee on Armed Forces and Society of the

International Political Science Association. A member of the International Institute for Strategic Studies and the Chicago Council of Foreign Relations, Dr. Sarkesian is former Chair of the Inter-University Seminar on Armed Forces and Society. His latest publication is *Unconventional Conflicts in the New Era: Lessons from Malay and Vietnam* (Greenwood, 1993). He served for over twenty years in the U.S. Army as an enlisted man and officer.

DON M. SNIDER is Deputy Director of Political-Military Affairs at the Center for Strategic and International Studies (CSIS). He served in the Office of the Chairman, Joint Chiefs of Staff before joining CSIS. The author of numerous articles on national security planning, defense policy, and military strategy, he is currently pursuing doctoral studies in national security policy.

WILLIAM J. TAYLOR is Vice President of International Security Programs at the Center for Strategic and International Studies. A former U.S. Army Colonel, he was Professor of Social Sciences, Director of National Security Studies, and Course Director for Middle East Studies at West Point. He is the author, with Amos A. Jordan and Lawrence J. Korb of the best selling third edition of *American National Security: Policy and Process*, and has written or edited more than 200 articles and 4 other books on international security affairs.

JOHN ALLEN WILLIAMS is Associate Professor and Chairman of the Department of Political Science, Loyola University of Chicago and Vice Chairman, Executive Director, and a Fellow of the Inter-University Seminar on Armed Forces and Society. Chairman of the International Security and Arms Control Section of the American Political Science Association, he is a member of the International Security and Peace Studies Section of the International Studies Association. A Captain in the U.S. Naval Reserve, his duties included service at the U.S. Naval Academy and the Naval War College and on the staffs of the Chief of Naval Operations (N3/N5), the Chairman of the Joint Chiefs of Staff, and the Office of the Secretary of Defense. His most recent publication (with Sam C. Sarkesian) is *The U.S. Army in a New Security Era*.